DATE DUE

DAWN OVER SUEZ

Steven Z. Freiberger

DAWN
OVER
SUEZ

*The Rise of American Power
in the Middle East, 1953–1957*

 CHICAGO · *Ivan R. Dee* · 1992

Library of Congress Cataloging-in-Publication Data:
Freiberger, Steven Z.
    Dawn over Suez : the rise of American power in the
    Middle East, 1953–1957 / Steven Z. Freiberger.
        p.   cm.
    Includes bibliographical references and index.
    ISBN 0-929587-83-9 (alk. paper)
    1. Middle East—Foreign relations—United States.
    2. United States—Foreign relations—Middle East.
    3. United States—Foreign relations—Great Britain.
    4. Great Britain—Foreign relations—United States.
    5. Egypt—History—Intervention, 1956. I. Title.
DS63.2.U5F74   1992
327.56073—dc20   91-46262

For Dr. Kurt Rosenbaum who, having survived a Nazi concentration camp, died much too young

Contents

Preface

The Suez crisis of 1956 was one of the most important
events of the Cold War era. The crisis evolved throughout the summer and fall of 1956, but the complex issues which
fostered the invasion of Suez by Israel, Britain, and France in
late October of that year had been simmering for years. An
inability to solve the deepening Arab-Israeli conflict; Western
fears of Soviet penetration of the Middle East; American frustration over the continued British imperial presence in the region;
the need to protect the West's oil lifeline; the instability provoked by regional nationalist forces—all these factors made the
area ripe for military coups and further violence. The complexity
and implications of these issues has fascinated historians, stu-
dents of foreign affairs, and other interested parties for the last
thirty-five years. Numerous historical accounts, memoirs, and
articles have explored the events leading to the crisis and the
crisis itself. But the documentation needed to prove their conclusions has been unavailable. Over the years, more primary
source materials were gradually released, but it was not until the
late 1980s that many of the most important materials appeared.

On January 1, 1987, the British Public Records Office made
available a considerable number of files pertaining to the Suez
crisis. These documents contain information which had been
closed for three decades and which now provided useful insights
into the many questions involving American and British policies
during the crisis. Since this release of British materials, the

United States government has begun to disseminate more of its own files on the crisis. For the first time one can almost fully document the events surrounding one of the most important conflicts of the Cold War.

The demise of the British and the American rise to power in the Middle East began not with the Suez crisis itself, as is commonly believed. It started in May 1953 when the Eisenhower administration developed a coherent strategy to reduce tensions in the Middle East by allaying Arab fears of British colonialism. This was to be a first step in the creation of an Arab-Israeli peace. Some historians have suggested this, but the importance of Anglo-Egyptian negotiations over the Suez Canal base, the creation of the Baghdad Pact (a British-dominated regional alliance), and the implementation of Project ALPHA (the Anglo-American effort to mediate the Arab-Israeli conflict) have received too little attention.[1] So has American annoyance with the British who sought to maintain their empire at all costs. After four years of intransigent British imperial policy, President Eisenhower used the Suez crisis to pressure Anthony Eden from office as prime minister. And with this the United States replaced the United Kingdom as the dominant power in the Middle East. The culmination of these events was the January 1957 announcement of the Eisenhower Doctrine, an American commitment to provide military and economic assistance to any Middle Eastern nation that felt threatened by communism.

While the United Kingdom and the United States shared similar concerns about Soviet encroachment in the Middle East in the years leading to Suez, their motivations and strategies were decidedly different. Politically the United States believed that any American initiative in the Middle East that did not conform to British desires would be blocked.[2] During the postwar decade there had appeared to be a basic similarity of outlook between the United States and Britain; this appearance justified the belief that their foreign policies substantially agreed on the important issues of the Cold War. Among emerging "Third World" nations, the price the United States paid for this assumption was the expectation that Washington would become the heir of European colonialism.

Most accounts of the Middle East between 1953 and 1957 focus on the 1956 Suez crisis as the major watershed in Anglo-American relations for the region.[3] The invasion of Suez is viewed as the primary cause for Washington's break with London. The Suez crisis was surely of great importance, but it was only the culmination of a process whose roots can be found in the Truman administration. In the early 1950s the United States came to believe that British imperial policies were hindering an improvement in Arab perceptions of the West. Washington began to pressure London to modify its policies. Under Eisenhower this strategy was continued, and the United States became increasingly irritated with British imperialism in the region.

The Anglo-American relationship in the Middle East during the 1950s leads to many important questions about Washington's role in the region. Did the United States actively develop a strategy to replace the British as the dominant power in the area? Did the Eisenhower administration follow a consistent policy toward the Third World? If so, how did this policy affect United States relations with the United Kingdom? Who was the guiding force in determining American Middle East policy, Secretary of State Dulles or President Eisenhower? Who was responsible for its ultimate failure? Did America sacrifice its NATO allies because it hoped to gain total domination of the region? Was the American aim of surrounding the Soviet Union with a Middle East Defense Organization an achievable goal? What was Washington's role in the immediate events leading to the collusion between Britain, France, and Israel in the fall of 1956? How effective were American policies designed to defuse the crisis? Finally, what were the philosophical underpinnings of American policy in the Middle East?

Exploring British policy toward the region, another series of questions presents itself. Did the Eden government pursue realistic goals considering the situation it faced in the Middle East? Did Prime Minister Eden follow a consistent policy toward the Third World? Did that policy affect London's relationship with Washington? Did the British understand that their obsession with the Baghdad Pact could ultimately destroy their position in the Middle East? Did the Eden government accurately assess its relationship with the United States? Did London suspect that Washington was actively trying to replace the British in the region? Why did the British pursue choices which led inexorably to the Suez crisis? And why did Britain create policies which, in the end, produced the results they were trying to prevent—the collapse of British power in the Middle East?

All these questions are part of the investigation that follows. My own judgment is that Washington's policies toward the region were more sophisticated than mere anticommunism. The Eisenhower administration developed a counterrevolutionary and antinationalist premise, focusing increasingly on the Third World and employing covert CIA operations. One can find this strategy in the CIA-sponsored Syrian coup planned for the end of October 1956, and in projects ALPHA and OMEGA, the latter of which strongly hinted that Nasser would be deposed or eliminated following Eisenhower's reelection in 1956.

What's more, there is ample evidence to conclude that the Eisenhower administration worked actively behind the scenes to force Anthony Eden from office in November 1956. Eisenhower's anger with Eden at that point was primarily because the Suez invasion had thwarted the CIA operation in Syria and ruined Washington's own plans to eliminate Nasser. The president further believed that Eden's actions cost him votes on election day.

Ostensibly the United States pursued an anticolonialist policy in the Middle East. In fact, this was only a mask used to replace the British and block Soviet expansion in the region. In the end, Washington's strategy was a failure. By misjudging Arab nationalism, the United States created a vacuum in the Middle East which Moscow used to its advantage.[4]

The British tried to maintain their position in the region at a time when their power and influence were waning. Clearly the Eden government was not of one mind with the Eisenhower administration. Eden sought to recapture the wartime relationship with Washington as a means of stopping the loss of British influence in the Middle East. But his definition of a proposed

Middle East Defense Organization differed markedly from Eisen-hower's. For the prime minister it was a way to foster an Arab alliance headed by Britain—a vehicle to maintain the position in the region which London had held since World War I. For Washington it was an organization designed to block Soviet encroachment, with no Western membership to rekindle Arab fears of colonialism. Any British hand in settling the Arab-Israeli conflict was designed, as London saw it, to set the stage for the United Kingdom to recoup its dominant role in the area. Eden and his government were out of step with an empire in decline. No matter which tactic London tried, the British smacked of colonialism, something they could never admit.

Following the Suez crisis, the United States replaced the British as the dominant Western power in the Middle East. But what appeared to be an American policy success was in truth a failure. The United States pursued a flawed policy in dealing with Arab nationalism; its subsequent military intervention in Lebanon and the overthrow of the Iraqi government by national-ist forces in 1958 reflected the failure of Washington's policies. By the late 1950s Americans had not only replaced the British but, in the eyes of the Arabs, had also inherited London's colonialist mantle. Washington's inability to alter its imperialist reputation in the Arab world caused it to lose interest in promoting negotiations to solve the Arab-Israeli conflict over the ensuing decades. Today, as a result, the Middle East is no closer to peace than it was thirty-five years ago.

Acknowledgments

This book was made possible by the understanding and support of a great many people. The services and advice provided by a number of archival and library staffs were invaluable. In particular I wish to express my thanks to the staffs of the Eisenhower Library, the Seely G. Mudd Manuscript Library of Princeton University, the Alexander Library of Rutgers University, and the Public Records Office, London, United Kingdom.

I am especially indebted to Lloyd Gardner, whose advice and friendship made the completion of this work possible. I also thank Victoria de Grazia, William O'Neill, and Frank Castigliola for their guidance and suggestions during the writing process.

Special thanks must go to several individuals who have aided me throughout the research and writing phases of this book: Mrs. Judith Rattner and Mrs. Helen Gardner, whose friendship was tested repeatedly as they reread and edited the manuscript; my editor, Ivan Dee, whose suggestions and support were greatly appreciated; Ronald Kanfer, a special friend, whose encouragement has always been a great asset; Arthur Ebeling, whose understanding and generosity facilitated my research; Dan and Marcia Breckenridge, who welcomed me into their home and whose sense of humor kept me going during the last phases of writing; and Professor Kurt Rosenbaum, of West Virginia University, whose life was cut short because of Nazi persecution, and who for years served as my intellectual model.

Most important, I thank my mother-in-law, Mrs. Ann George, without whose unselfish help this project would never have been completed. My wife Ronni tolerated my absences and assumed the burden of family responsibility during crucial stages of my research. I owe my children, Ashley and Joshua, many trips to the movies, plays, museums, and sports events.

                                                                S.Z.F.

Rindge, New Hampshire
January 1992

DAWN OVER SUEZ

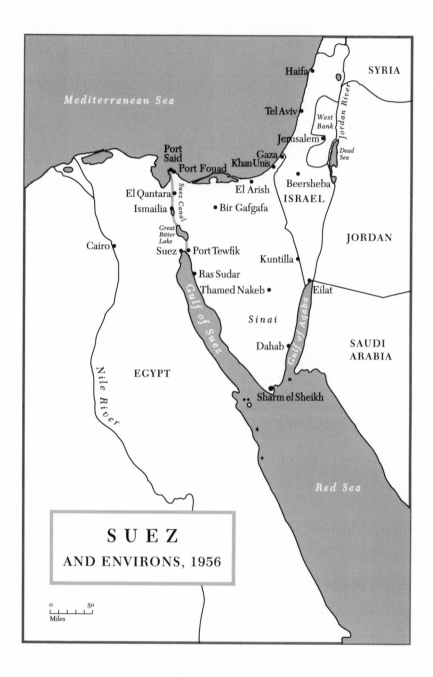

SYRIA

Mediterranean Sea

Haifa

Tel Aviv

West
Bank

Jordan River

Jerusalem

Dead
Sea

Port
Said

Port Fouad

Gaza

Khan Unis

El Arish

Beersheba

ISRAEL

El Qantara

Ismailia

Suez Canal

Bir Gafgafa

JORDAN

Great
Bitter
Lake

Cairo

Suez

Port Tewfik

Kuntilla

Ras Sudar

Thamed Nakeb

Eilat

Gulf of Suez

Sinai

Gulf of Aqaba

Dahab

SAUDI
ARABIA

Nile River

EGYPT

Sharm el Sheikh

Red Sea

SUEZ
AND ENVIRONS, 1956

0   50
Miles

1 *The Truman Background*

The administration of Dwight D. Eisenhower brought to Washington a new strategy for coping with the perceived worldwide threat of the Soviet Union. This so-called New Look sought, somewhat arbitrarily, to limit defense spending to $38.5 billion per year. Reducing the military budget for conventional weapons and land-based units forced strategists to rely on nuclear weapons, which became the centerpiece of the "massive retaliation" policy set forth by Secretary of State John Foster Dulles. Eisenhower described this in his 1954 State of the Union Address as getting "more bang for the buck." With increasing reliance on the nuclear option, Eisenhower sought to improve national security by establishing alliances beyond the traditional interests of the United States.

As a consequence, the Eisenhower administration became the first to focus on the Middle East as a prime region for American foreign policy concerns. Although the United States aimed to produce a coherent program of global, regional, and local objectives, its Middle East policy which emerged between 1952 and 1956 failed to support these goals.

Until the early 1950s American strategists had recognized the United Kingdom as the preeminent power in the Middle East. How the Anglo-American relationship affected the region in the years immediately preceding the Eisenhower administration are an essential background for understanding the new initiative.

* * *

In the spring of 1950 the administration of Harry S Truman found itself involved in a full-scale debate over the implementation of National Security Council paper 68 (NSC-68). This document called for a radical shift in United States global defense doctrine and capabilities, with large increases in military expenditures. The Pentagon asserted that should war with the Soviet Union occur, the United States would be unable to help the British protect vital military bases in Egypt and Iraq.[1]

Britain's strategy for the Middle East called for an Anglo-Egyptian partnership designed "to assist the defense of the Near East in case of Soviet aggression." Eventually the plan would bring other Arab states and Israel into a Middle East defense arrangement—and thus recognized that a resumption of the Arab-Israeli conflict must be prevented.[2] Truman's secretary of state, Dean Acheson, sensing the anti-Israeli bias of British recommendations, sought to reduce domestic political fallout as well as congressional opposition by issuing a public nonaggression declaration blocking the use of force against any Middle Eastern country.[3] But in April 1950 Truman and his advisers accepted British plans for the region.

At the London Conference that same month, British Foreign Secretary Ernest Bevin proposed that the Arabs and Israelis be allowed to purchase arms for "internal security." Bevin realized that if the Western powers refused to sell arms to Middle Eastern states, the Soviet Union would surely do so. His government could not sell weapons to Israel for fear of alienating the Arabs; and the United States would seek to limit Arab strength because of domestic political pressure. The result was a British Foreign Office draft combining the American desire for a nonaggression statement and the British desire for a joint declaration on arms.[4]

On May 17, 1950, President Truman was presented with the concept of an agreement between the United States, the United Kingdom, and France. It called for "formal assurances" from Middle East nations receiving Western military equipment that it would not be used against other states in the area.[5] On May 25 the U.S., U.K., and France issued the Tripartite Declaration to this effect.[6] While it mollified the domestic political fears of the Truman administration and satisfied the foreign policy goals of the Atlee government, the declaration also legitimized the supply of arms to countries of the Middle East, particularly Egypt, in pursuit of British imperial and American Cold War goals.[7]

Neither the Arab states nor Israel were consulted in the discussions which led to the Tripartite Declaration—not the last time such an omission would defeat British and American initiatives. In the early fifties Britain and the United States mistakenly assumed that the Arabs and Israelis would support any initiative. Their error meant that the Tripartite Declaration failed to alter Western arms policy toward the Middle East. Britain sold weapons to the Arabs; the United States refused to sell arms to Israel. The Arabs, and especially Egypt, were angered because they could not purchase American weapons, while the Israelis grew more suspicious of Western intentions.[8] Despite British and American agreement in the Tripartite pact, their differences over Middle East policies began to crystallize by the fall of 1950. The British, obsessed with retaining their position in the region, sought total control over their large Suez Canal base, without interference from the Egyptian government on troop movements or weapons disposition. The Foreign Office wished to use the Tripartite Declaration as a negotiating tactic with Egypt. This move highlighted the differing approaches of the U.S. and the British in the region, and presaged a later American preference for what became known as the "northern tier" strategy. Britain, with sagging remnants of its once-proud military domination located at the core of the Middle East, was most concerned with the "inner ring" of the area—Egypt, Jordan, and Iraq. The United States, obsessed with the containment of the Soviet Union and concerned about oil resources in areas where a Cold War vacuum existed, preferred to leave Egypt to the British while concentrating on the "outer ring" of the area—Iran, Turkey, and Iraq along the north, and Saudi Arabia.[9]

The Korean War had proved to be a watershed in the Anglo-American approach toward the Middle East. Lack of Arab support in the fight against North Korea reflected the Arab world's indifference toward communism; the Arabs still viewed the machinations of Britain and France as a greater threat. Aside from underlining the strength of Arab nationalism, the Korean War accented the strategic importance of the Middle East for the West. The Soviet Union might easily take advantage of an unpoliced power vacuum in the Turkish Straits and in the Suez Canal area.[10]

The key to the Anglo-American response, aside from making arms purchases easier and showing the flag in the region, was the establishment of a "combined US-UK command structure to stimulate cooperation among the Near Eastern states."[11] A direct relationship between the American and British command and the Arab states and Israel would thus be made more attractive to Arab and Israeli military authorities. George C. McGhee, assistant secretary of state for Near Eastern, South Asian, and African affairs, went a step further in a memorandum prepared for Acheson. He recommended a "combined US-UK responsibility and active US-UK cooperation in the development and implementation of plans [to] replace Great Britain as the primary responsible power."[12]

As intelligence reports pointed to a growing fear of Soviet encroachment in the Turkish Straits and Suez Canal area in 1951, the Truman administration took a fresh look at extending NATO instead of creating a regional defense pact in the Middle East. As early as 1949 Gordon P. Merriam of the State Department's policy planning staff had argued that the creation of a Middle East pact demanded area-wide cooperation—a precondition made unlikely by unresolved Arab-Israeli hostility. Moreover, this course ran the risk of exposing Anglo-American differences over the Arab-Israeli problem.[13]

By early 1951, however, American concern was growing that Turkey would abandon the West for neutralism or an accommodation with the Soviet Union.[14] In February Acheson accepted the recommendation of his Middle Eastern ambassadors to create an Eastern Mediterranean pact, rather than extend NATO. But the Joint Chiefs of Staff opposed Acheson and offered to extend NATO to include Turkey and Greece. The

Pentagon argued this would be the best way to supplant the United Kingdom, appease the Turks, and prevent the loss of the Turkish Straits to the Soviet Union. On April 30 Truman approved NATO membership for Turkey and Greece.[15]

Britain supported Turkish membership in NATO in return for Ankara's adherence to the concept of an Anglo-American Middle East Command (MEC).[16] That plan would serve as a means to solve the Anglo-Egyptian dispute over the Suez Canal base. Herbert Morrison, British secretary of state for foreign affairs, hoped to replace British control of the Canal Zone with a multinational operation that would include Turkey and Egypt, thus satisfying Egyptian national aspirations.[17]

There were a number of stumbling blocks to gaining Egyptian support for the MEC. The Israeli issue was avoided as Tel Aviv was excluded from the command. Because membership would have aggravated her relations with the Soviet Union, which was considering allowing substantial Jewish emigration to Israel, the Israeli government accepted this decision. But strained Turkish-Egyptian relations could not be easily overcome.[18] In their Cold War orientations, neutral Egypt and pro-Western Turkey competed for the leadership of the Arab world. The Arab states had not forgotten centuries of Ottoman rule. In addition, Turkey had recognized Israel, was involved in a border dispute with Syria, and was highly critical of Egypt's negotiations with the United Kingdom over the Suez Canal base. The Anglo-American failure to recognize Egyptian nationalist feelings helped discredit the MEC in Egyptian eyes.

On October 13, 1951, the U.S. and Britain presented the MEC proposal to the Egyptian government. The proposal addressed only the "single issue of how to keep the Canal Zone in western hands by preventing the abrogation of the 1936 Treaty which had legalized the British presence in the area." The offer did "not consider the command structure other than to assure the Egyptians that they would have a position of high authority and responsibility within the Allied Middle East Command."[19] It also failed to address the sticky problem of the MEC's relationship to NATO. The Egyptian government, with the full support of the Arab states, rejected the proposal.[20]

At once the British position hardened. London wished to develop the MEC without the Arabs as a means of pressuring Cairo over the Suez Canal base negotiations. This tactic, along with the failure to check Arab neutralism, led the United States to consider charting a separate course from its ally.[21]

The eventual extension of NATO to include Greece and Turkey checked the Turkish drift toward neutralism and retained control of the Straits. But the failure of the MEC left the British with a Suez Canal base problem. The entire episode demonstrated Truman's desire to avoid direct American political and military involvement in the Middle East as well as the administration's poor understanding of the region's problems. It further reflected growing differences between the United States and the United Kingdom, a development not overlooked by Egypt.

Egyptian abrogation of the 1936 treaty with the United Kingdom and the 1899 Sudan Agreement soon followed. Sudan had been a source of friction between Egypt and Britain for a number of years and by 1945 had become a British protectorate. Cairo objected to London's plan to grant the Sudan independence and self-government. Egyptian nationalists, who wanted Sudanese resources, demanded political union between Cairo and Khartoum and resented British attempts to demonstrate the benefits of colonialism. The Egyptian actions raised an immediate storm with American officials, overshadowing Egypt's rejection of the MEC.[22]

U.S. debate on Middle East defense continued during the late fall of 1951. The logic motivating American policy ran something like this: The Soviet Union had designs on the region, particularly its oil; Egypt and the Suez Canal were pivotal prizes in the strategy of Soviet expansion; it did not matter that the Soviets had not yet taken an active interest in the area. Egypt was incapable of defending the Suez Canal; its defense had to be maintained by outside powers—hence the MEC. As Geoffrey Aronson notes, "British imperatives demanded a continued aggressive pursuit of Egypt, if not for collective defense, then to create a dependable economic and political client in the heart of the region."[23]

Washington wanted the British and the Egyptians to solve

their problems in Suez and the Sudan, for it feared that continued friction between the two would encourage the rise of distasteful Arab neutralism. Harold B. Hoskins, acting regional planning adviser for the State Department, warned that "the need for harmony with our western allies must not blind us to the urgent need for reform in some of the colonial or foreign policies of our allies." Hoskins argued that the United States should make it clear to the British there was little to gain from repressive politics, especially in relation to Suez. If antagonisms in the area festered, these areas would become less useful to the West, even if they did not eventually fall to communism. Hoskins recommended that Washington pressure its NATO allies to alter their antinationalist policies and give them less support if they failed to do so.[24]

With Cairo's rejection of the MEC, the new Churchill government in London hardened its negotiating position. The consequence in Washington was a reappraisal of American Middle Eastern policy. A new NSC policy statement set forth "United States Objectives and Policies with Respect to the Arab States and Israel."

Unlike previous NSC statements on the Middle East, this one rightly identified the major danger facing the West in the area, arising "not so much from the threat of direct Soviet military attack as from acute instability, anti-western nationalism and Arab-Israeli antagonism which could lead to disorder and eventually to a situation in which regimes oriented toward the Soviet Union could come to power."[25] The document recognized the controversy between Britain and Egypt and the continuing Arab-Israeli tensions as basic issues which required American initiatives. The report recommended that the United States take an increased role in the area while simultaneously giving Britain as much support as possible.[26] Although primary responsibility for regional defense should still rest with the United Kingdom, for the first time the NSC suggested the dispatch of token American forces if this action would help promote regional acceptance of MEC or facilitate the resolution of the Anglo-Egyptian crisis. In short, the United States and its allies must show "the peoples and governments of the area that their interests and aspirations can best be furthered by association with the West," and, in the event of outside aggression, that the West would come to their aid.[27]

One month later a policy planning staff memorandum, while arguing that the Middle East was primarily a British responsibility, noted that British capabilities were "inadequate to defend the Middle East against Soviet aggression." The memorandum concluded that "without suggesting any derogation of [the] U.K. ... it would appear that the U.S. will have to provide more assistance and bring its influence to bear if we are to look foward to a significant strengthening of the situation in the Middle East."[28] The blueprint for American policy in the Middle East— its relationship with the United Kingdom, the Arab-Israeli conflict, and the Soviet threat—was now articulated. Over the next four years the United States rarely deviated from it. One could argue that the consistency of Washington's policies should have allowed the British to predict the response of the Eisenhower administration during the Suez crisis in 1956.

Lack of progress in negotiations over the Suez Canal base and the Sudan increased Egypt's sense of frustration with British imperialism.[29]   In July 1952 a group of young army officers, known as the Free Officers group, overthrew the Farouk regime in Cairo.

The military coup in Egypt influenced American policy in a variety of ways. There is some evidence not only of Washington's participation in the coup but of attempts by the United States, without the knowledge of the British, to reorient Egyptian politics.

In late 1951 Secretary of State Dean Acheson had "borrowed" Kermit Roosevelt, a CIA agent, to head a special committee of experts from the State and Defense departments to study the Arab world and its conflict with Israel, and propose possible courses of action. As Acheson stated, "The possibility of some unconventional activity to help along the natural forces was at least worth considering."[30]

By early 1952 it was decided that Washington was ready for "an operation." Egypt was chosen as the target because of its influence in the Arab world. Roosevelt's group insisted on the need for a man who would have more power "in his hands" than any other Arab leader to make "the unpopular decisions." This person would retain power by using the fear of an outside threat to Egypt, i.e., the Arab-Israeli issue.[31]

In March 1952 Roosevelt held three meetings with Gamal Abdel Nasser, the most influential member of the Free Officers group, and other military figures. At the second meeting Roosevelt is said to have given Nasser $3 million to implement a coup. In June Roosevelt returned from Cairo and informed Acheson that there was no likelihood for a popular upheaval in Egypt and that the army would be the driving force behind any coup. Roosevelt assured the secretary of state that the Free Officers held no outlandish hopes about regaining Palestine or using Arab nationalism to generate a revolution. He was convinced that once in power the Free Officers would adopt a more flexible policy toward the Suez and Sudan issues.[32] The Truman administration responded favorably to the prospect of a coup and hoped it would help resolve the Anglo-Egyptian crisis and bring Egypt into the regional defense group.

Two days after the successful coup in Cairo, in a memo to Assistant Secretary of State Henry Byroade, Harold Hoskins warned that the "tides of neutralism and communism continued to rise" and that "distrust of the motives of the western powers" in the region was mounting. Hoskins was concerned because of the lack of progress in talks between the United Kingdom and Egypt concerning Sudan and the Suez Canal base. In addition, American influence throughout the Muslim world had weakened because of "our continuing moral, material and military support of Israel." The Hoskins memo accurately concluded that the basic problem behind America's position in the region was its continued middle-of-the-road policy between the United Kingdom and France, on the one hand, and the Afro-Asian states on the other. Afro-Asian mistrust of NATO was growing, and U.S. inability to influence the British or French called for a policy reassessment before the Soviets might take advantage of an expanding vacuum in the region.[33]

Meanwhile, the British embassy regretted that the State Department was supporting the military regime in Cairo. American support for the new Egyptian government was based on principles of reform, not personalities. British Foreign Secretary Anthony Eden realized that the United States wished to "stand well" with General Mohammed Naguib, head of the new Egyptian regime, but he feared that Naguib would soon be controlled by extremists. Eden worried that if the United States and United Kingdom looked to be "out of step," extremist elements against London would be encouraged.[34]

On September 18, 1952, Lieutenant Colonel Abdel Amin of the Free Officers group visited Jefferson Caffery, the American ambassador to Cairo, with a message from General Naguib. During the conversation Amin stated that Egypt was "completely on the side of the United States and unalterably opposed to communism." The problem was to "sell the United States to the Egyptian public and educate the average Egyptian on the dangers of communism." To accomplish this, Egypt needed military and financial assistance from the United States. In exchange, Egypt was prepared to provide secret commitments "concerning long-term objectives of movement including MEDO [a Middle East Defense Organization] and or partnership with the U.S." Amin reiterated more than once that Egypt did not intend to renew hostilities with either the British or the Israelis. At the conclusion of the conversation, Caffery repeated that the ultimate objective was the realization of a Middle East Defense Organization and that it could not be accomplished without British participation. Amin "made noises about evacuation, but in essence agreed."[35]

Twelve days later Acheson instructed Caffery to tell Naguib of America's desire for cooperation. Caffery would determine Egypt's precise economic and political needs, and gain Cairo's commitment for a MEDO and a settlement of the Suez problem. Egypt was encouraged to look to the British for military and economic assistance because the United States would not undertake a purely bilateral program.[36]

In late October Nasser presented Assistant Secretary of Defense William Foster with a $100 million military shopping list. Nasser shortly sent his trusted aide, General Ali Sabry, to Washington for arms talks. The United States agreed to sell

Egypt $10 million in equipment and reached a vague under-
standing that this would be the first of several purchases. But
the next day the State Department withdrew the American
offer.[37]

The United States canceled the deal because General Naguib
refused to provide the secret assurances that Amin had promised. In addition, the United States and Egypt could not agree
whether concrete pledges by Cairo and public gestures regarding adherence to the MEDO would precede or follow arms
sales.[38] Nasser and Naguib continued their hostile statements
toward the United Kingdom in a mid-November interview in
the *New York Herald Tribune*. Nasser remarked that while there
would be no formal declaration of war, guerrilla activities would
continue, and "there will be much terror, we hope, it will
become far too expensive for the British to maintain their
citizens in occupation of our country."[39] The United States feared
that if it were to provide military aid to Egypt, American
weapons might be used against the British. Although Washington had begun to reassess its Middle East policy and its association with the British in the region, the U.S. was not yet ready to
follow a course that London totally opposed.

Despite this setback, Acheson, in a January 7, 1953, meeting,
made one final attempt to persuade President Truman to support
an arms agreement with Egypt which would "support and
strengthen" the Naguib government. Acheson argued, futilely,
that Naguib and his regime were the best hope for a favorable
Western orientation in Egypt and the creation of a Middle East
Defense Organization which would stabilize the region.[40] Truman concluded that "it would not be wise for him to make the
finding of eligibility for Egypt for military grant assistance."[41]
The president reached this decision in part because of his own
lame-duck status and the strong opposition of the United Kingdom.

The State Department disagreed with the Churchill government's view that the United States should give economic aid
priority over arms sales to Egypt. Acheson argued that Cairo was
a military regime which evolved from the reform of the Egyptian
armed forces. If the Naguib regime was to remain in power,

Western military weapons had to be forthcoming. Acheson opposed dividing the responsibility for military and economic aid
between the United States and United Kingdom, believing that
Egypt would then expect both types of aid from each country.[42]
Hence Washington and London failed to agree on military aid to
the Naguib government and later to the Nasser regime.

The new Egyptian government which came to power on July
23, 1952, created a unique opportunity for the United States to
move on a number of important Middle East issues. While
reassessing its relationship with London over the Suez Canal
base negotiations, the Sudan, and MEDO, the United States
was not yet ready to force a break with the Churchill government. Foreign Secretary Eden nonetheless epitomized British
resentment toward the "arrogance of American pressure" and
promised that his government "would not keep the Egyptian
government alive by feeding the Sudanese to them."[43]

Obstacles presented by the British competed with another
major problem facing American policymakers who sought to take
advantage of a new government in Egypt: the attitude of the
Israeli government and the widening Arab-Israeli conflict. A
related major deterrent was the tension between Washington
and London over the Palestine issue which had emerged after
World War II. Truman's January 1949 decision to extend de jure
recognition to the new state of Israel had been greeted with
disdain in London. This British displeasure grew as American
economic aid poured into Israel between 1949 and 1952. Israel
had just emerged from a destructive war and lacked the infrastructure to feed and clothe thousands of new immigrants.
American assistance may have been pivotal in the Israeli government's ability to care for its growing population.[44] By 1952 an
influx of 686,748 immigrants had increased Israel's population by
120 percent since its statehood was declared.[45]

After the July 1952 coup in Egypt, Israeli Prime Minister
David Ben-Gurion told the Knesset that "the events that have
taken place in Egypt during the past few weeks should be
welcomed. . . . There is not now any cause or basis for strife
between Egypt and Israel."[46] Despite these public remarks, the

Israeli government privately was deeply concerned about events in the region.

On January 5, 1953, Abba Eban, Israeli ambassador to the United States, visited Secretary of State Acheson and voiced Israeli concerns. Eban complained that in November 1952 the British had announced their willingness to sell more jet aircraft to Egypt, Iraq, Syria, and Lebanon. Although Israel was included in possible British arms sales to the region, he argued that it was difficult for Tel Aviv to keep up with the arms race without diverting funds needed for economic development. He concluded that the Tripartite Declaration was being ignored. Further, he complained that the U.S. and the U.K., in a note to Israel on November 11, 1952, "implied that the refusal of the Arab states to negotiate a peace settlement with Israel had no effect on the fitness of those states to receive shipments of arms from the very Western Powers which strongly believed that a peace settlement should be negotiated."[47]

Israeli concerns had been exacerbated by a series of Arab actions. In September 1952 Egypt had declared that Cairo remained in a state of war with Israel; in November Cairo had threatened West Germany for providing reparations to Holocaust survivors. In December the Arabs had opposed a United Nations resolution calling for negotiations between Israel and the Arabs, and Egypt had refused to end its naval blockade of the Gulf of Aqaba, which violated the September 1, 1951, UN Security Council resolution. Acheson's response to Eban did not soothe Israeli sensitivities:

> ... Our purpose is to provide Gen. Naguib with a foundation of military assistance—to encourage him and get him into a position where he will be with us, and not out of control. ... We see no threat to Israel—or at most only a "paper" or theoretical threat, as Gen. Naguib's army is not very good and our military aid will be so modest it could not cause any upsetting of the balance of Power in the Near East.[48]

Israel concluded that it could not survive if it stood idly by in the ongoing Cold War. Worsening Soviet attitudes toward Zionism and Israel during 1952 strengthened Tel Aviv's conviction that it must look westward for its security. The hope that guided Israel's foreign policy shift toward a stronger pro-Western stance was that its security would be enhanced by being part of a regional security system. But this new perception did not fit the developing American and British plan for a Middle East Defense Organization that excluded Israel. The State Department and the Foreign Office began to recognize that a settlement, or at least a reduction of tension, between Israel and the Arab states was a prerequisite for the implementation of their goals.

But how to convince the Israeli and Arab governments to take part in substantive negotiations? The fear of a renewal of full-scale war—or, at the very least, increasing border infiltration by both sides—was apparent. Monnet B. Davis, the American ambassador to Israel, argued that the key to any area defense required the liquidation of the Arab-Israeli conflict. He warned that the United States must make clear to both sides that we would not allow the destruction of either. In addition, the U.S. must be careful because the success of its policy "will be jeopardized if a psychology of desperation and panic should develop in Israel," if Israel came to believe there was no hope for peace.[49] Tel Aviv was especially upset that General Naguib and Colonel Adib Shishikli, the new Syrian leader, both seen as conduits for peace, were now bowing to Arab nationalist pressure.

The Arabs believed that their economic blockade, which forbad any Arab state to trade with Israel, was making it difficult for the Israelis to support their new immigrants. As the Eisenhower administration prepared to assume office in 1953, the Arabs reasoned they could bring Israel to its knees by continuing to use the economic weapon.[50] For Israel the battlefield might be the only alternative. American and British diplomats were fully aware that if they were not able to defuse the tension between Arabs and Israelis, any hope of the United Kingdom retaining its Middle East position and the United States creating another front to contain the Soviets would be lost.[51]

As Eisenhower prepared to assume the presidency, the Middle East was churning. The Churchill government and the Truman administration, instead of achieving peace, had left a smoldering Arab-Israeli hostility. Rather than providing security by aligning Arab states with the West, they bequeathed a growing anti-Western and neutralist movement which invited Soviet penetration. Arab leaders had labeled the United States pro-Israel in Palestine and pro-British in the Suez Canal base talks, thus making Arab-Western cooperation against Soviet adventurism unlikely. Now a new American administration would attempt to develop another "tier" to surround the Soviet Union while the Conservative government in the United Kingdom confronted Egyptian nationalism and aimed to retain its "imperial position." Both Washington and London had important practical and ideological reasons for seeking to impose their own visions on the region.

2 *The Eisenhower Initiative*

The advent of the Eisenhower administration brought to the fore British and American diplomatists who had been influenced by similar historical experiences. In the United States, Dwight D. Eisenhower and John Foster Dulles had been swayed by Wilsonian assumptions, the Munich appeasement legacy of the 1930s, Soviet actions during and immediately after World War II, and a deep-seated concern about European "colonialism." For the British, Winston Churchill represented Pax Britannica with its overly facile assumptions about the empire, British power, and its wartime relationship with the United States. Churchill and his foreign secretary, Anthony Eden, were intellectual victims of appeasement. Because of his personal feelings toward John Foster Dulles, Eden was not as sanguine about joint policies with the United States. To understand the evolution of Anglo-American policy toward the Middle East, it is important to be aware of the intellectual predispositions of the major statesmen as they came to office.

Following World War II, containment became the cornerstone of American Cold War policies. In the United States the liberal internationalist establishment hoped for "a postwar world which rested upon collective security, free trade, national self-determination, and the rule of law under American leadership."[1] Soviet *nyets* in the United Nations and Russian militarism in

Eastern Europe assured that containment would become a strategy of choice for the United States. To save American postwar goals, the communist world must be roped off.

The "free world," that area lying within the protective wall of containment, would reflect American values. State Department planners realized that not all the nations within the wall reflected democratic values; it was Washington's goal to allow them freedom of conduct without fear of intervention by "socialist internationalism." Support for our colonial allies fit this strategy because rapid decolonization would open the emerging countries to victimization by Marxism-Leninism. Containment was designed to create a stable and hospitable environment for growth and prosperity for the United States, its European allies, and their former colonies. The Soviet Union would consequently realize the futility of trying to subvert these areas, and the Kremlin would then be ready to negotiate with the West.[2]

After the Soviets' detonation of an atomic bomb in August 1949, Washington debated whether or not to respond by building a far more powerful hydrogen bomb. On January 30, 1950, after considerable debate within his administration, President Truman authorized a study to develop a thermonuclear weapon and called for the State and Defense departments to review American defense policy.[3]

By April this review was completed, its results embodied in National Security Council paper 68. The report, written mostly by Paul Nitze, director of the State Department policy planning staff, predicted prolonged global tension, Soviet expansion, and relentless communist aggression. It made sweeping assumptions about Soviet motives and capabilities and proposed overwhelming American military superiority. NSC-68 argued against negotiations with Russia. Instead it called for U.S. development of hydrogen bombs and a rapid buildup of conventional American military forces.[4] Because of the appearance of a shift in the world balance of power with the loss of the American nuclear monopoly, Truman and Acheson were no longer satisfied with a policy of containment. Both wanted Soviet withdrawal and absolute victory in order to preserve America's credibility in the world. "By stressing the importance of perceptions and images in world politics, NSC-68 vastly expanded the number of American interests," Richard Melanson has suggested. The key to implementation of the new strategy was long-term economic growth. An expanding U.S. economy would overcome anticipated short-term budget deficits and allow the United States to increase defense spending.[5]

Both Truman and Acheson were hard-headed Wilsonians who appreciated power but believed that it must be guided by moral purpose. Americans would support a diplomatic strategy only if it defended and exported liberal democratic values. If the United States were to resort to power politics, the American people would eventually turn against it as they had in the Korean War.[6]

Upon entering the White House, Dwight Eisenhower sought to reconstruct the "containment strategy" which by 1952 had been seriously weakened. Robert Griffith characterizes Eisenhower as a proponent of the "international corporate commonwealth," a man upset by the industrial strife, increasing inflation, and growing partisanship that he associated with the Truman administration. Eisenhower feared corporate competition and private self-interest, stressing cooperation to achieve national goals.[7] Like Truman and Acheson, he believed that the United States had a moral obligation to use its power to contain communism, strengthen economic and political ties within the free world, and protect American institutions from the uncertainty of international instability.[8] The president accepted Wilson's world outlook—"a pluralistic international order respectful of national self-determination and democratic institutions, committed to collective security, animated by free trade, and underwritten by American moral, political, and economic leadership."[9] In short, as one observer put it, Eisenhower "combined domestic conservatism with international liberalism, mixing Hoover with Wilson to produce a vision of enormous appeal to cold war America."[10]

Deeply affected by his wartime and NATO experiences, Eisenhower became a committed internationalist for several reasons. First, he believed the 1930s had shown that isolationism could not be a sound basis for foreign policy. Second, the determination of the Soviet Union to develop long-range nuclear striking power made it imperative that the United States have reliable allies to intercept Soviet assaults from forward bases. Third, the United States could not afford to lose Western Europe to communism. The resulting loss of markets and investment opportunities would shift the world balance of power in favor of the Soviet bloc.[11]

These views had to be reconciled with Eisenhower's fiscal conservatism. He believed that Truman's national security strategy, with its nuclear and conventional force buildup, would bankrupt America and destroy its social fabric. Eisenhower sought a preparedness program which would retain Truman's definition of American interests and the Soviet threat while exploring new ways to reduce defense costs and avoid bankrupting the treasury.[12]

While Eisenhower endorsed the broad outlines of the containment strategy, he doubted the American economy could tolerate the defense expenditures required to implement NSC-68. The president feared that such an increase in defense spending would batter the American economy and eventually plunge its allies into recession. The alternative was to reassert the containment strategy by developing a conventional, proportional military response wherever communism threatened to expand. Eisenhower offered a "dual-track response"—first, the "New Look" of atomic weapons, "taking advantage of our atomic and aerial superiority," and second, expanded activities for the Central Intelligence Agency. Eisenhower hoped to implement this strategy by using the threat of massive nuclear retaliation to control communism. In addition, he hoped to construct an atomic umbrella around the Soviet Union and its communist periphery with a series of regional defense pacts which "placed the primary responsibility for conventional defense in indigenous hands."[13]

On assuming the presidency Eisenhower immediately began to implement a policy based on his belief that failure to oppose communism everywhere would eventually defeat his conservative vision of America. His deeply held anticommunist convictions prevented any major alteration of the Truman-Acheson strategy for the Cold War.

During Eisenhower's first term in office, administration policy toward the Middle East fit this developing ideological mind-set. Resting on Eurocentric priorities, Eisenhower believed that Middle Eastern oil was essential for the economic and military health of America's Atlantic allies. This view led the president to be overly concerned with the effect of Middle Eastern events on his allies while neglecting the feelings and aspirations of the Arabs themselves.[14] The key for Washington was to deny the area to the Soviet Union and continue to make oil available to its Atlantic allies. The dilemma lay in reconciling Eisenhower's fundamental Eurocentrism with a policy of accommodating Arab nationalism. The administration's lack of insight into the political and social problems of the Arab world precluded any such reconciliation.

Until 1955 American policymakers encouraged the British and French to pursue aims which would help to stabilize the Middle East. Heavy American commitments elsewhere restrained Washington from becoming the dominant power in the area. The United States and United Kingdom, for a time, were tied together in a mutual strategic dependence.

Reliance on its colonial allies produced contradictions in American policy. Fully aware of the power of modern nationalism, Eisenhower realized that American support for Britain and France was detested in the Arab world and could only embarrass the United States. The American dilemma was heightened by its support for Israel. Fearful of Soviet inroads into the region, Washington would in theory support anti-imperialist causes and try to break the identity which the Arabs had established between Washington and its NATO allies. Rather than upholding the old imperial order, the United States would sometimes offer vocal encouragement to genuine Arab nationalism in order to appear as a true friend of the Arabs. This was theory; in reality the Eisenhower administration believed that its only choice was to oppose Arab nationalism in the interests of Western Europe. Washington's belief that Soviet goals in the region coincided with radical Arab nationalism led the United States to defend the conservative status quo in the region.[15]

America could not escape its economic interdependence with

a Europe that needed Middle Eastern oil. In a March 13, 1956, diary entry, Eisenhower noted that if Europe were cut off from Arab oil sources its economy would collapse and "the United States would be in a situation of which the difficulty would scarcely be exaggerated."[16]

At the outset of his presidency, Eisenhower began expanding the American commitment in the Middle East, not to diminish London's influence but to compensate for British decline in the region. He stated clearly in his diary on January 6, 1953, that supporting the British in the newly emerging Third World could cause Washington a good many problems. Commenting on the situation in Iran and the future of the Anglo-American relationship, which Prime Minister Churchill hoped to restore to the "euphoric days of World War II," Eisenhower wrote, "Nationalism is on the march and world communism is taking advantage of the spirit of nationalism to cause dissension in the free world." Moscow, the president continued, wished to take advantage of the situation to spread the Kremlin's domination. "In this situation the two strongest Western powers must not appear before the world as a combination of forces to compel the adherence to the status quo."[17]

The Eisenhower administration was fully aware of the problem presented by Third World nationalism. Upon returning from a fact-finding mission to the Middle East, Secretary of State Dulles reported on June 1, 1953 that

> ... most peoples of the Near East ... are deeply concerned about political independence for themselves and others. They are suspicious of the colonial powers. The United States too is suspect because, it is reasoned, our NATO alliance with France and Britain requires us to try and preserve or restore the old colonial interests of our allies. ... Without breaking from the framework of western unity, we can preserve our traditional dedication to political liberty.[18]

American policymakers had somehow to establish an effective working relationship with Arab nationalism while seeking a way to influence and stabilize the movement and contain it. When the essential neutralism of Arab nationalism emerged, it precluded any possibility of continuing Western influence in the region.

* * *

Eisenhower's secretary of state, John Foster Dulles, was deeply influenced by his religious background and the Wilsonian concept of liberal internationalism. He believed the United States to be an ethical role model for the postwar world. By the time he became secretary of state in 1953, Dulles's anti-Soviet worldview blinkered him to the changes already taking place in the Third World and especially in the Middle East.

Former presidential assistant Emmet Hughes has characterized Dulles's conduct of diplomacy in courtroom terms—he saw himself as "the prosecutor assigned to the historic labor of arraignment, condemnation and punishment of the Soviet Union for crimes against freedom and peace."[19] At the conclusion of World War I Dulles had been a member of the American delegation to the Versailles peace conference. There he had witnessed the aftermath of the Russian Revolution through the flow of diplomatic dispatches that crossed his desk. The men surrounding him at the conference were repulsed by the Bolsheviks, who were regarded as threats to Western civilization. Dulles was involved in numerous policy debates designed to develop a strategy to crush the Bolsheviks, which reinforced his anticommunist bias.[20]

During the interwar period Dulles rarely commented on events in the Soviet Union. But with the outbreak of World War II he began to perceive Soviet communism as a rival "faith." As the war continued he saw the Soviet Union as a powerful nation whose existence and diplomatic policies were virtually straightforward functions of a controlling ideology.

By 1943 Dulles realized that after the war sharp differences would quickly emerge between the United States and the Soviet Union, each representing opposing ideologies.[21] His fears were confirmed in 1944 by the Soviet Union's actions in Eastern Europe. "The foreign policy of the USSR today," Dulles wrote at the time, "is that of Peter the Great." He understood the Soviet need for security, but he was becoming deeply concerned about Soviet consolidation of a sphere of influence in Eastern Europe.[22]

Despite his feelings toward Moscow, Dulles's public remarks

were restrained. He was still able to draw a distinction between communism as an ideology and the Soviet Union as a nation-state.

Dulles's perspective was greatly altered upon his return to government service in April 1945. As an adviser to the American delegation to the San Francisco conference which saw the founding of the United Nations, he came in contact with Soviet delegates for the first time. These meetings, in conjunction with the London foreign ministers conference in September and October 1945 and the opening UN General Assembly meeting in January 1946, affected him greatly. Dulles came to perceive the Soviet Union as led by ideologues bent not just on maintaining Russian domination of Eastern Europe but on revolutionary meddling in every part of the globe.[23]

The future secretary's first article for *Life* magazine in June 1946 provides insights into his developing attitude. In the Soviet mind, Dulles wrote, the establishment of peace and security meant the "eradication" of peace and security in the free world. "World harmony, in the Soviet understanding of the term, will only come into existence through the creation of a great political calm which will be Pax Sovietica."[24]

Dulles's antidote to Soviet expansionism was for Americans to reeducate themselves "to the faith of their fathers" and a "good old fashioned spiritual revival"—thus American freedom as a kind of law. This theme would often dominate Dulles's justification for refusing further cooperation with the Soviet Union. He preferred an American commitment to freedom which could not be broken by communism.[25]

In the late 1940s Dulles attended three foreign ministers conferences and two General Assembly meetings of the United Nations. Each of these head-to-head encounters with the Soviets stiffened his world-view; overlooking instances of American greed in world affairs, he could see only the moral expression of the free world as the true moral law. Ignoring imperfections and immoralities in America's past, Dulles told Americans to remember that they were "predominantly a moral people, who believe that their nation has a great spiritual heritage to be preserved."[26]

From 1949 on Dulles believed that the Soviet Union had merely shifted its attention away from Western Europe, where the Kremlin had encountered persistent opposition, to East Asia and North Africa where conditions for communist expansion were more favorable. Therefore, strategies such as regional alliances, which had worked earlier in blocking Soviet expansion in Western Europe, must now be undertaken in other parts of the world.

In *War or Peace*, published in 1950, Dulles stressed the importance of understanding the Soviets' ruthlessness and limitless ambition.[27] As he universalized the conflict between the Soviet Union and the United States, he saw two ideologies vying for world domination. Since the position of the United States was a moral one, with no "lust" for power but only a desire "to safeguard institutions that respected human liberty," whatever policy choices Washington developed would be right on ethical grounds. Thus the nations of the world "must reject neutrality and prefer to stand together against aggression, direct or indirect."[28] To accept neutralism in the worldwide struggle against communism was heresy. As Dulles commented in a 1955 address, "The United States does not believe in practicing neutrality. Barring exceptional cases, neutrality is an obsolete conception. It is like asking each community to forgo a police force."[29]

As secretary of state, Dulles sought to expand Washington's focus beyond Europe to the Middle East. European stability, he believed, would allow the United States to devote greater energy to areas of Soviet threat. With the British seemingly unable to manage a retreat from colonialism in the Middle East, Washington would likely have to assume greater responsibilities in the region.[30]

As Geoffrey Aronson has observed, Dulles's preoccupation with the Soviet Union and his failure to recognize the anti-Western sentiments expressed in Arab nationalism "reflected a long-standing American intellectual bias." The failure of any country "to stand up and be counted" on the side of "free world democracy" had always been a "sin" of great magnitude.[31] In Dulles's case the "sin" was compounded when it was applied to new areas of American interest such as the Middle East. After the secretary visited Arab capitals in May 1953 he freely admitted that he saw no basis for an overall defensive arrangement. Dulles learned during his tour that the Arab world saw Israel, not the Soviet Union, as its chief threat. Returning to Washington, he was convinced that a new strategy was needed to block Soviet encroachment in the area.

Aside from the moral strain in Dulles's intellectual development, one cannot ignore the influence of the Wilsonian concept of liberal internationalism.[32] Dulles's ideological mind-set after World War II focused on reestablishing the economic health of the United States and preventing another worldwide depression. To accomplish this Dulles, just as Wilson before him in Paris, had to balance the threat of communist expansion with the desire of America's Atlantic allies to recoup their colonial empires. Should these colonies be returned, and later revolt, they would create a great opportunity for the Soviet Union to fill a newly created political vacuum. The preeminent U.S. fear was that those markets once tied to Britain and France would eventually be lost to "international socialism." The goal was to maintain European economic recovery.[33]

Even with European recovery, Dulles was aware that the resurgence of the decolonization problem could undo much of the economic achievement. As early as 1942, in a conversation in London with British Foreign Secretary Anthony Eden and Colonial Secretary Lord Cranborne, Dulles offered the following advice: "What you have got to do is... pocket [your] pride in order to secure American postwar collaboration in the development of the great colonial areas of the world."[34] By 1953, however, the British had yet to follow this suggestion. After the secretary of state returned from the Middle East in May 1953, the Eisenhower administration's Wilsonian dilemma became more acute than ever.

Dulles's goal was a Middle East free of European colonialism or remnants of imperialism represented by the outdated policies of the Churchill government in Egypt, Iraq, and Jordan, and the French in Syria and Algeria. Continuance of these traditional spheres of influence could create a tinderbox for the sparks of revolutionary socialism. In addition, Dulles had to deal with competing problems of self-determination involving the Palestinian Arabs and Israeli nationalism.

Dulles's course of action shows how he endeavored to reduce tension in the Middle East. He set out to defuse the Arab-Israeli crisis, gain British withdrawal from the Suez Canal base, and construct a regional defense network which would be supported by Egypt. The desired result would be a region free from Soviet threats to European oil supplies, and the creation of new markets and stable trading partners for the United States. British-French colonial policy could not be allowed to jeopardize this scenario; Dulles, like Wilson, felt he knew best what was good for his allies, and he would help save them from themselves. In the end, Dulles's anticommunist dogma, like Eisenhower's, overcame his theoretical model.

Comparing the ideological frameworks of Eisenhower and Dulles, one finds general agreement on Middle Eastern issues. The question still debated is which of the two was the dominant partner in the conduct of American Middle East policy.

After his election in November 1952, Eisenhower delayed for three weeks before naming Dulles secretary of state. The president selected Dulles only after his advisers warned him that "the Taft wing of the Republican Party would accept no one else."[35] Thus it was largely politics, "not intellectual affinity," that created the Eisenhower-Dulles partnership. In the conduct of American Middle East policy, it was Dulles who determined the "nature" of administration strategy—the selection of responses to international events. But Eisenhower possessed the keener "sense" of strategy—how responses were to be correlated with fundamental interests. The president retained ultimate authority, overriding Dulles when he felt it was appropriate.[36] Dulles never enjoyed the latitude in foreign affairs that Truman had accorded Dean Acheson after 1949. Despite the argument developed by Herman Finer in *Dulles Over Suez*, for example, it was Eisenhower who controlled American policy during the 1956 Suez crisis.[37] According to historian Richard Immerman, Dulles showed virtually all his draft speeches to Eisenhower, and it was not unusual to find the president's suggestions incorporated verbatim into the final text.[38]

Historian Barton J. Bernstein called the president a "shrewd administrator, a man skilled in directing men and organizations while quietly maintaining his dominance and authority."[39] Despite the leeway Eisenhower provided Dulles, the president controlled major policy decisions. Eisenhower once confided to an aide that "Dulles knows more about foreign affairs than anyone I know, but there's only one man I know who... knows more... that's me."[40]

When Winston Churchill formed his second government in October 1951 there were few indications as to how long he would remain in office. Churchill immediately appointed Anthony Eden as his foreign secretary, but the smoothness of their wartime relations would not be resumed. Eden was the heir apparent, and Churchill himself spoke of handing the government over to his foreign secretary within the year. Eden was fully aware that Churchill's interests did not lie in domestic affairs. While he greatly respected and admired Churchill, Eden was determined to maintain control over foreign affairs. Eden expected that he would soon take up residence at Number 10 Downing Street. He never anticipated that Churchill would literally hang on to the prime minister's office until April 1955.[41]

Churchill was not the only obstacle Eden had to overcome. His own ill health plagued him throughout the rest of his career. A diagnosis of gallstones in early April 1953 resulted in surgery. During the operation Eden's biliary duct was accidentally cut. The resulting high fever and loss of blood necessitated another surgical procedure to save his life. But the duct remained blocked and jaundice reappeared. An American specialist took over the case and Eden was flown from London to Boston for a third operation. To Eden's dismay, in his absence the seventy-nine-year-old Churchill took over the Foreign Office.[42]

On May 11, 1953, while Eden was awaiting his third operation, Churchill, without consulting the cabinet or his close advisers, spoke before the House of Commons and called for an immediate great-power summit between himself, the new Soviet leaders, and President Eisenhower. The prime minister announced that the meeting should have no agenda or preparatory talks; it would be an attempt to reinstate the "Grand Alliance" of World War II. Eden was appalled and totally against such a strategy. Although more pragmatic about the Soviets than the elderly Churchill, Eden's distrust of Moscow remained strong despite the recent death of Stalin. Further, Churchill's approach reminded Eden of the tactics that had been such a failure under Neville Chamberlain in the 1930s.[43]

When Eden finally returned to the Foreign Ministry in October 1953 he found unresolved most of the problems he had left behind six months before. Difficulties in the Middle East were Eden's topmost concerns. Talks with Egypt about the replacement of the Anglo-Egyptian Treaty of 1936 had made little progress during his absence.

General Naguib's revolutionary government was encountering new internal difficulties, and Egyptian nationalism was steadily rising. The main difficulty for the British was the future of the Suez Canal base, on which Churchill and his supporters refused to compromise. Evelyn Shuckburgh, Eden's private secretary, in his diary entry of January 29, 1953, provides a useful insight into the predicament of the British foreign secretary.

> But when the Prime Minister got back and A.E. went to see him at noon today, Jock Colville came to me in a great state of agitation. He said there was going to be a row. The latter was in a rage against A.E., speaking of "appeasement" and saying he never knew before that Munich was situated on the Nile. He described A.E. as having been a failure as Foreign Secretary and being "tired, sick and bound up in detail." He positively desired the talks on the Sudan to fail, just as he ... hoped we should not succeed in getting into conversations with the Egyptians on defence which might lead to our abandonment of the Canal Zone.[44]

The situation in Iran was no better. Britain had had no diplomatic representation in Teheran since terminating relations in 1952. The summer of 1953 had witnessed the flight of the shah, the CIA-arranged overthrow of Mohammed Mossadegh,

and the return to power of the shah. Yet British oil installations
in Iran remained nationalized, with British and American oil
companies disagreeing over how to reactivate the oil fields. In
addition, Eden also faced a crisis in relations with Saudi Arabia
which had occupied the Buraimi Oasis.[45]

Eden's intellectual makeup may not have prepared him to
deal effectively with these problems. His temperament inhibited
his appreciation of the importance of ideology, symbols, and
rhetoric in mass politics. And the logic he applied to diplomatic
situations tended to ignore the internal character of the governments with whom he was negotiating.[46]

Eden's inability to understand the behavior of dictators, and
his disrespect of ideology, led him to characterize men such as
Egypt's Nasser as a dictator, a "madman," a "gangster," or the
reincarnation of Mussolini. Eden's own aristocratic background,
with its sense of pomp and honor, were inadequate to deal with
authoritarian regimes. He had a low tolerance for treaty viola-
tions and broken promises, the standard tactics of emerging
Third World dictators. Instead he was affronted—unlike a more
cynical Churchill in dealing with Stalin in 1944. Churchill had a
more realistic understanding of power than Eden, who had to
pretend to be a practitioner of power politics. As a result, Eden
would often call for resolute action rather than accept the fact
that he led a government which could no longer impose its will
on other nations.[47]

In effect, Eden became a prime minister in charge of a
declining nation whose position in the Middle East was eroding.
Still smarting from losing India and Palestine after World War II,
both Eden and Churchill felt the British had to prove they could
act decisively. In addition, Eden intensely resented the United
States' effort to usurp British power in the Middle East.[48]

Despite his limitations, Eden appeared to be highly self-con-
fident. He kept to himself and remained aloof from colleagues
and subordinates. He was a diligent worker who frequently
pushed himself to exhaustion. When Eden felt he was correct he
exhibited a dogged determination which lay at the root of his
difficulties with Secretary of State Dulles.

Eden had an early premonition that Dulles would be difficult to work with. He tried, soon after Eisenhower was elected, to lobby against Dulles's appointment to head the State Department. Eden and Dulles had disagreed over numerous issues in the past. During the Korean War, Eden had sought to minimize the risk of possible war with China as he feared for Hong Kong and a Soviet move in Eastern Europe. Eden had resented Dulles's pressure on the new Japanese government to recognize Chiang Kai-shek's government on Taiwan. Further, Eden had opposed the ANZUS pact (the regional alliance for the Pacific between Australia, New Zealand, and the United States) unless the United Kingdom was accorded membership. The foreign secretary was against British membership in the European Defense Community, which Dulles favored, as Eden wanted Britain to remain a global power, not a regional one. Finally, in Egypt Dulles favored a British withdrawal from the Suez Canal base in order to create a new relationship with the revolutionary regime in Cairo.[49]

Eden's distrust of Dulles was fully reciprocated. Dulles believed that Eden's leadership epitomized the United Kingdom's colonial past. As former Assistant Secretary of State Robert Murphy wrote, ". . . the Prime Minister had not adjusted his thoughts to the altered status of Great Britain, and he never did."[50] Eden wished to turn the clock back, Dulles felt, or at least slow it down. Dulles must have resented the fact that despite Eden's old-fashioned ideas about the Middle East, Eden had a sharper sense of the future as it applied to Eastern Europe, the Soviet Union, and Communist China. Eden recognized these new forces and realized that the Poles, Russians, and Chinese had their own vital interests which Dulles refused to acknowledge. Shuckburgh points to what appears to have been the basic problem in the Eden-Dulles relationship:

> They were like two little strings whose vibrations never coincide. . . . The trouble I think was due to the fact that Master and Foster do not really understand one another. Foster talks so slowly that Master does not wait to hear what he has to say, while our man talks in so roundabout and elusive a style the other, being a lawyer, goes away having failed to make the right guesses. . . .[51]

Dulles sought to shape the world in America's vision and

wanted the United Kingdom to accept its role as a regional power. Eden wished to maintain the trappings of empire in Egypt, Jordan, and the Persian Gulf for as long as possible. His overestimation of British power and influence in the region led the United States to reassess its own Middle Eastern policy and resulted in Dulles's fact-finding mission to the region in May 1953.

While the Eisenhower administration faced no immediate threat to its interests in the Middle East in early 1953, the continued decline of British power in the region was becoming troublesome. It signified the removal of a major obstacle to Soviet penetration. A second area of concern was the growing rift between Israel and the Soviet Union. The U.S. feared that Moscow, in shifting its sympathy from Israel to the Arab states, would seek to play upon Arab resentment of American support for Israel. A third vexing problem was the escalation of the Arab-Israeli conflict. Frontier incidents were increasing as Arab attacks across the 1949 armistice lines provoked retaliatory Israeli raids. Hostility in the Arab world was fueled by public statements of Arab leaders reaffirming their refusal to accept Israel's existence and calling for its destruction. These tensions and the domestic instability they engendered in several Arab states provided the Soviet Union with ample opportunity to spread its influence into the Middle East.[52]

Before his fact-finding mission, a March 31, 1953, State Department memorandum advised Dulles that "the governments of General Naguib in Egypt and Colonel Shishikli in Syria probably cannot last more than six months after Dulles' visit, unless the United States does something affirmative in the period."[53] The memo recommended that "a definitive termination should be brought about of the war now existing between Israel and the Arab states." Further, "the problem of the Arab refugee should be solved, either by repatriation, by just compensation, or by resettlement." The memorandum urged that "the United States convince the Arab states that its policy was not designed to increase the state of Israel at the expense of its neighbors and the creation of a Middle East Defense Pact."⁵⁴

Eisenhower thought Egypt could be the key to the Middle East. The president feared that Israel had become a rallying point for Arab leaders, distracting them from pursuing a more moderate policy. American aid to Israel might allow the Jerusalem government simply to avoid facing the issue of peace. American aid to Cairo, on the other hand, could help improve Egypt's economic base and allow the Egyptians to make peace with Israel.⁵⁵ A further analysis prepared before Dulles's trip warned of the possible outbreak of open hostilities between Egypt and the United Kingdom if the British did not commit themselves to eventual withdrawal from their Suez Canal base. The new Egyptian leader, General Naguib, was "unwilling to commit his government openly for defense arrangements with the West at this time because of public opinion." But Naguib promised "on his word of honor to cooperate with the United States, as soon as better feelings exist with the British and others." "Naguib feels moving forward on arrangements with Israel [would] not be difficult once he solved his problem with the British."⁵⁶ In fact, Naguib's position in his government was slipping due to his cautious pro-Western stance. Younger officers of the revolutionary command council, such as Colonel Nasser, argued that the United States was losing its prestige in the area by its support of the British and its inability to provide aid to Egypt.

After his visit to the region in May 1953, Dulles concluded that the American position in the Middle East was weak. On May 18 Dulles cabled Eisenhower from Baghdad that "bitterness toward the West, including the United States [is] such that while Arab goodwill may still be restored, time is short before [its] loss becomes irretrievable." Any hope placed on the new American administration will soon be lost "unless our acts seem here to show a capacity to influence British and Israeli policies," which were now seen by the Arabs as entering a new phase of aggression. The Anglo-Egyptian situation was the most dangerous of all, Dulles observed, and if it remained unresolved we will "find [the] Arab world in open and united hostility to the West and in some cases receptive to Soviet aid."[57]

The State Department analysis prepared after Dulles's trip recommended that the United States "seek every possible means to allay fear in the Arab world over future Israeli objectives and to convince the Arab world that the United States is operating upon a policy of true impartiality."[58] This effort was designed to undo the damage caused by President Truman's immediate recognition of Israel in May 1948. In coping with the problem of colonialism, the report suggested that American policy reflect sympathy for the legitimate aspirations of the people in accord with the United States' own historical traditions, and further pressure the French and British to move in this direction. But the Arab states had to be "steadily reminded of the philosophy of the Kremlin, which gives clear indication that Soviet strategy plans to use extreme nationalism for its own purposes."[59]

During his journey Dulles found that despite establishing a promising relationship with Naguib, he "could not correct the deep Egyptian distrust of the British, a distrust which seemed to override any fear they might have of the Soviets."[60] At his meeting with Nasser on May 11 Dulles was told that the "Arab Mutual Security Pact was directed solely against Israel." When Dulles replied, "You are threatened by the Russians," Nasser argued that he "couldn't see the Soviets attacking the heartlands of the Middle East except in the event of a global war."[61] It was increasingly clear to Dulles that the Egyptian leadership saw a Middle East Defense Organization as a vehicle to retain Britain's position in the region; their major concerns were not the Soviet Union but the United Kingdom and Israel. Dulles realized that a regional security system could not be an immediate prospect, for any such system would have to "grow from within out of a sense of common destiny and common danger."[62]

If Dulles had reached these conclusions, he nonetheless continued to pursue the creation of an anti-Soviet alliance which totally disregarded increasing pan-Arabism and fears of Western imperialism. At the meeting of the National Security Council on June 2, 1953, Dulles reiterated his dim view of American prestige in the Middle East and the problem of ties to British and French imperialism. But in testimony before the Senate Foreign Relations Committee the next day, the secretary of state argued that aid to Egypt would not convince Cairo to become the "cornerstone of some kind of Mideast Defense Organization."[63] As an alternative, Dulles now proposed the "northern tier" option, arguing that Pakistan and Turkey could be made strong allies. Syria and Iraq could also be induced to join. Countries further south were too ignorant of the Soviet menace to offer any prospect of becoming dependable allies. In Iran, anti-Soviet sentiment must be immediately exploited "to concentrate on changing the situation there." Dulles believed a fresh start was needed, and "the only concept which would work was one which was based on the contribution of the indigenous peoples."[64]

While Dulles had altered some of his basic perceptions of the Middle East, he still refused to see the numerous conflicts within the region as functions beyond the American-Soviet struggle. In his Cold War tunnel vision, the Soviet Union was behind all problems in the region. Dulles was not oblivious to the Anglo-Egyptian and Arab-Israeli problems, but for him they were transitory, of interest only insofar as they affected American efforts to win the Cold War.

On July 9, 1953, the National Security Council adopted NSC-155/1, "The U.S. Objectives and Policies with Respect to the Near East," as the basis for Washington's new Middle East policy. This document, which reflected the findings of the Dulles mission, became the basis for American policy for the next four years.

The most important recommendations of NSC-155/1 were to "assist in finding solutions to local problems in the area which involves its relations with the United Kingdom" and to help settle "the outstanding issues in the Arab-Israeli conflict." These two problems, if they remained unresolved, were seen as openings for the Soviet Union to extend their "control and influence by means short of war." With the removal of these obstacles, the United States could develop secret plans for the defense of the area with the "United Kingdom, Turkey and such others as is desirable."[65]

The State Department's attitude toward Israel and the United Kingdom were paramount. The United States must make it clear to Israel that she would not receive preferential treatment over any Arab state and that "our goal is to show our interest in the well-being of all Arab states and Israel." The Israelis must agree to boundary concessions as well as repatriation and compensation for Palestinian Arabs, and curtail the large influx of Jews into Israel.[66]

For the moment, the attitude toward the British was spelled out as:

> ... U.S. security interest is for the U.K. to continue to assume much responsibility as is feasible under present conditions.... Although the trend is for the U.S. influence to replace British influence in the area as a whole, British ability to aid in the preservation of western security interests in the area should not be minimized.[67]

The United States would work to obtain a solution to the Suez Canal base problem which would allow "adequate arrangements ... for the effective use of the base for the defense of the area as a whole." But "we must realize that the continuation of British forces on Egyptian soil is an impossibility." NSC-155/1 concluded that unless these issues were resolved, "the Near East may well be lost to the west within the next few years."[68]

Washington immediately renewed its behind-the-scenes efforts to bring England and Egypt back to the negotiating table to resolve the Suez situation. Eisenhower administration officials hoped that once the Suez Canal base issue was settled, the Egyptian government would prove more receptive to American suggestions on other key issues.

3 *The British Withdraw from Suez*

After World War II, long-standing differences between Britain and Egypt intensified, especially the criteria for British evacuation of its military facilities in the Suez Canal Zone. These facilities consisted "of no less than ten airfields, 34 military stations, railways, roads, ports, flying boat stations, and a vast array of communication networks, including a local radio station." Another major issue was whether the Sudan should be reunited with Egypt or allowed to become an independent state. The United States sought a speedy resolution of these issues because they threatened to weaken Britain's role in Middle Eastern defense. If unresolved, these problems would further encourage Arab neutralism. The British, however, were determined to maintain their dominant position in the region, even if their negotiating policies sometimes appeared self-defeating.[1]

Until late 1951 the Truman administration had supported the British negotiations with Egypt without carefully weighing the consequences of their action. Washington encouraged Cairo to reach a settlement on British terms and rejected Egyptian calls for American mediation. When British policy proved bankrupt in the wake of the Egyptian rejection of the Middle East Command in October 1951, and Churchill's new Conservative government adopted a harsher position toward Cairo than had the previous Labor government, the United States finally began to reassess its policy.[2]

* * *

Throughout early 1950 Anglo-Egyptian talks concerning both the Sudan and the Suez Canal base remained stalled. By fall Britain coerced the Egyptians into a more cooperative attitude: the Foreign Office in September canceled Cairo's order for sixty-five jet fighters and delayed delivery of sixteen Centurion tanks which had already been paid for.[3]

On November 16 the Egyptian government responded to British intransigence. In the annual speech from the throne, Egyptian Prime Minister Nahas Pasha declared that the Anglo-Egyptian treaty of 1936 would no longer serve as the basis for Anglo-Egyptian relations. A new foundation would have to be laid, one which included the unity of Egypt and the Sudan under the Egyptian crown and the total and immediate evacuation of British forces. As Nahas spoke, violent riots erupted throughout Cairo protesting British imperialism.[4]

Throughout early 1951 the Egyptians insisted that British forces immediately evacuate the Suez Canal Zone. The British refused to withdraw until Egypt agreed to join a regional defensive alliance. On the sidelines, the United States feared that cessation of the talks would jeopardize ongoing discussions with Egypt regarding a mutual security program, and that soon the Suez Canal base would become more of a liability than an asset.

Following a bellicose speech by British Foreign Secretary Herbert Morrison in the House of Commons on July 30, 1951, Egypt broke off further talks. As pressure against domestic failures and corruption intensified in Cairo, Nahas Pasha's government found what it needed to divert public attention.[5] In a message to the Egyptian parliament on October 7, King Farouk abrogated the 1936 Anglo-Egyptian Treaty and the 1899 Condominium concerning the Sudan.[6]

Despite Egypt's action, and against the advice of their respective ambassadors, the United States and the United Kingdom decided to proceed with the formation of the Middle East Command.[7] Without consulting the Egyptian foreign minister in advance, London and Washington expected Cairo to support the MEC proposal. Instead it was immediately rejected. The pro-

posal ran counter to Egypt's basic national aspirations of independence and sovereignty. The MEC was viewed in Cairo as
merely a new version of the 1936 treaty, a new form of Western
control to replace British domination.[8]

The new Churchill government refused to recognize Egyptian
actions. A war of words ensued, and violence increased against
the British in Cairo and in the Canal Zone. The United States
recognized that its support for Britain had not prevented the
Egyptian government from rejecting the MEC or its abrogation
of the 1936 Anglo-Egyptian Treaty and the 1899 Condominium.
From this point the United States sought to chart a separate
course from its British ally.

Throughout 1952 the new Egyptian government, which had
overthrown the Farouk regime, realized it was imperative to
reach some sort of agreement with the British. In order to gain
popular support, General Naguib's government was willing to
pay a high price to secure a final British evacuation from the
Suez Canal base.[9]

The change in governments also improved prospects for spreading Egyptian influence over the Sudan as Cairo's southern
neighbor approached self-government and independence. Naguib no longer insisted on unity with Egypt for the Sudanese.
He aimed at winning over Sudanese parties to the Egyptian
viewpoint for future elections.

This change in the Egyptian position resulted in an agreement
between Britain and Egypt on February 12, 1953, on Sudanese
self-government and self-determination. The treaty provided for
self-determination and a new government in Khartoum at the
end of three years. In the interim, supreme constitutional
authority would be exercised by the British governor-general
aided by a commission of two Sudanese, one Briton, one Egyptian, and one Pakistani. An international commission of seven
would prepare and supervise elections in 1955.[10] The Sudan
settlement now created an opportunity to solve the more difficult problem of the Suez Canal base.

For the British, the Suez Canal base was of declining strategic
importance in an age of atomic warfare. In December 1952 the
British government had already moved its joint headquarters for

the Middle East from the Suez base to Cyprus. This decision flowed naturally from the development of the hydrogen bomb and the political conclusion that a vast, sprawling target such as the Suez base was a financial drain as well as a strategic liability. The new base in Cyprus was envisaged as a vital link in the NATO bomber and interceptor chain stretching from Germany through Greece to Turkey.[11] The Turks had decided to play a more active part in the defense of the Middle East after they joined NATO in September 1952.[12]

British goals in the Suez negotiations were outlined by Foreign Secretary Anthony Eden in a memo prepared for the British cabinet on February 17, 1953. Eden contemplated a general settlement with Egypt comprised of a phased withdrawal of troops and the maintenance of a military base in the Canal Zone which could immediately be put to use in the event of war. Further, the memo called for an Anglo-Egyptian organization for the air defense of Egypt, Cairo's adherence to a Middle East Defense Organization (MEDO), and an Anglo-American military-economic assistance program for Egypt. It was important, Eden stressed, for London to receive "effective assurances that the Canal Zone Base be readily available to us in a future war." In addition, "technicians and others who would run the installation [would] be members of the armed forces entitled to wear uniforms and carry personal arms." Eden stipulated that the United Kingdom would not withdraw until a "MEDO was a concrete reality."[13] The foreign secretary, having accepted the inevitability of British military withdrawal, wanted the creation of a MEDO to counter Tory opposition to the British concession.

Discussing Eden's proposals, Prime Minister Churchill reiterated the need to be sure that "we have the full sympathy and support of the United States. They [the U.S.] should realize we will not be bullied or cajoled into leaving until we have obtained a useful agreement."[14] An understanding with Washington on procedure was necessary before London would reveal its criteria for resuming negotiations with Egypt.

In moving toward an agreement, the British sought to retain their influence in Egypt and their position in the Middle East. In London's view, the greatest obstacle to an evacuation agreement on its terms was not the Egyptian desire for sovereignty and independence but American designs. Eden suspected a tacit alliance between Washington and Cairo aimed at supplanting American for British influence in the area. He could not allow that the new government in Cairo would avoid agreement with a foreign power which could in any way be seen as an abridgement of its sovereignty; any continuation of British troops on Egyptian soil would always be a reminder of Egypt's colonial past.

In general, the United States accepted the view that any settlement between the United Kingdom and Egypt would involve an agreement concerning the Suez base and an evacuation formula. Egypt would also be expected to participate in some form of MEDO. In return, a program of military and economic assistance would be made available to the Egyptians. The area of deepest concern was the Egyptian attitude toward a regional defense organization.[15]

The British position, which called for Egyptian adherence to a MEDO before evacuation, was opposed by the Naguib government. On November 11, 1952, General Naguib had proclaimed that future membership in a defense organization depended on the "effective withdrawal of British forces from Egyptian territory." Although the British acknowledged that "considerable concessions will have to be made to secure Egyptian goodwill," the State Department was deeply distressed over the course of events in Egypt.[16]

Behind this unease was the belief that Egypt was the key to the Arab states and therefore to the problem of area defense and the solution of the Arab-Israeli conflict. The emergence of General Naguib was seen as "perhaps the first real opportunity for a reasonable settlement of the problems which threaten the stability of the Near East."[17]

At the time of Eisenhower's inauguration the British had 81,000 troops in the Canal Zone, despite the 1936 treaty limiting British troops to a level of ten thousand. General Naguib "indicated that he would permit a certain number of technicians to remain in the Canal Zone to maintain the installations if the bulk of British forces were withdrawn and other conditions met."[18] But British insistence that Egypt agree to participate in

a MEDO before evacuation became a major obstacle in negotiations.

American aid to Egypt now became a source of friction
between the United States and the United Kingdom. Washington had planned to offer Egypt a small military aid program, but
not until an agreement in principle was reached between Cairo
and London.[19] The British objected to the timing of any aid
package to Egypt. They wished to maintain a "phased release of
arms" to Cairo "as an effective bargaining weapon in extracting
from Egypt some sort of package deal on evacuation and Egyptian participation in a MEDO." Jefferson Caffery, the American
ambassador to Egypt, warned that Washington's approach was
self-defeating and that if it were pursued there was danger of an
"open Anglo-Egyptian blowout."[20]

In January 1953 Henry Byroade, assistant secretary of state for
Near Eastern, South Asian, and African affairs, was sent to
London to try to work out Anglo-American differences over the
Suez negotiations. The British position was broken down into
three cases, called A, B, and C. Case A called for the Canal
Zone to be handed over to Egypt and the base area placed under
Egyptian control. The depots and installations would act as a
working maintenance base for a portion of the Middle East land
forces in peace. "The Army would retain not more than 5,000
personnel to run these installations and the R.A.F. not more
than 2,000 for the same purposes." The rationale being, "The
allies would be assured of having a working maintenance base in
peace to which they could return and operate immediately in
war."

The lesser position, from the British view, was Case B. It
would allow the base to remain in Egypt and be placed under
Egyptian control. The Egyptians "would take over such depots
and installations [and assume] full responsibility for keeping all
communications, &c. . . . .and maintaining Allied war reserves
and heavy workshops in a state to be reactivated at short notice."
To assist the Egyptians in this task, "a rather smaller number
than under Case A of allied supervisory and technical . . . personnel would be required." The implication was that during
peacetime it would take sixty days to reactivate the base.

The ultimate fallback position was Case C. The base would remain under Egyptian control, and Cairo would assume the same responsibilities as in Case B. Britain would retain the right of periodic inspections of reserves and installations. The military personnel who would carry out these inspections would be based in Egypt, but if Cairo was adamant on this point, civilians stationed outside Egypt could be used. In these circumstances, the British estimated that "it would take at least 90 days to reactivate the base."[21]

Byroade's meetings with Foreign Office officials during the first week of January 1953 highlighted the basic differences between the American and British approaches. Byroade stressed that the Egyptians "should be made to feel equal to us," particularly in regard to the use of foreign technicians and supervisors. The British felt they must take total responsibility for the air defense of the base. Byroade expressed general agreement with most of the British points but doubted whether Case A could be achieved. And he was against establishing a regional defense organization as part of a "package" deal including evacuation and military and economic assistance. Byroade argued that evacuation at best could elicit Egyptian agreement in principle on common defense planning.

The British were concerned that American military aid would damage London's bargaining position, have a negative effect in Parliament, and cause difficulties with Israel.[22] Foreign Secretary Eden argued that the United States should concentrate on economic aid and leave military aid to the British. In this way, the United Kingdom could use military aid as leverage in its negotiations with Cairo.[23]

The United States was against providing London with veto power over any type of aid to Egypt. The State Department was "convinced that an immediate interim response to General Naguib's request for aid was essential to reduce Egyptian military opposition to Naguib and set the stage for negotiations over the Suez Canal base. The United States hoped to provide Egypt $10 million in arms and equipment, reassuring the British that the equipment would not be conducive to guerrilla attacks against British forces in the Canal Zone. The United

States would also encourage Cairo to pursue its "habitual arms sources," namely the British.[24] Although Washington was sensitive to Foreign Office concerns, Byroade rejected the idea that the United States be excluded from supplying weapons to Egypt.[25]

On January 14, 1953, Eden, trying to create the illusion of American support, falsely reported to the British cabinet that Washington agreed that Case A should form the basis of negotiations. The foreign secretary stated that the United Kingdom would not agree to troop withdrawals "until the Egyptians have indicated their willingness to cooperate in a regional defense organization." Also, the United States should withhold weapons from Egypt until they "have shown themselves ready to cooperate in the MEDO."[26] Here Eden completely misjudged the American position. After encouraging Naguib on military aid, Washington felt that if it were to withdraw its proposals, the Egyptian government would lose whatever faith it had in the United States. The State Department feared that if it allowed the British veto power over aid, there would never be a MEDO, that the Egyptians ultimately would expel the British from the Canal Zone and incite a revolt in the Sudan.[27]

On January 23, 1953, Dulles, newly sworn in as secretary of state, informed the American embassies in London and Cairo that it would be unwise to link the interim aid program for Egypt with Middle East area defense negotiations. Therefore the United States would proceed with the development of an aid program.[28] Despite further British objections, on February 19 the State Department informed the Egyptian government that it qualified to receive military aid specifically limited to training.

Upon the Eisenhower administration's taking office, Churchill had written a series of letters to the new president calling for a clarification of the American role in the Anglo-Egyptian talks. Eisenhower and Dulles now informed the British that they supported the Truman administration's position that the United States not take part in direct talks between the British and the Egyptians. Washington would become involved once negotiations began concerning a defense structure for the region and possible military and economic aid for Egypt.[29] Churchill at once dispatched Eden to meet with Eisenhower and Dulles to smooth over their disagreements.

Eden arrived in Washington during the first week in March. His goal was to overcome what he felt was "an American policy [which] seemed to be conditioned by a belief that Egypt was still a victim of British colonialism and as such deserving of American sympathy."[30] Eden hoped to convince the United States to participate in negotiations with Egypt because an American presence would induce the Egyptians to accept a package deal which combined evacuation, aid, and a regional defense organization.

On March 6 Eden indicated that the British cabinet would not go beyond Case A except for minor modifications. His government would rather remain in the Canal Zone than relinquish treaty rights in exchange for an arrangement which provided no base or an inoperative base in time of war.[31] Dulles urged greater flexibility, arguing that Egypt would certainly reject Case A. He suggested that Case B be substituted.[32] Dulles made it clear that American participation in the negotiating process was contingent upon Egyptian invitation.

Despite Dulles's negative attitude on the point, Eden insisted that the MEDO be included in a package deal with Egypt. Rather than rejecting it outright, Dulles politely pointed out that the new administration required additional time to study the regional defense proposal.[33]

Eisenhower agreed to send Lieutenant General R. A. Hull to Cairo to assist British negotiators and to support the introduction of Case A. Eden departed for London, realizing that his visit had been less than successful. He had been unable to win American approval for his MEDO, for control of aid to Egypt, and for Washington's participation in the negotiations without Egyptian approval.

Yet upon his return to London, Eden deluded himself: he informed his colleagues that he had reached full agreement in Washington on the Egyptian negotiations. In his memoirs Eden later confessed, "We were not prepared to discuss our exodus in isolation. There was, in consequence, no basis on which to begin negotiations." He complained

... it was unfortunate that the United States government was not prepared to put any pressure upon the Egyptians to bring about their participation. ... The Egyptians were left to act as they wished and they preferred to divide both the discussions and the allies.[34]

The fundamental difference in approach was the American view that the United States and United Kingdom must avoid any "charge of forming bilateral combinations" in order to pressure the Egyptians. This is exactly what Eden hoped to achieve with American compliance.

London failed to recognize that Gamal Nasser, who was emerging as the real power in the Egyptian government, and the revolutionary command council were more interested in defending themselves from the British than in protecting their country from the Soviet Union. Nasser wanted no part of a MEDO, nor did he care whether or not the British had bases in the Middle East. Nasser needed American military aid. After the 1948 defeat by Israel, Nasser aimed to restore pride in the Egyptian army and use it as the mainstay of his internal security system. If his army was to have any military mission at all, it would be used against Israel or uncooperative Arab countries, not against the Soviet Union or any European power.[35]

According to Miles Copeland, a CIA operative with close ties to Nasser, the British and the Americans were under no illusions about the Egyptian leader's attitude which was "spelled out in detail in contemporary national intelligence estimates."[36] But the British, and to a lesser extent the Americans, ignored this estimate in a doomed attempt to proceed with negotiations. Their fears of Soviet penetration of the region were paramount; information which cast doubt on policies of containment was disregarded.

The failure of Eden's visit increased Churchill's frustration with Washington. Responding to Churchill's letter of March 18 which rebuked the United States for its lack of support, Eisenhower claimed to be puzzled by Churchill's attitude.[37] The president wrote the prime minister that the United States did not disagree with British plans for the Canal Zone. Rather, Washington was concerned with "the appearance of ganging up on the Egyptians."[38] Dulles told Eisenhower that Churchill "seems to think we are trying to run out on him whereas the facts are just the contrary." Eisenhower and Dulles were annoyed that Churchill's letter seemed, by innuendo, to suggest that United States failure to help the British in the Middle East would bring a loss of British support in Korea.[39]

After more than two months of persuasion by Jefferson Caffery, the Egyptian government moderated its position. Nasser informed the American ambassador that if the British agreed to withdraw, Egypt was prepared to discuss arrangements for maintaining the Suez base and guaranteeing its availability to the West in the event of future hostilities.[40]

On April 12 Nasser announced that Cairo was willing to discuss how the efficiency of the base might be preserved after evacuation. He acknowledged that the base was a complex one and that British technicians would be needed. But while he refused to have his country linked to NATO, he did not refuse to cooperate with "friends" once the evacuation was completed. Nasser also indicated that Egypt would maintain the base in readiness for war, but he rejected the idea that Egypt's ties to a Western defense organization should be a condition for withdrawal.[41]

Despite this "slight" softening in the Egyptian position, the British approach remained constant. Churchill agreed to renew the talks but instructed his negotiators to proceed on the basis that "it was the Egyptians who desired to resume negotiations" and that discussions should be based on Case A.[42] Despite these differences, negotiations were renewed on April 26—and soon collapsed as both sides hardened their positions.

The Egyptians may have known that the Dulles fact-finding mission to the Middle East was imminent and may have hoped they could convince the United States to apply greater pressure on the British. But Dulles soon made it clear that the United States was not prepared to support Egypt completely. The secretary of state suggested that the Suez base should remain in good working order and be available for immediate use in the event of future hostilities.[43]

On May 12 Dulles met with Naguib and presented him with a

pair of plated .38 caliber pistols from President Eisenhower. The negative symbolism of a gift of pistols created a stir in both Tel Aviv and London. Naguib promptly expressed the historical distrust which the Arabs felt toward the British and suggested that a defense arrangement would be possible only when Arab suspicions were allayed. Naguib would accept British technicians only until Egyptians were trained to replace them. After these issues were resolved, the Arab-Israeli problem and a MEDO could be considered.[44]

Dulles responded that the United States had not sent him to arbitrate the Anglo-Egyptian stalemate. The secretary lost no time stressing the danger that communism presented for the Middle East. He conceded that Washington had paid too much attention to Israel in the past and now wished to approach the Middle East evenhandedly, favoring neither Arab nor Israeli. For Washington the outcome of the Anglo-Egyptian talks was of deep concern: a change in the status of the Suez Canal base must not create a power vacuum, and the base must be instantly available at a high level of efficiency in the event of war.[45]

Naguib and Egyptian Foreign Minister Mohammad Fawzi assured Dulles that they too believed in instant availability. They were confident that Egyptians could be trained to maintain the base adequately. Dulles departed Cairo aware of "complete distrust and ill will" between London and Cairo; he saw no "easy way to break the present deadlock without the loss of face for one side or the other."[46]

After Dulles's departure the situation in Cairo worsened as Naguib announced the breakdown in negotiations in an inflammatory speech. The Naguib government was clearly under great pressure from extremists and those who were waiting for land reform at a time when world cotton prices were declining. With the danger of guerrilla warfare in Egypt growing stronger each day, the United States was in a quandary as to how to proceed. The British, meanwhile, blamed Washington for failing to join in negotiations. London believed that had the United States allied with them, the Egyptians would have been compelled to accept British terms.

Dulles was fully aware that the British "package proposals" were unobtainable. It was obvious that Egypt would accept only a little more than Case C. In Dulles's view, the best possibility was a written commitment from the Egyptian government that when the evacuation of British troops was accomplished, Cairo would negotiate and conclude a regional defense agreement with the United States and United Kingdom. An agreement would solve three problems. It would provide the new Egyptian government with a political victory; Cairo would receive American economic and military aid; and the issue of a regional defense organization would be indefinitely deferred.[47]

Dulles's approach again ignored the one issue which Egypt cared about most, its national sovereignty. For Cairo the British were the main enemy; the Soviet threat was remote. While the State Department believed that London would support Dulles's proposals, it overlooked Egyptian pride, which would remain a major stumbling block.[48]

Dulles returned to Washington and reported to the National Security Council on June 2 that Naguib "was a front," that the revolutionary command council, under Nasser's influence, was the real power in Egypt. Even if the administration solved Anglo-Egyptian difficulties, he said, the larger problem of political and economic stability in Egypt would remain for years to come. Dulles now believed that "we must abandon our preconceived ideas of making Egypt the key country in building the foundations for a military defense of the Middle East.[49]

Yet by mid-June the situation in Egypt seemed to be improving. The Egyptians knew that in early July the United States and the British planned talks in Bermuda. To gain American support, the Egyptian government therefore agreed on June 11 to tone down its criticism of London and to stipulate that the Canal Zone would be available to "Egypt's allies and the allies of Egypt's allies in case of a land attack on the frontiers of any Arab nation." In return, Cairo expected a public announcement that the United States and United Kingdom would begin economic and military talks with Egypt.[50] There now appeared to be a basis for agreement between Washington and Cairo, but this informal understanding was unknown to the British.

On the eve of Anglo-American talks in Bermuda, the British position had not changed. Churchill told Winthrop Aldrich, the American ambassador to London, that he still hoped to reach a settlement based on Case A.[51] But as the Bermuda meetings approached, the American position was closer to Egypt's than to its ally's. Eisenhower believed that Naguib's flexibility was greatly hindered by "local circumstances of which the most important [was] Egyptian nationalism." Churchill clung to the belief that it was the duty of the United States to support its Western ally, and that if it did, Egypt would succumb to British demands.[52]

Meeting with Lord Salisbury, Britain's acting secretary of state for foreign affairs, at Bermuda on July 12, Dulles discovered that Britain's position had not changed. Salisbury argued that the essential features of Case A must be maintained, and was adamant that the base must remain under British control. In addition, Turkey and Iran were to be part of a list of countries which, if attacked, would trigger reactivation of the base.[53] Many British cabinet members, sensitive to the lack of American support which they believed the British government deserved, complained they "were being manoeuvered into a position whereby the United States would act as an intermediary between themselves and the Egyptians."[54] Should that take place, Washington might even side with the Egyptians!

The Bermuda talks ended inconclusively. The major sticking points were whether British technicians at Suez could remain in uniform following evacuation, the conditions for availability of the Suez base, and the duration of the agreement.

After Bermuda, the British showed a greater willingness to return to the negotiating table with Egypt. They were bolstered by an impending treaty with Libya which would permit London to maintain its military establishment there for twenty years.[55] But the British nonetheless refused to reconsider any major points. London offered Egypt a ten-year arrangement for the Suez base with a phased withdrawal of technicians over the period; but on other critical issues such as uniforms, the right to carry personal weapons, and availability of the base should Turkey or Iran be attacked, the British remained adamant.[56]

The Egyptian position regarding Turkey was that the Turks

were not Arabs. Nasser believed that availability of the base should not involve nations other than those in the Arab League Collective Security Pact, of which neither Turkey nor Iran were members. Cairo altered its views about duration, proposing five years, with the technicians allowed to remain for three, and possibly for the last two in "the way of disguise or inspectors."[57]

Despite Egyptian responses, the British pushed for a seven-and-a-half-year term and insisted on the provisions for Turkey and Iran.[58] The Foreign Office refused to believe that the Egyptian offer was close "to being the maximum politically feasible." Dulles informed the British ambassador, Roger Makins, that from an American standpoint "the poker game" was just about played out. The Egyptians had gone as far as possible on duration, and from a military viewpoint the "present Egyptian position was satisfactory."[59]

On September 24 the Egyptians walked out of their meeting with British negotiators without setting a date for another session. Nasser was most upset over British insistence on seven years' duration after he had raised his offer to six and a half years and agreed to military uniforms for technicians rather than civilian clothing. The British also raised a new point of controversy: they wished to include a reference to freedom of transit through the Suez Canal in the preamble to any agreement. Pressure from Conservative members of Parliament was responsible for British recalcitrance because many believed that London was giving in to American demands.[60] British intelligence advised London that the Egyptian government would not last much longer, therefore the longer negotiations were stretched out, the better. On October 2 the British government decided "to make no further attempts to compromise with the Egyptians."[61]

The internal political situation in Cairo was directly responsible for British intransigence; a power struggle had developed within the revolutionary command council. Even before Nasser had become vice premier in June 1953, he had intervened in administrative affairs and dealt with ministers over Prime Minister Naguib's head. Suspecting that Naguib and his civilian ministers were actively working to frustrate the purposes of the revolution, Nasser believed that he and the council alone could initiate the social and economic reforms needed so desperately by the Egyptian people.[62]

Unable to share the radical fervor of his younger colleagues, Naguib felt most at ease with the ultra-conservative Wafdists and the Muslim Brotherhood. Naguib sometimes told his council associates that there was no great urgency in getting the British to withdraw their troops. Such talk was, of course, anathema to the revolutionary command council. As the months passed, Nasser and his allies overruled Naguib with increasing frequency. Naguib sought to marshal the government, where the majority supported him against the council.[63] This apparent upheaval within the Egyptian government, and British intransigence, led the State Department to believe that the Egyptians had gone far enough to meet British demands. If negotiations failed, the blame would now fall on London.[64]

Throughout the remainder of 1953, domestic politics in Egypt and Britain greatly affected negotiations. In the United Kingdom a large section of the Conservative party was opposed to the evacuation of Suez. It would weaken the defense link with the Commonwealth countries and constitute a blow to British prestige and, consequently, British power in the world. Ambassador Aldrich alerted Washington that the British government might fall over this issue. To avert a political disaster, the British government believed that any agreement must make the Suez base available "in circumstances more consistent with western defense requirements than merely attacks on members of the Arab League Collective Security Pact."[65] Therefore the Churchill government saw itself on politically tenuous grounds over the entire negotiation issue.

In Egypt the power struggle between Nasser and Naguib erupted on February 25, 1954, when the Egyptian prime minister submitted a letter of resignation. The next day Nasser was proclaimed chairman of the revolutionary command council and prime minister, and Naguib was placed under house arrest. A state of emergency was declared throughout Egypt.[66]

In early March the council announced new elections for July 23. Nasser soon organized a sit-down strike by the army against

Naguib and a strike by transport workers which paralyzed Cairo. This action was designed to crush whatever support for Naguib remained in the Egyptian military. By March 28 it was clear that Naguib was defeated and that Nasser held complete power. Yet while he no longer depended on majorities in the revolutionary command council, Nasser realized that most Egyptians did not support him.[67] Thus negotiations over the Suez Canal base were of paramount importance in consolidating his rule.

Domestic considerations also influenced the Eisenhower administration's position toward Anglo-Egyptian negotiations. The president viewed a settlement of the base issue as a first step toward a lessening of tensions between Israel and the Arab states. If Egypt's nationalistic sensitivities concerning the Suez base could be satisfied, Cairo might support a peace initiative designed to solve some of the outstanding issues between Israel and her neighbors. If peace could be attained in the region, the Jewish lobby in Washington would no longer oppose America's supplying weapons to the Arabs as part of a larger policy of denying the area to the Soviet Union.

Aside from disagreement over the Suez base negotiations with Egypt, the issue of aid to Cairo remained a major stumbling block between the two Atlantic allies. Based on their concessions at the bargaining table, the Egyptians believed they were entitled to American aid. Complicating the situation was a recent release of $26 million in American aid to Israel. Henry Byroade proposed an aid package of $20 million to $27.5 million for Egypt, the military portion to be withheld until the Suez base negotiations were completed.[68] Eden denounced this proposal as "deplorable" and argued that it would provide the Egyptians with evidence of a "major divergence of British and American policies," warning that "it would remove an important inducement [for Cairo] to reach an agreement with us.[69] The British foreign secretary was also concerned about how the Iraqi government, an important ally of London's in the region, would react to further Western aid to Cairo. The Baghdad regime saw itself as the leading spokesman for pan-Arabism in the region and greatly distrusted the new Egyptian government.

When the issue was raised at the Bermuda conference between the U.S. and the U.K. in December 1953, Dulles had assured Churchill and Eden that Washington would withold economic aid from Egypt until the new year.[70] Upon returning from Bermuda, Churchill received a letter from Eisenhower which sympathized with his political problems but stated that since allocations to Israel were part of a congressionally approved Middle East aid program, "we have little excuse avoiding aid to an Arab country." Eisenhower added that in regard to "Egypt, [we] have gone to great lengths to meet your convictions and opinions. We certainly want to continue to do so. We think we proved it in Persia [Iran]."[71] At a time when Eisenhower was becoming increasingly frustrated with the British, he was sending the wrong message. It reassured Eden that no matter how London behaved, the United States would eventually support her. This belief was reinforced by the 1953 CIA-supported coup in Iran, and it shaped Eden's strategy during the continuing struggle with Egypt.

As 1954 began the British looked more positively toward a settlement with Egypt. In a paper prepared for the cabinet, dated January 7, Eden argued that a successful treaty would have a marked influence on British relations with other Arab countries. London needed to secure the eastern flank of NATO, shield oil interests, protect the use of the Suez Canal, and in general assist in "ensuring the stability of the area." Eden was freshly motivated by a number of factors. First, the chancellor of the exchequer had called for a 10-million-pound reduction in defense spending for 1955–1956. Eden could either reduce the British contribution to NATO or cut back on Middle East expenditures. The latter was seen as the less dangerous option. Second, should the British decide to remain in the Canal Zone, force would be necessary to cope with increasing Egyptian hostility. Third, if an agreement were not reached, London would lose support in the United Nations and weaken the regional balance of power. Fourth, it was obvious that the United States would not provide the support in the negotiating process that London felt it deserved. Taking all this into account, Eden recommended that the United Kingdom try to reach a settlement based on "present terms."[72]

Eden's position was strengthened in the British cabinet by a January 9 defense memo, prepared by the chiefs of staff, which recommended approval of the foreign secretary's views.[73] The full cabinet met on January 12 and endorsed Eden's plan.[74] While it now appeared that the British were more willing to negotiate, in fact they only agreed to settle with the Egyptians based on their October 21, 1953, proposals—which were unsatisfactory to Cairo. The British concurrently were talking with Turkey about joint defense of the area. London's willingness to reopen talks with Cairo was in part predicated upon a hope that Turko-Pakistani talks for a mutual defense pact would be successful. Thereafter, Iraq and Britain could join to create a "northern tier" defense to replace the Suez Canal base. Once these ideas were communicated to Washington, Eden hoped the Americans "would bring strong pressure on Cairo to persuade them to accept the terms."[75]

The British proposals that arrived in Washington in mid-January were essentially a restatement of previous positions. When shown the British proposals on January 24, Nasser was not enthusiastic, but he did agree to recommend to the revolutionary command council that the availability formula be extended to Turkey in the event of an attack. But he continued to reject the formula pertaining to uniforms and personal weapons.[76]

By early March Nasser agreed to the "automatic reactivation of the base in the event of an attack on Turkey . . . if Her Majesty's Government will make a concession on the question of uniforms."[77] Nasser's new reasonableness in part reflected the domestic political struggle being waged with Naguib. Nasser wanted a quick agreement, undercutting Naguib's chances of presenting himself to the Egyptian people as the "one member of the RCC who wished to adopt a firm attitude toward the British."[78]

Instead of accepting Nasser's offer, the British now raised the ante. Eden was willing to concede on the uniform issue, but, due to domestic political pressure, he raised the duration from seven years to twenty. In addition, London sought new assurances for the Sudan where unrest against the British was growing. In return the Foreign Office was willing to withdraw its own technicians and use civilian contract labor to maintain the base.[79]

The political situation in Egypt soon altered Cairo's negotiating strategy. At the end of March the revolutionary command council announced it would transfer power to an elected constituent assembly on July 24, and considered the revolution ended. The newly elected assembly would elect a president for the republic. This decision helped to obscure the appearance of an internal crisis. Nasser apparently allowed the political situation to deteriorate in order to inspire a counterreaction in the armed forces. He was then able to point to an impressive demonstration of army solidarity, seemingly without having sought it. On April 17, following Naguib's resignation, Nasser assumed the prime minister's office. Despite the reorganization of the Egyptian government, Washington realized that achievement of its Middle Eastern goals depended upon convincing the British to soften their negotiating stance toward Cairo.[80]

Washington again pointed out to London that Nasser's position was sufficiently secure to sign an agreement. The State Department recommended that the British propose an agreement of ten years' duration with complete withdrawal of British forces within twenty-four months. Availability would include attacks on Egypt, any member of the Arab Collective Security Pact, or Turkey. After British withdrawal the Egyptian government would be responsible for the base: a "civilian entity acceptable to both sides would maintain the base under Egyptian authority."[81] In mid-June Dulles voiced concern over the British delay in accepting and executing the American proposals which they approved.[82]

In London the cabinet was slowly coming around to the American viewpoint. More and more the British realized that redeployment of their troops was necessary and that commitments elsewhere made a "rapid and large reduction in the Canal Zone essential." They accepted the fact that "the Egyptian government [had] its house in order and were anxious to reach an agreement." If they waited too long to reopen talks, the Egyptian government might not be able to prevent a deterioration in the situation in the Canal Zone which would make a resumption of negotiations impossible.[83]

The major stumbling block was now Churchill's insistence that the United States be involved in a final settlement. Eden was against overt American involvement in the negotiating process. The foreign secretary had little faith in the American secretary of state and was especially annoyed by Dulles's insistence that American aid must be provided to Egypt by June 30. As always, Eden believed that American aid to Egypt would lessen Cairo's willingness to compromise. He favored a strong American endorsement of British proposals, a link between a new defense agreement and American aid to Cairo, and a clause in the agreement assuring freedom of navigation in the canal.[84] On June 22 the British cabinet approved Eden's strategy.

At the end of June Eden and Churchill arrived in Washington for discussions with Eisenhower and Dulles. The president and his secretary of state were skeptical of the British; Dulles was sure they would try to convince the United States that their colonialism was different from that of the French. Eisenhower agreed, remarking, "Sure, the British always think their colonialism is different and better. Actually what they want us to do is go along and help them keep their empire."[85] The Atlantic allies met at the White House on June 26 and endorsed two separate agreements, with no legal connection between the two—a Suez Canal Base Agreement and a United States Aid Agreement. The British agreed to make new proposals to Cairo in the "immediate future."[86]

On July 7 Eden related his Washington talks to the British cabinet and observed that "the United States government had come to meet our requirements as we could reasonably expect." Eden falsely stated that "United States aid was dependent on [a Suez base] agreement," when in fact the two were not linked. Churchill finally voiced his approval, stating that "withdrawal can [now] be justified on military grounds," and the cabinet authorized a resumption of negotiations.[87]

On July 11 British Ambassador Ralph Stevenson met with Nasser, and the Egyptian prime minister remarked that "with amendments" the drafts "might be a basis for agreement."

Nasser did insist on a seven-year duration and a fifteen-month evacuation period, which he correctly argued had been previously agreed.[88] Two days later he accepted the British proposals save for these two points.[89] On July 27 the British, under American pressure, finally accepted a seven-year duration, and Cairo agreed to a twenty-month evacuation. Later that day British and Egyptian negotiators initialed an agreement.[90]

From August until the final signing of the treaty on October 19, 1954, a number of major points in the agreement demanded clarification. Nasser was under considerable pressure from the Muslim Brotherhood, which openly opposed the agreement. Clashes between the Brethren and government forces were commonplace throughout September and October. With pressure on his government rising, it appeared to the British that Nasser was dragging his feet in reaching a final settlement. Anthony Nutting, an under secretary of state, was dispatched by the Foreign Office on September 28 to conclude the negotiations.[91]

On October 5 Nutting informed Eden that great progress had been made and that all outstanding issues had been settled.[92] On October 19, 1954, a final treaty was signed.

Dulles immediately issued a statement supporting the agreement.[93] Washington was relieved that the tortuous negotiations were finally completed. British distrust of American goals in the region had been exacerbated, but Washington's relationship with Cairo was intact, and this was vital for the next step in the larger American plan for the Middle East—the reduction of tensions between Israel and the Arab states. Israeli reaction to the Anglo-Egyptian treaty, however, now created a major roadblock for American policy.

Throughout the long negotiating process for the Suez Canal base treaty, the Americans and the British believed it unwise to mix the intractable Arab-Israeli conflict with the already complex base evacuation issue. Both agreed that Israeli concerns would be addressed after the conclusion of an agreement.

To placate the Israelis during the negotiating process, the Atlantic allies reassured Tel Aviv that its security would not be jeopardized by the British evacuation from Suez. For the Foreign Office, Israel's interests were peripheral. Its main goal was to gain Arab adherence to a British controlled MEDO, not to worry about Israeli insecurities. The British did try to convince the Israelis that greater confidence between the Arab states and the West would facilitate solutions of other major problems in the area. Further, they told the Israelis that the agreement contained a clause in which both parties agreed to respect the Suez Canal Convention of 1888 in relation to free passage through the canal. Concerning items in the base which were to be turned over to the Egyptians on July 12, 1954, Selwyn Lloyd, British under secretary of state, informed the Israeli government that there was no thought of handing over large quantities of armaments.[94] Despite their pretensions to the contrary, the British were fully aware that the Suez base agreement altered the regional balance of power and that Israel had legitimate reasons for concern.

If the Americans supported British attempts to calm Israeli fears, Henry Byroade's remarks to a Jewish audience in Philadelphia on May 1 only increased Israeli anxiety. Byroade stressed the need for Israel to abandon the

> attitude of the conqueror and the conviction that force and a policy of retaliatory killings is the only policy your neighbors will understand. . . . It is, for instance, a concern to us that Israel is prone to see dangers to herself in such a process and to exaggerate far beyond what seems to us to be the realities of the situation. . . . Israel should see her future in the context of a Middle Eastern state and not as headquarters of a world-wide grouping of peoples of a particular religious faith who must have special rights within and obligations to the Jewish state.[95]

The Israeli government protested Byroade's remarks, which also suggested that Tel Aviv change its open-door immigration policy to Jews from anywhere in the world. Not only did Byroade question the philosophy upon which the Israeli state was founded, his characterization of Israel as "a conqueror" was an insult to Tel Aviv. This speech, the developing arms programs to Iraq and Egypt, and the deteriorating border situation reinforced Israeli fears that the State Department was shifting from an evenhanded attitude toward the Arab-Israeli conflict, to one which was pro-Arab.[96]

The approaching British evacuation of Suez deepened Israel's sense of insecurity and isolation. Israel viewed the transfer of the base to the Egyptians as the first of many Western accretions to the Egyptian military, which was perceived as a greater threat than infiltration of Israeli borders from Jordan. The crux of the concern for Israel was British evacuation, leaving communication lines for Egypt unencumbered and making it easier for Egyptian troops to mass on the Israeli border. There would no longer be a Tripartite army close enough to alter an Egyptian attack. In addition, there would be a massive transfer of weaponry from Britain to Egypt, including 70,000 tons of equipment, 14,000 vehicles, an infrastructure for 81,000 soldiers, ten airfields, and three radar stations.[97]

In the agreement itself were three clauses that caused the Israelis further consternation. First, Israel was omitted from any contingency plans regarding base availability should a war result in an attack on its territory. Second, the agreement recognized the Arab Collective Security Pact, which Israeli Prime Minister Moshe Sharett characterized as "an instrument of waging war against Israel." Finally, there was nothing in the agreement to enforce Israel's right of navigation in the Suez Canal as specified in a 1951 UN resolution.[98]

A cabinet meeting in Tel Aviv on July 15 discussed Egypt's noncompliance with the UN resolution and the fact that the "Heads of Agreement" (the preliminary Anglo-Egyptian accord for the Suez base) did little to ameliorate the situation. The cabinet decided to challenge the Egyptians by sending an Israeli vessel, the *Bat Galim*, into the canal. By this action Israel hoped to embarrass the Egyptians and provoke a situation which would prevent or delay British withdrawal from Suez. The ship, with a crew of ten and a cargo of meat, wood, and hides, set sail from Massawa to Haifa during the first week of September. On September 28 the *Bat Galim* entered Port Tawfiq at the southern entrance to the canal. After proceeding for an hour, the ship was stopped by an Egyptian patrol boat. The crew was arrested, the boat and cargo were confiscated.[99]

The British were embarrassed as the seizure coincided with Anthony Nutting's arrival in Egypt for the final drafting of an agreement. London and Washington were furious, believing the Israelis aimed at thwarting the final Anglo-Egyptian treaty.

Israeli anxiety over the removal of the Suez Canal base increased as the signing of the treaty appeared imminent. In another attempt to embarrass the Egyptian government and delay British withdrawal, Israeli intelligence implemented a series of sabotage acts directed against Western embassies and other institutions in Cairo such as libraries, cultural centers, and consulates. The Israelis hoped that the British would blame these acts either on the Egyptian government itself or on the fanatically nationalist Muslim Brotherhood. In either case, the attacks would demonstrate that Nasser's regime was weak, incapable of maintaining order, and not to be relied upon to keep the agreements it signed. The British government would be obliged to reconsider the evacuation plan or even cancel it. But this elaborate plan failed and resulted in the capture of Israeli agents by Egyptian police. Ten Israelis were tried in Cairo in December 1954; two were acquitted, six were sentenced to long prison terms, and two were executed.[100]

With the signing of the Anglo-Egyptian treaty, Egyptian hopes for American assistance increased. In August 1954 Nasser suggested a basis for American-Egyptian cooperation in an interview with *U.S. News and World Report*. "He favored an independent Arab bloc that would receive Western arms alongside a separate Northern Tier pact without any Arab members."[101] At this point Washington set aside $20 million in economic aid, a figure substantially lower than the $100 million Nasser had requested. Although it would be difficult to provide weapons for Egypt and none for Israel, Dulles agreed to try. He decided that aid could be used as an inducement to achieve an Egyptian-Israeli agreement in the same way that the Anglo-Egyptian settlement had been reached. Because Nasser refused to accept an American Military Assistance Advisory Group (MAAG) which was to accompany any American arms shipment, as stipulated in the Mutual Security Act of 1954, Dulles's ploy failed. Nasser rejected any compromise on this issue because of potential domestic opposition and as an affirmation of Egyptian sovereignty.[102]

This should have been a clear warning to Dulles that Nasser would not tolerate any regional pact designed to further American interests. Instead, Dulles appointed Henry Byroade, a former army general and State Department officer, as American ambassador to Cairo. Since Byroade was a military man and about the same age as the Egyptian leader, Dulles hoped the two would get along well and that Nasser would be more amenable to American goals. But Cairo's refusal to accept MAAG and Dulles's continued hopes of mediating the Arab-Israeli conflict led him to decide by the end of December 1954 not to sell weapons to Egypt.[103] He could not tolerate Nasser's neutralist position in the Cold War. Although Dulles's policy was designed to pressure the Egyptian leader, it created an opening for the sale of Soviet weapons.

Meanwhile, Dulles was having problems reaching agreement with the Israelis on how to break the impasse in Tel Aviv's conflict with the Arabs. After two meetings with Abba Eban, the Israeli ambassador to the United States, Dulles wrote a memo to Byroade dated August 9, 1954, in which he expressed increasing sensitivity toward Israeli security.[104] To try to alleviate Israeli anxiety, Dulles asked Byroade to consider supporting an administration request for increased military aid for the Israelis in the 1955 appropriations legislation about to go before Congress. Throughout 1953 and 1954 American initiatives in the Middle East had been confined to the reduction of border strife through the promotion of an agreement for the development and distribution of the Jordan River.[105] Dulles now appeared to recognize that Israeli insecurity would have to be further as-suaged if successful negotiations were to be possible.

According to Nadav Safran, as 1954 drew to a close the root of the problem between Israel and the United States lay in their differing assessments of Arab attitudes and the possibility of modifying them. Dulles believed that American military and economic cooperation would restrain the Arabs and perhaps induce them to come to terms with Israel. Meanwhile, it was in Israel's best interest not to interfere, not to press the United

States to identify openly with Israel, and not to protest every American gesture toward the Arabs.

The Israelis, however, believed that the Arabs cooperated with other powers to acquire weapons and strengthen themselves for an eventual showdown with Israel. They did not share Dulles's confidence in his ability to influence the Arabs decisively toward peace. Tel Aviv was convinced that the Arabs would interpret American efforts to court them as an abandonment of Israel and would therefore encourage their intransigence. For these reasons the Israelis would take action against the Arabs when they saw an opportunity to do so, resorting to violence if necessary.[106]

As 1954 drew to a close, British policy in the Middle East faced numerous obstacles. Clearly, the British position in the region was weakened with the signing of the treaty with Egypt. Redeploying military forces to Cyprus was proving an entirely unsatisfactory substitute in the absence of funds to create adequate naval facilities. In addition, Foreign Secretary Eden faced pressure from Conservative ranks where hostility to his "scuttle" at Suez was so intense that it constituted a major threat to the government's survival should the Egyptian gamble fail. To avoid this possibility, Eden decided to proceed as rapidly as possible to conclude negotiations—by this point well under way—for a British-dominated defense pact for the area.[107] Egypt was already opposed to involving any Arab state in this project, but it was the American attitude that presented enormous difficulties.

The Eisenhower administration was increasingly preoccupied with the communist threat in Europe and the Far East. This fact, along with Dulles's inability to achieve any common ground with either the Egyptian or Israeli governments, reduced United States Middle East peace initiatives and overt American involvement in a regional defense pact. Soviet inroads in the region were most important to Washington. This was why the U.S. had pressed the British to withdraw from the Suez Canal base, and why it began to oppose the evolution of Eden's "security blanket," the Baghdad Pact.

4 *The Pursuit of the Baghdad Pact*

There is no settled interpretation of the origin of the Baghdad Pact, the agreement among Turkey, Iraq, and Britain. Did the initial suggestion come from Secretary of State Dulles, who then used Turkey as a vehicle for its implementation? Or did the proposal originate with Foreign Secretary Eden, who sought collusion between Turkey and Iraq in order to maintain London's role as a Middle Eastern power? Evidence suggests that Britain stood to benefit from the pact far more than the United States.[1] An examination of the evolution of the American concept of the "northern tier," from Dulles's mission to the Middle East in May 1953 until the announcement of British adherence to the Baghdad Pact in April 1955, supports this premise.

Upon returning from the Middle East in June 1953, Dulles was still determined to organize a new anti-Soviet grouping of Middle Eastern states. But as a result of the trip, his emphasis shifted. The State Department became convinced that the "political situation is such that the Arab states will not, at this time, openly join defensive arrangements with a combination of western powers."[2] Dulles believed that the United States must abandon its hope "of making Egypt the key country in building the foundations for a military defense of the Middle East."[3] On June 1 he reported to the National Security Council:

The general concept [is] that . . . Pakistan could be made a strong
loyal point. So, obviously, could Turkey. Syria and Iraq realized their
danger, and could probably be induced to join us. As for the
countries further south, they were too lacking in the realization of
the international situation to offer any prospect of becoming dependable allies. Iran . . . was the obvious weak spot in what could become
a strong defensive arrangement of the northern tier of states: Turkey,
Iraq, Syria, and Pakistan.[4]

To accomplish this arrangement, Dulles would have to pursue
a policy independent from Britain's Suez-centered strategy. If
London failed to come to a rapprochement with Cairo, the Arab
world would continue to associate the United States with British
colonialism. While Dulles realized that too heavy a reliance on
Egypt made no sense, he hoped that should Cairo solve its
difficulties with the British, and the revolutionary command
council consolidate its position, Egypt could help persuade other
Arab nations to join a U.S.-sponsored anti-Soviet grouping. But
if London and Cairo remained at loggerheads, any hope of
drawing Egypt into a regional defense organization would be
lost.

Dulles's new tack satisfied many of Washington's simplistic
anti-Soviet goals while confusing the Egyptian government. On
the one hand the United States pressured the British to conclude an evacuation agreement with Egypt. At the same time
Washington tried to organize Arab states, which Egypt sought to
lead, into an anti-Soviet alliance. The problem throughout the
period was Dulles's inconsistency; burgeoning Egyptian nationalism limited his options with Cairo, but he nevertheless wished
to use Egypt's control over Suez and Nasser's influence in the
Arab world.

Egypt responded to Washington's actions by developing a
united front of neighboring Arab states. After negotiations, on
June 17, 1953, Cairo issued a decree bringing the Arab League's
Collective Security and Economic Pact into force. This would
supposedly satisfy Dulles's desire that a regional defense force
"would grow from within," and it offered Egypt the opportunity
to spread its influence within the larger Arab world.[5] Miles
Copeland, the CIA's main operative in Egypt and a Nasser

confidant, later reported that the Egyptian leader believed the United States would give him time to develop an Arab-based regional defense organization. Not linked to the West, this grouping would be constructed to fall quickly into line with Western plans should a common danger arise. It was highly unlikely, however, that Dulles would support Nasser's goal of organizing the Arab states into a "union of positive neutralists." As time passed, the secretary of state began to suspect that Nasser hoped to balance the great powers against each other and gain the most advantageous deal.[6]

Before July 1954 and the signing of the Heads of Agreement, the British held fast to a Suez-centered strategy for the creation of a MEDO, or Middle East Defense Organization. Following the drawn-out negotiations to achieve the Anglo-Egyptian Suez Canal base agreement, London realized that Cairo could not be relied upon to help Britain maintain its declining position in the region. After the final treaty was signed, London shifted its military forces from Suez to Aden, Kenya, Cyprus, and Iraq. Headquarters for the Middle East Land Forces moved to Cyprus, a strategic location for air support of the northern tier, and a position from which the forces could maintain security between Greek and Turkish factions on the island. The shift of defense concepts from Suez to the northern tier made Iraq the logical alternative for maintaining a strong British presence in the area.[7]

For years Nuri al-Said, the Iraqi premier, had favored the United Kingdom and had worked to maintain close relations between London and the ruling Hashemite family of Iraq. After World War II this policy was actively denounced by Arab nationalists who pressed Nuri to turn against the 1932 Anglo-Iraqi treaty of alliance. For Nasser, Israel was the major threat to the Arab world; but for Nuri, Russia appeared to be an equal or even greater threat. He was determined to join a Western-sponsored security system, but he also wished to rid Iraq of its unequal treaty with Britain. He wanted ties with London, in other words, but on an equal basis. To end the Anglo-Iraqi treaty and force the British to evacuate Iraq would be a major national accomplishment. Yet Nuri refused to reject the security that the British alliance offered. If he could transform it from a bilateral relationship with London into a regional pact with Britain as one of a number of powers, Iraq would retain the support of the United Kingdom against the Soviet threat.[8] Well aware of his opposition and the nationalist aspirations that would be "contained," especially Nasser's, Nuri was nonetheless convinced that leftists and communists, supported by Moscow, formed the major threat to his government.

The Iraqi premier's mind-set coincided with the goals of the British Foreign Office. As a result, Eden saw the Baghdad Pact as a means of maintaining and reinforcing British power in the area. By concentrating on Iraq, Eden hoped to isolate Nasser in the Arab world; and by including northern-tier countries who were encouraged by Dulles to form an anti-Soviet regional alliance, he would eventually convince the United States to join.[9] If Dulles developed the northern tier scheme, Eden, with Nuri's compliance, attempted to use it as a vehicle to retain British hegemony in the Middle East. This British strategy rested in large part on maintaining the Hashemite dynasty of Iraq.

During the summer of 1953 the Korean armistice, the impending French collapse in Vietnam, and Soviet explosion of a hydrogen device convinced American planners that Moscow would make a major push in the Middle East. In June the State Department decided it would be best to "work individually with those states which seemed most disposed to cooperate with the west. These included Iraq, Syria, and Pakistan."[10] The goal was a separate bilateral arrangement with each of these countries. Dulles believed the policy was modest but realistic, and more apt to produce results than a MEDO based on a NATO model. With more favorable political conditions, any successful American bilateral arrangements could be turned into a larger multilateral grouping for the region. This would allow an American-supported area defense arrangement to "arise from within," and Washington would assume the role of a weapons supplier.[11]

American plans for the Middle East called for the United Kingdom and Turkey to support this phased approach to a regional defense organization. The United States wanted a grouping in which the Western powers would be associated, one "designed to influence the political orientation, increase the internal stability, and strengthen the defense of the area." The State Department realized that "the political base for such an organization [did] not exist and must first be brought into being." The United States sought the support of certain "Asian and African states, particularly Pakistan, as might contribute to the security and stability of the Near East."[12]

By September Pakistan announced its support for a "northern Middle East defense pact" which included Turkey and Iraq. But the Pakistanis made it clear that in return they expected economic and military assistance.[13] On October 12, 1953, Assistant Secretary of State Henry Byroade, meeting with General Ayub Khan, commander of Pakistani field forces, presented America's plan for a program of military assistance to begin before the end of the fiscal year.[14]

The United States viewed its weapons relationship with Pakistan as a first step in developing a MEDO of Turkey, Iraq, Pakistan, and Iran. Success of "an association of indigenous forces under an indigenous command" would not hinge upon a satisfactory resolution of the Anglo-Egyptian and Arab-Israeli differences.[15] There would be "no direct or overt western participation and no Arab state would be allowed to join except for Iraq."[16] This idea would become a major source of friction between American and British policymakers. The British wished to adhere to the pact themselves and to encourage other Arab states, particularly Jordan, to join as a vehicle to maintain their presence in the region. The State Department sought to keep the Western role covert and not pressure the Arabs to adhere. Washington correctly believed any such pressure on Arab nationalists would backfire and create an opening for the Soviet Union in the Middle East.

On November 30 the Turkish government informed the American ambassador, Avra M. Warren, that it would welcome defense talks with Pakistan.[17] At this juncture the United States worked behind the scenes to bring Turkey and Pakistan closer together.

88 DAWN OVER SUEZ

A favorable defense agreement between the two countries could serve as a model for other bilateral treaties in the region.

Meanwhile, negotiations between Britain and Iraq had reached a standstill. The Iraqis expected to revise their treaty with Britain along the lines of the arrangements that emerged from the Anglo-Egyptian talks.[18] The prime minister, Dr. Fadjil-Jamali, explained there was great opposition in the Iraqi parliament simply to revising the Anglo-Iraqi treaty. He wanted the treaty liquidated altogether, with the status of the military bases at Habbaniya and Saibba to be based on the same formula that emerged from the Anglo-Egyptian negotiations.[19] While opposed in principle to the revision of the treaty, the Foreign Office was aware that the Iraqis viewed British presence at the military bases as "an infringement of their sovereignty." It was obvious that no Iraqi government could allow this situation to reappear in a new treaty.[20]

Aware of American-Pakistani discussions, Nasser's aggravation with Washington mounted because his aid was not forthcoming. Lack of progress in the Anglo-Egyptian talks in late December 1953 moved Nasser to recall his ambassadors from the United States, India, Pakistan, and the Soviet Union. On December 27 Egyptian Foreign Minister Fawzi announced that Cairo would now pursue a policy of "noncooperation in the cold war," which included improved relations with the communist bloc.[21] On January 9 the Egyptian government went a step further and announced that its foreign policy would now be based on "the establishment of an Arab bloc, free from imperialist influence, to protect the interests of Islamic, Asiatic and African peoples." In addition, Nasser called for "an African bloc which would include all African countries still under the imperialist yoke." Despite the rhetoric, Egyptian neutralism was still more an expression of a desire for national independence than a militant weapon in the Arab world.[22]

As 1954 dawned, Dulles realized that Turkey and Pakistan presented the only chances for bilateral defensive arrangements in the Middle East. Based on State Department reports, Washington saw no serious obstacles to an agreement between Turkey and Pakistan. Any agreement between the two would provide for joint consultation and defense planning and would prohibit the participation of the U.S. or any other Western power.[23] By January 1954 the Eisenhower administration had decided to proceed with military aid to Pakistan as part of the ongoing process of achieving a Turkish-Pakistani pact.[24] As negotiations continued, the behind-the-scenes role of the United States increased.

The British were displeased by the course of Turkish-Pakistani talks and the possibility of American military aid for Pakistan. The Foreign Office felt it had greater expertise in the region and resented what appeared to be an American "show." In early January the State Department responded to a number of British concerns. Washington informed the Foreign Office that it was proceeding with the Turkish-Pakistani talks to develop a pact which would make it easier to gain the adherence of Iraq and Iran at a later date. Placing American aid in the context of a defensive alliance would help offset criticism from India and the Arab states. Creating a regionally based alliance without Western membership would avoid one of the major obstacles that had caused previous MEDO failures. The State Department hoped that other states would choose to adhere to a newly created MEDO.[25] Despite British reluctance to accept this rationale, the State Department proceeded with the talks.[26]

By the end of January the Turkish government accepted American plans, especially the idea that any defense arrangement should not appear to be instigated by Washington.[27] The State Department feared that once the Turkish-Pakistani pact was complete, the British, as a Commonwealth member with Pakistan, might insist on broadening the pact. So Washington made it clear to London that it was being informed, not consulted, on the negotiations, particularly regarding military aid to Pakistan, which was seen as a bilateral arrangement.[28]

Once the British were "informed," they advised Turkey to delay concluding any agreement with Pakistan, again arguing that the Western powers should be included.[29] Ignoring British advice, Turkey and the United States agreed in February on all significant points of procedure in Turkey's negotiations with Pakistan and on the subsequent American aid agreement. [30]

On April 2, 1954, Turkey and Pakistan concluded a Treaty of Friendly Cooperation. The agreement provided for:

> Consultation on international matters of mutual interest; continuing cultural, economic; and technical cooperation; consultation and cooperation on certain defense matters; and accession of any state whose participation is considered by the contracting parties useful for achieving the purposes of the present agreement.

The accord was to last five years and be automatically renewed for additional five-year periods unless denounced a year before each such period ended. [31]

Among all the Arab countries, only Iraq reacted positively to the Turkish-Pakistani agreement. The British responded with continued resentment against the perceived American encroachment in London's sphere of influence. The Foreign Office feared that if Iraq adhered to the pact it would receive overt support from Turkey and Pakistan, and with the United States in the background, "they would either refuse facilities, [or] at least take a less compliant line than they would feel able to at present" in Anglo-Iraqi treaty talks. London also feared that Iraq would ask Washington to take part in its negotiations with the Foreign Office resulting in American pressure on London, just as they were being pressured to conclude a deal with the Egyptians. The British resented being *informed* about events in the region; they wished to be consulted. They did not welcome Washington's incursion. [32]

To understand the full measure of British anger one must recall that in April 1954 the battle of Dienbienphu had reached its final phase, and the French collapse in Indochina produced far-reaching consequences. Anthony Eden later claimed that the United States approached the French and British concerning an "ad hoc coalition, comprising the United States, France, the United Kingdom, Australia, New Zealand, Thailand, the Philippines and the three associated states of Indochina" to warn the Chinese about intervention and in the future serve as the basis for a collective defense organization for Southeast Asia. Eden feared that such a warning would only aggravate the Chinese, "might lead to a world war," and would be militarily ineffective. The Foreign Secretary wished to do nothing that might interfere with the Geneva Conference on Indochina due to open at the end of April.[33]

Dulles began working to settle the membership for his new South East Asian Treaty Organization (SEATO) in advance of the Geneva Conference. Eden, unable to gain American support for a MEDO which he favored, resented Dulles's pressure for a defense organization in yet another region. Eden's bitterness is evident in his memo to Roger Makins, the British ambassador to Washington.

> Americans may think the time past when they need to consider the feelings and difficulties of their allies. It is the conviction that this tendency becomes more pronounced every week that is creating mounting difficulties for anyone in this country who wants to maintain close Anglo-American relations.[34]

The Turkish-Pakistani agreement brought a favorable reaction from Iraq despite British resentment. Nuri al-Said immediately informed Burton Y. Berry, American ambassador in Baghdad, that "The regent and I are 100% for it, and of course the King." Nuri also stated that he had planned from the beginning that Iraq should be a member, "for how else could Pakistan assist Turkey except through Iraq." Ever the realist, the Iraqi premier tempered his enthusiasm by stating, "Of course we will join, but first we have to meet the problem of neutralizing Middle Eastern public opinion on the Palestinian issue."[35]

Despite the appearance of full Iraqi support, remarks made by an Iraqi representative at the April 1 Arab League meeting in Cairo angered Dulles. Publicly denying that Baghdad had been invited to adhere to the Turkish-Pakistani pact, the Iraqi delegate asserted his country had not considered membership, nor had it considered receiving military aid from the United States.[36] Washington demanded a clarification of Baghdad's position, including public assurances that Iraq supported the Turkish-Pakistani pact. Concerned that Israel's friends in Congress would block military aid to Iraq, the State Department asked Baghdad to tone down its support for the Arab states' anti-Israeli statements.[37]

On April 18, faced with the possible suspension of military aid talks with the United States, Prime Minister Mohamed Fadjil-Jamali reassured Ambassador Berry that Iraq wished to receive American aid and that adherence to the Turkish-Pakistani pact would "come at a proper time."[38] The next day Dulles agreed to renew the talks if the "character, timing and amounts" of aid were predicated on "international developments in the area," and that once completed, the agreement would be publicly announced.[39] On April 20 Baghdad and Washington agreed to all points for a military aid package, and on the 25th it was publicly announced. The agreement was soon followed by a May 19 announcement of a similar American package for Pakistan. It was becoming difficult for the United States to maintain a "covert" role in the construction of bilateral arrangements for the region.

The predictable Egyptian reaction to the Iraqi arms agreement came on April 2 when Nasser commented that "no Arab country should join the alliance. It is a defensive pact which ignores the interests of the Middle East, and at the same time aims at frustrating the work of the Arab League."[40] Failure to conclude his own agreement with Washington exacerbated Nasser's opposition. After initialing the Heads of Agreement in July, Nasser decided to pursue an even greater pan-Arabist foreign policy, ultimately revealing his rivalry with Nuri al-Said and creating further roadblocks for American and British interests in the area.

With the region in flux and the initialing of the Heads of Agreement between Egypt and the United Kingdom imminent, the Eisenhower administration decided to take stock of its Middle East policy. In Istanbul in early May, the State Department convened a meeting of its mission chiefs from the region. This conference reflected the continuing American fear of Soviet encroachment in the area. Despite the success of the Turkish-Pakistani pact, Washington had to be careful not to overemphasize the agreement as a Western initiative, a tactic which had caused the failure of earlier MEDO attempts. The mission chiefs suggested that Washington not pressure Iraq or any other Arab country to adhere to the newly signed pact. American diplomats were well aware that Egypt would resent any arrangement for the Middle East in which Cairo did not play the central role.[41]

Because the Egyptians regarded themselves as indispensable to the defense of the Arab world, the mission chiefs believed that the United States must convince Cairo that the northern tier did not detract from the importance of Egypt. In addition, the diplomats advised the State Department to work out differences with the British in order to guarantee their approval for the northern tier arrangement.

Concern about political trends in Israel and its increasing frustration over a settlement with the Arabs, especially at a time when Egypt was about to inherit the military benefits of the Suez Canal base, clouded the efforts of the conferees. The Israeli inclination was that matters would become much worse before they would improve. The State Department feared that with increasing military aid for the Arabs, the Israelis would choose a more aggressive policy.[42] A peace initiative would soon have to be attempted before the situation was out of hand.

By the end of June American intelligence estimates concluded that recent events in the region were favorable to the U.S. but that the immediate effects of the Turkish-Pakistani pact were psychological and political rather than military. The pact would not reduce tension or the instability of regimes in the area. While the region remained militarily vulnerable, the pact did create an opportunity to improve military deficiencies. A National Intelligence Estimate warned the United States to proceed slowly to avoid arousing strong Israeli opposition and a resulting escalation in Arab-Israeli and inter-Arab hostilities.[43]

In July these estimates were brought together in a National Security Council Paper, NSC-5428, "United States Objectives and Policies with Respect to the Near East." NSC-5428 reached many of the same conclusions as had NSC-155/1 a year earlier. It reiterated the northern tier as the best prospect for creating an indigenous regional defense arrangement for the Middle East, and noted that the adherence of Iran and Iraq mandated an improvement in the political climate of these states. The paper also warned that until the problems of the region were settled it was unlikely there would be further adherence by any other Arab country. In the interim, the planners called for the United States to develop secret plans for the defense of the area with the United Kingdom, Turkey, and other interested parties. The paper stressed, too, that the northern tier concept must be developed as "an indigenous movement, not linked formally... with the western powers or with western defense organizations except through the participation of Turkey." The NSC recognized the importance of the United Kingdom in the region and the need for cooperation with Great Britain. It urged the administration to increase U.S. responsibility in the region, act in concert with London when possible, but reserve the right to act with others or alone.[44] The paper demonstrated the NSC's increasing awareness that the northern tier concept could not be developed without resolution of the tensions caused by the Arab-Israeli conflict. Therefore the NSC strongly recommended greater United States involvement in promoting peace proposals between Israel and the Arab states.[45]

While the United States was reassessing its Middle East policy, the United Kingdom was finishing its negotiations with Egypt and proceeding with similar discussions with Iraq. Foreign Secretary Eden, realizing the unpopularity of the existing treaty with Baghdad, recommended that London proceed with negotiations. As with the negotiations with Cairo, Eden was motivated by a fear of Washington. He told the British cabinet that if events ran their course, the Iraqis might believe that London was leaving it to the United States to "make the running of that part of the world."[46]

With the announcement of the Heads of Agreement in July, public pressure in Iraq increased, calling for a new Anglo-Iraqi treaty similar to what the British were negotiating with Egypt. On July 28 Prime Minister Fadjil-Jamali informed the Foreign Office that the United Kingdom should return the military bases at Habbaniya and Shaibba to Iraq, with arrangements for British access to their remaining property whenever they desired. Jamali stressed the Iraqi government's desire to cooperate, but it must be careful "not to create the appearance of a fait accompli to the Iraqi people."[47] Nuri assured the British in early August that he would not abrogate the Anglo-Iraqi treaty. He favored an agreement which called for a British maintenance staff and Royal Air Force use of the bases by invitation from a joint Anglo-Iraqi defense board.[48]

With the commencement of Anglo-Iraqi talks, Baghdad's differences with Cairo widened. Traditionally, Iraq had little faith in the armies of her Arab neighbors and closer relations with Turkey and Iran. Iraq viewed both the Arab League and the Arab Collective Security Pact (ACSP) as little more that Egyptian tools to dominate the Arab world, which Iraq considered its legitimate sphere of influence. Historically, Nuri supported the Hashemite desire to achieve union with the Fertile Crescent (that area containing parts of Israel, Lebanon, Jordan, and Iraq), which Cairo's appeal to Arab nationalism had destroyed. Nuri did not believe that Iraq could defend itself without Western support. He further understood the need for close relations with Turkey and Iran in order to contain the Iraqi Kurds and thus ensure Iraq's internal unity. Most important, Nuri viewed the defense debate in the Arab world as a chance for Iraq to recapture from Egypt the initiative in Arab affairs.[49]

For Nuri, Dulles's northern tier concept was not entirely satisfactory. The British were opposed to it, and the forward strategy of the northern tier did not provide for extensive Arab membership. Iraq wished to lead the Arab world, not be cut off from it. Baghdad's adherence to the Turkish-Pakistani pact could result in Iraqi isolation from the Arab world. Thus Nuri sought to develop a formula whereby Iraq would serve as the link between the Arab world, its northern neighbors, and the Western powers.[50]

Nuri's hand had been strengthened by the Heads of Agreement. In the document Egypt agreed to the reactivation of the Suez base in case of attack not only on any ACSP member but on Turkey as well, thereby establishing a connection between Cairo and a future MEDO. Nuri believed that "Nasser had compromised the exclusive Arab nature of the ACSP, and by indirectly linking it to the evolving northern tier group, he had opened the door to Iraqi domination of ACSP." Nuri immediately threatened to adhere to the Turkish-Pakistani pact if steps were

not taken to achieve a unified Arab command for ACSP, a step he
knew Nasser would reject because it would result in placing
Egyptian soldiers under an Iraqi command. By linking the
Heads of Agreement to ACSP, ACSP itself became a stumbling
block for Nasser. Washington and London believed that Iraqi
adherence to the Turkish-Pakistani pact would force Egypt to
withdraw from ACSP because of its hatred for Iraq. Thus isolated, Egypt could be more easily lured into a MEDO with
promises of Western aid.[51]

Nasser refused to acquiesce to Nuri's plans. On August 13 he
dispatched Major Salah Salim, the Egyptian minister of national
guidance, to Baghdad to try to dissuade Iraq's collaboration with
the West on regional defense planning. The two sides met at
Sarsank and discussed a wide range of issues, including the
communist threat, Iraq's traditional fear of the Turks, the Palestinian problem, and the British role in the region.[52] At the
conclusion of the meeting, Nuri convinced Salim to agree to
joint Iraqi-Egyptian leadership of a new Arab pact whose foundation would be closely coordinated with Britain and the United
States. Salim also agreed to work secretly for a settlement of the
Arab-Israeli conflict.[53] When Salim returned to Cairo, Nasser
disassociated himself from any agreement which may have been
reached. His anger stemmed not from Salim's acceptance of
Nuri's proposals to end the Arab-Israeli conflict, but from his
agreement to coordinate regional defense planning with the
West.[54]

On September 15 Nuri visited Cairo in an attempt to reverse
Nasser's reaction to the Sarsank talks. Nuri told Nasser that Iraq
could not rely upon the Arabs for protection, and that the only
way to defend Iraq was to enter into an alliance with the West.
Nasser responded that he wished to conclude negotiations with
the British and then wait two years until the situation crystal-
lized. Nasser concluded, "We shall continue with our policy and
the future will judge between us."[55] The split between Iraq and
Egypt was now inevitable.

Nuri's new strategy emerged during his October visit to
Britain and Turkey. In London he proposed an alternative to the
northern tier alliance and suggested that ACSP be strengthened

by including Turkey and with aid from the United Kingdom and the United States. Eden warmly received the idea as a device to recapture control of regional defense planning from the United States and block Washington's attempt to supersede Britain's position in the Middle East.[56]

The key to such strategy was to draw Turkey away from its recent agreement with Pakistan. The Turkish foreign minister, Fuat Koprulu, was inspired by a vision of a vast grouping of all Arabs under Turkish leadership, and Ankara contemplated negotiating bilateral agreements with individual Arab states.[57] The United States did not enthusiastically support these developments. Dulles favored closer cooperation between Iraq and Turkey and hoped Baghdad would be brought into the framework of the Turkish-Pakistani Pact. But Dulles also feared that Iraq was being used by the British as a means to enlarge ACSP, as a basis for Middle Eastern defense, and as a replacement for the proposed Suez base agreement with Egypt and the Anglo-Iraqi treaty.[58] As a result of Nuri's visit to Turkey on October 23, the Iraqi premier agreed to work out a Turkish-Iraqi agreement along the same lines as the Turkish-Pakistani pact.[59]

Nuri informed the British in early January 1955 that he expected no specific agreement to emerge during the upcoming visit of Turkish President Adnan Menderes. He wished to work out the details for regional defense with both the United States and the United Kingdom before any agreement with Turkey was concluded. Once this agreement was reached, he would then terminate the Anglo-Iraqi treaty.[60] When Nuri met with the Turkish delegation, however, most major points were accepted, and on January 13 Iraq and Turkey concluded a treaty whereby both sides agreed to "undertake to cooperate, in conformity with Article 51 of the United Nations Charter, against any aggression against them from any quarter, whether it comes within the Mid East region or from outside." The treaty was still to be drawn and would be signed "in the very near future."[61]

Britain and the United States welcomed the agreement, but for different reasons. The State Department was pleased that another piece of its northern-tier puzzle had been secured, and Foreign Office reaction centered on the fact that a member of

ACSP had adhered to an expanding MEDO. As expected, the Egyptian government condemned the agreement. The Egyptian press attacked Iraq for its bad faith and for destroying the efforts of Egypt and the Arab states toward a cohesive policy.[62]

Further, the Egyptian government now summoned Arab prime ministers to a conference in Cairo for January 22. Nuri's agreement on a pact with Turkey incensed Nasser and weakened his bargaining position with the West. The Egyptian leader wanted the full weight of Arab support in his negotiations with the United States and United Kingdom, and Nuri had broken ranks and threatened to carry other Arab states with him.

Despite British advice, Nuri refused to attend the Cairo conference, citing ill health. Instead he sent Prime Minister Fadjil-Jamali. Meanwhile, the Muslim Brotherhood in Egypt opposed the Suez Canal base agreement, adding to British concern about Nasser's internal position. The Foreign Office hoped to prevent Nasser from isolating Iraq at the conference, but they did not wish to weaken the Egyptian leader's domestic political support.[63] At the conference, supported by Saudi Arabia alone, Egypt insisted on passing a resolution not only condemning the Turkish-Iraqi pact as contradicting ACSP but also precluding any agreement with states who were not members of ACSP. The Egyptians were taken aback by the lack of support, particularly from Jordan, Lebanon, and Syria. At the second session Nasser exploded:

> If Egypt has to go it alone it will do so, but I shall tell the Arab [people] that the rest of you are not willing to cooperate with us. Egypt will not be intimidated. We shall carry on even if the Arab necklace is broken and all the beads scattered. Egypt will continue to champion the cause of the Arabs even if the rest have become slaves of the West and the Turks.[64]

Despite Nasser's admonition, the conference adjourned on February 6 without reaching a decision or issuing a joint statement.[65] Yet the next few weeks proved to be propitious for Nasser as well as a turning point on the road to the 1956 Suez War.

Nasser's opposition to the Turkish-Iraqi treaty went beyond its threat to his hope of pan-Arab leadership. He believed it narrowed his slim chances of acquiring modern military equipment from the West. The United States and United Kingdom, having endorsed the Turkish-Iraqi alliance and supplied arms to both partners, would find it embarrassing to arm simultaneously an Egyptian-led coalition of Arab states. Should other Arab states adhere to the Turkish-Iraqi pact, Egypt's isolation would increase.

In London Foreign Secretary Eden, with President Eisenhower's support, continued to work for a "defensive alliance among Britain, Turkey, Pakistan, and the Arab nation of Iraq, to strengthen those countries near the Soviet Union's southwestern boundary."[66] In pursuing regional designs, neither leader realized that intra-Arab divisions were as great an obstacle to such plans as the Arab-Israeli conflict.

With Turkish-Iraqi negotiations drawing to a conclusion, Nuri began to push for immediate British adherence to the pact. The Foreign Office was fully aware that should the United Kingdom adhere to the Turkish-Iraqi pact anytime soon, "the price to be paid was Egypt." Also to be reckoned with was a new Anglo-American peace initiative, code-named Project ALPHA. A major component of ALPHA was the use of Egypt to achieve an Arab-Israeli peace.[67] Despite Egypt's importance in the developing peace process, the Foreign Office favored British and American adherence to the Turkish-Iraqi pact as original signatories. Whitehall reasoned that the resulting Egyptian resentment was worth the price, for failure to support Nuri "would endanger the Turkish-Iraqi agreement and consequently our best interests in the Middle East."[68] The British acknowledged that American adherence presented a major stumbling block. First, the United States had no existing commitments to Iraq and thus would be extending the scope of its military obligations. Second, pro-Israeli public opinion in the United States would vigorously oppose American participation. Finally, such adherence would need congressional approval, and for political reasons the Eisenhower administration was not willing to seek it.[69]

The State Department now began playing a two-sided game with the British over the proposed pact. For a year and a half it had opposed the creation of a regional pact for the Middle East with overt Western participation. Suddenly American policy appeared to do an about-face. On February 9 Washington announced its strong support for the pact and reiterated its reluctance to take any action that might suggest outside direction. But Washington informed the Foreign Office that "the United States understands that [if] the United Kingdom prefers to accede after [the] signature of the proposed pact, the United States concurs in this view."[70]

It appears that the American reversal resulted from a desire to maintain as much policy flexibility as possible in the region. In any event, Washington's attitude caused the British to assume that they had sufficient American support to expect U.S. adherence to the emerging Baghdad Pact soon after London joined. The continuing problem was that the British were engaged in wishful thinking. The United States did not wish to participate overtly in the Baghdad Pact; but the British had convinced themselves that Washington would join. The growing rift between the two allies was now certain to widen.

At 11:30 p.m. on February 24, 1955, the Turkish-Iraqi pact was signed. Eden, enroute to Bangkok for the first SEATO conference, decided to visit Cairo and talk with Nasser personally. Eden realized there was little possibility of persuading Egypt to join the pact; nonetheless he met with the Egyptian leader at the British embassy on February 26. As expected, the meeting produced nothing but recriminations. Nasser argued vehemently against the Turkish-Iraqi pact. Eden tried to persuade the Egyptian leader to stop his verbal attacks on Nuri al-Said and the Hashemite kingdom, the centerpieces of British Middle East strategy. Eden refused, moreover, to accept Nasser's assertions that he was a spokesperson for the entire Arab world. For Nasser, Eden was the embodiment of all he disliked in the British; Eden reciprocated this dislike and distrust.[71] More important, each seriously underestimated how strongly the other held his views, a misperception which was to lead to disastrous consequences.

After his meeting with Eden, events of the final week of February 1955 brought further pressure on Nasser. Looking back one can clearly see why Egyptian anxiety increased daily.

During the evening of February 23 a group of Egyptian infiltrators crossed the border from the Gaza Strip, broke into the guardroom of an Israeli scientific institute, and stole documents stored there. The Egyptians then ambushed an escaping cyclist and murdered him. Another group of infiltrators ran into an Israeli patrol and were killed. A search of one attacker's clothing revealed a report on traffic patterns and highways in southern Israel. On February 27 David Ben-Gurion, who a few weeks earlier had replaced Moshe Sharett as defense minister, met with his chief of staff, Moshe Dayan. They suggested a retaliatory strike against the Egyptian base at Gaza, which Dayan estimated would result in the death of ten enemy soldiers. Later that day Prime Minister Sharett gave his approval.[72]

The dimensions of the Israeli operation grew unexpectedly because of Egyptian reinforcements. Israel reported eight Egyptians killed in the clash on February 28, and the following day Egyptian radio reported thirty-eight dead and more than thirty wounded. Overnight the Gaza raid sharply escalated military tensions between Egypt and Israel.[73] The raid also had a marked impact on Nasser. Until then the border with Israel had been relatively quiet, and according to *New York Times* reporter Kennett Love, the Egyptians had been lulled into a state of security. Believing the border safe, Nasser had reduced military expenditures at a time when his regime was struggling to remain in power.[74] Both Love and Donald Neff, in his book *Warriors at Suez*, argue that until the Gaza raid Nasser was willing to consider peace, that the attack transformed him.

Nasser perceived the attack as a signal that Ben-Gurion (through Dayan and Shimon Peres of the Israeli defense ministry) was reviving the policy of large-scale reprisals combined with the threat of war in the hope of forcing a peace settlement. Nasser concluded that it was now imperative for Egypt to develop a reliable source for modern weapons.[75] The Egyptian army was deeply shaken by the raid. Because the army was the mainstay of the regime, something must be done to restore its morale. Nasser immediately ordered a major increase in the military budget and established suicide units *(Fedayeen)* to launch raids from Gaza into Israel.

The Israelis, as expected, had not reacted favorably to the signing of the Turkish-Iraqi pact. In assessing the reasons behind the Israeli attack on Gaza a few days later, one must consider Tel Aviv's preoccupation with its increasing isolation and the fact that one of its bitterest enemies, Iraq, had joined an alliance with one of Israel's few active supporters, Turkey. The Israeli government viewed the terms of the pact as proof that the West, as represented by Turkey, would always be ready to appease the Arabs at Israel's expense. The Turkish move was a considerable blow to Prime Minister Sharett, the most dovish member of the Israeli cabinet, and strengthened the hands of those who argued that Israel's interests would always be ignored unless it exploited its nuisance value by adopting an aggressive policy.[76]

Yet the raid itself backfired. For months the Israelis had sought a bilateral agreement with the United States to insure their security. On March 6, Deputy Assistant Secretary of State John D. Jernegan, talking before a Jewish audience in Washington asserted that Israel's inclusion in any defense arrangement would depend on an easing of border tensions. A week later Dulles informed his ambassador in Tel Aviv that all discussion of a bilateral treaty was suspended because of the raid.[77]

Many historians have argued that the Gaza raid was a turning point in Israeli-Egyptian relations. An examination of the military and political climate of the period shows this argument to be oversimplified. The decisive events that motivated Nasser to seek arms and political support from the Soviet Union were the signing of the Turkish-Iraqi pact, subsequent British adherence, and Nasser's inability to obtain weapons from the United States. The Gaza raid only added urgency to Nasser's search for new allies and weapons sources.

On February 26 Nasser dispatched Salah Salim to Damascus to begin discussions for a new Arab pact whose main thrust would be directed against Israel. By the end of March Syria had agreed to a unified command with the Egyptian army; although Lebanon and Jordan delayed in deciding on membership in the organization, Saudi Arabia and Yemen quickly announced their intentions of adhering to the treaty. With this diplomatic triumph, Egypt began to reverse the events of the previous month.[78]

On March 11 Nasser met for two hours with Henry Byroade, who had succeeded Jefferson Caffery as the American ambassador to Egypt. For two months, as crucial events were unfolding in the Middle East, the United States had been without appropriate representation in Cairo. During the meeting with Byroade, Nasser professed to be both confused and suspicious about the course of American policy. He based his objection to the Turkish-Iraqi pact on Iraq's long-held ambition to draw Syria into a federation. Nuri's invitation to Damascus to adhere to the Turkish-Iraqi pact was further proof. Nasser saw this as part of Iraq's attempt to isolate Egypt in the Arab world. His response was to develop an Egyptian-sponsored regional defense pact to protect the Arab states from Nuri's machinations.[79]

Nasser also presented Byroade with a long list of urgently needed weapons. The Egyptian leader's apprehension over weapons had grown because of reports of a secret arms deal between Israel and France.[80] Eisenhower characterized the contents of Nasser's arms request as "peanuts," but the U.S. took no prompt action.[81]

The major obstacle in concluding an arms deal between the United States and Egypt was Nasser's resistance to receiving American military advisers along with weapons shipments. In addition, Dulles sustained the hope that by stalling on arms for Egypt, he could force Nasser to agree to join an American-supported regional defense pact. The secretary totally misjudged Nasser, and American actions—or, rather, lack of action—on his military needs soon drove Nasser closer to the communist bloc.[82]

By the time the British joined the Baghdad Pact in April 1955, hopes that the pact would provide Nuri with a leadership position in the Arab world and retain British dominance in the region had vanished. The Egyptians remained uncompromising, and the center of pan-Arabism resided in Cairo. Why then did the British—and the United States by indirectly supporting London's decisions—pursue a policy which was self-defeating?

The British were wary of Nasser's "little Arab League" which excluded Iraq. British concern focused on Baghdad and Amman.

Jordan was the home of the Arab Legion and central to British plans to expand the Baghdad Pact. British policymakers believed that Nasser's new pact was not viable without Amman, and the Foreign Office was convinced that the only way to thwart Nasser was to gain Jordanian adherence to the Turkish-Iraqi pact.[83] British adherence was seen as easing Jordan's decision, especially since Nasser had warned the British on March 14 that should Jordan join the Turkish-Iraqi pact, it would be subject to the same "propaganda barrage" as Iraq. That would further inflame Arab nationalist opinion in Jordan against the British.[84]

In addition to this crucial relationship with Jordan, the British respected their obligation to Nuri and were concerned about his domestic position and Iraq's weakening role in the Arab world. Adherence to the Turkish-Iraqi pact, Eden argued, could solve a number of problems pertaining to regional defense, including restructuring of the Anglo-Iraqi Treaty of 1930, thus reassuring Britain's own position in the area. Eden believed it was beneficial for the United Kingdom to join despite the reluctance of the United States or any Arab government to do so.[85]

The British foreign secretary felt strongly that he could not abandon Nuri who was willing to deemphasize the American northern tier alliance in favor of a scheme designed superficially to protect British interests in the Arab world. Further, a Conservative government in Britain could not even contemplate disengagement in Iraq when it was still preoccupied with charges of a "scuttle" over Egypt in the ranks of Eden's own supporters.[86]

British policymakers also had to consider the increasing importance of Persian Gulf oil. At least three-quarters of Europe's oil supplies came from the region, and it had been calculated that two-thirds of the world's oil reserves were located there. With the recent Iranian example (in 1953 the British, in collusion with the CIA, had overthrown Iranian Prime Minister Mohammed Mossadegh, whose nationalization policy was viewed as a threat to Western oil sources), the military benefits provided by acceding to the Turkish-Iraqi pact could not be used to protect the vital oil lanes of the Persian Gulf. These factors, the Foreign Office argued, made the political risks of accession worthwhile.[87]

The political gamble was great. With plans to develop an

Arab-Israeli peace proceeding behind the scenes (Project AL-PHA), aggravating Egypt was not in the best interest of any Arab-Israeli rapprochement. Although Nasser had informed the British that "he accepted the concept of a northern defense in which Britain would take part," he was pleased, he said, that he had London's assurance not to press other Arab states to join.[88] It was obvious that the Egyptian leader would work to destroy what the British felt they had achieved.

On March 30 the British and Iraqi governments reached an agreement on a new defense treaty. The British would be allowed to maintain their stocks of equipment in Iran but ceded ownership of their air bases at Habbaniya and Shaibba.[89] On April 4 the British officially acceded to the Turkish-Iraqi pact and the Baghdad Pact was born.

The pact was another jolt to Israeli feelings of insecurity. Prime Minister Sharett informed the British ambassador that the Turkish-Iraqi pact, by excluding Israel, had "an unbalancing effect on Israel's status within the region . . . [and with] Britain's accession . . . has aggravated that disequilibrium."[90] With Anglo-American plans for a peace initiative for the Arab-Israeli conflict under way, one of the project's main participants was again feeling insecure.

Contemporary British analysis of Israel's position reflected how often unrealistic were London's views. Some in the Foreign Office even suspected State Department officials of feeding Israeli insecurity in order to create opposition to the Baghdad Pact.[91] The British seemed to ignore all U.S. attempts to notify them that it had no intention of adhering to the pact. The State Department, meanwhile, worked diligently to create a Middle East defense grouping. Washington consistently rejected the membership of any Western power in such an organization. Dulles firmly believed that if either Britain or the United States adhered to such a pact, it would suffer the same Arab rejection as had the MEDO project in the Truman administration. Later, when the United Kingdom joined, the British were bitterly disappointed that the United States did not follow their lead. Eden commented in his memoirs:

The United States sometimes failed to put its weight behind its friends, in the hope of being popular with their foes.... Having played a leading part to inspire the project, the United States government held back while Britain alone of the western powers joined [the Baghdad Pact]. Worse still, they tried to take credit for their attitude in capitals like Cairo, which were hostile to the pact.[92]

Washington's motives for staying out of the pact were numerous. First, with the degree of Egyptian opposition now manifest, Washington wished to maintain as much credibility as possible with Arab nationalists. Because he was considered the focal point in any lessening of tension in the area, the State Department sought to avoid further estranging Nasser. Second, military assessments of the pact by the Joint Chiefs of Staff concluded that it lacked the necessary defensive depth to be a factor against the Soviet Union. Third, Washington was concerned with the deteriorating relationship between Britain and Saudi Arabia over the Buraimi Oasis.[93] The approaching expiration of the lease for the American air base at Dhahran and the quantity of Saudi oil reserves made the United States wary of further association with Britain's colonialist image in the region. Finally, with Israel's opposition to the pact the Eisenhower administration was unwilling to pay the domestic political price for adhering to it— likely to consist of congressional hearings, an Israeli demand for a mutual defense treaty, and political fallout for the upcoming 1956 presidential election. Eisenhower's frustration with London is obvious in a remark in his diary on December 16, 1955: "The British have never made any sense in the Middle East."[94]

The Baghdad Pact, in retrospect, was a failure. The American decision to be only an observer left all who had joined with a feeling they had been deceived. Iraq was isolated in the Arab world. Warranted or not, the British felt betrayed by their Atlantic ally. Egypt, which was to be assuaged by the absence of American membership, moved closer to the neutralist bloc in order to combat the pact. The entire process of setting up the Baghdad Pact with Western participation added yet another obstacle to reducing tensions between Arabs and Israelis. With both Israel and Egypt rejecting the Baghdad Pact, the development of Project ALPHA now signaled a shift in Anglo-American strategy for the region.

5 The Search for Peace: The ALPHA Project

By the spring of 1955 it was apparent to the British that any hope of expanding the Baghdad Pact into a regional defense alliance depended upon rapprochement between the Arabs and the Israelis. Neither the United States nor the United Kingdom had shown strong interest in becoming directly involved in a Middle East mediation effort. By mid-1955, however, both seemed suddenly almost obsessed with the possibilities of a peace initiative. A number of mediation efforts overlapped during 1955–1956; the most important was the ALPHA project. This was an Anglo-American-sponsored mediation effort designed to foster a peace treaty between the Arab states and Israel. London and Washington thereby hoped that a reduction of Arab-Israeli tensions would promote Western goals in the region. The State Department and the Foreign Office were heavily involved in planning the mediation effort, but each had different motives.

London believed that a Baghdad Pact without full American participation would remove British influence among the Arab states. There was one other means to strengthen the pact: induce other Arab states to join, particularly Jordan. But London knew that further attempts to gain Arab adherence to the pact would exacerbate intra-Arab rivalries. Nonetheless, Britain's insistence on a strong Middle East position caused the

Foreign Office to ignore intelligence reports that contradicted its intentions. For the British, the ALPHA project could be used as a vehicle to foster American support for the Baghdad Pact. For if ALPHA succeeded, the Foreign Office believed the United States would be unable to use the Arab-Israeli conflict as an excuse for not adhering to the pact. And with American membership, London hoped to preserve its position in the Middle East.

For its part, the United States recognized that continued British pressure to gain Arab adherence to the Baghdad Pact would increase regional hostility toward British colonialism. Too much British pressure would also reinforce Nasser's neutralist tendencies and threaten the entire Western position in the region. After the February 1955 Israeli raid on Gaza, Secretary of State Dulles, in order to proceed with ALPHA, sought to overcome the British by somehow restoring Nasser's prestige and confidence. A focal point was to encourage Israel's Arab neighbors, particularly Jordan, *not* to adhere to the Baghdad Pact. Foreign Secretary Eden pursued the opposite course, which Dulles feared would ultimately create a political vacuum in the area to be filled by the Soviet Union. Dulles reasoned that British pressure would produce an Arab backlash led by Egypt, with a turn toward Moscow.[1]

With Europe increasingly dependent on Middle Eastern oil, State Department officials warned that a Soviet foothold in the Middle East could bring an energy crisis to Western Europe. Reduction of Arab oil shipments to the West would also bruise an American economy which had already entered a sharp recession. The Eisenhower administration was convinced that an effort must be made to reduce tensions in the area, and that some accommodation must be reached between the Arabs and Israel. An Arab-Israeli peace might make Egypt more cooperative in furthering Arab support for a regional alliance. It would also reduce tensions between the British and certain Arab states and secure Western oil supplies. And the Arab world would see that the United States, not the Soviet Union, could bring stability and economic development to the area. Unfortunately, during 1955–1956 Washington had little time to accomplish its aims. The approaching 1956 election and fears of a continuing recession mandated a peace initiative by January 1956 if American domestic politics were not to interfere.

In 1954 the State Department had begun to accept the idea of American involvement in a comprehensive peace initiative for the Middle East.[2] By that summer the United States was pursuing a policy of impartiality toward the Arabs and Israel. In United Nations Security Council debates dealing with such issues as the Israeli raid on Qibya, Israeli plans to divert the water of the Jordan River at Banat Ya'qub, Egyptian restrictions on Suez Canal transit, and the debate on the border situation, Washington showed a more evenhanded approach than it had in the past.[3] Despite this new strategy, America experienced only marginal success in reducing tension between Israel and the Arab states. The only positive development was the ongoing Johnston mission, an effort to obtain an agreement between Israel and the Arab states to develop the Jordan River Valley.[4]

By July 1954 the National Security Council argued that it was time to try to alleviate Soviet-generated tensions in the area. Success depended upon the reduction of border tension between the Arab states and Israel. Because the United Nations was unable to cope with the problem, the NSC argued that the United States was "impelled to assume responsibility in developing solutions and insuring their implementation." Increasing unrest would "provide the Soviet Union with manifold opportunities for improving its position."[5] The NSC favored cooperation with the United Kingdom in any initiative to bring about "indigenous participation in collective security arrangements against the Soviet Union."[6]

British concerns about Arab-Israeli tensions focused on how the states of the region would react to the Anglo-Egyptian Suez Canal base agreement which was about to be concluded. Although the Foreign Office was annoyed with the Israelis because of the *Bat Galim* affair, it nonetheless sought to reassure them that the forthcoming agreement with Egypt would not affect

Israeli security. Despite these assurances, Tel Aviv insisted on
face-to-face negotiations between Israel and the Arab states—
which the Arabs refused. The British hoped that upon concluding an agreement with Egypt, prospects for a peace initiative
would improve.[7]

As 1955 approached, the Foreign Office believed that prospects for an effective mediation attempt were poor. The only way
to improve upon them was to alleviate Israel's insecurity vis-à-vis
the Arab states. Tel Aviv must be guaranteed security, but
neither London nor Washington was willing to make such assurances. With the Israelis convinced that the balance of power in
the region was being altered to their detriment, Tel Aviv would
refuse the necessary territorial concessions that would make
negotiations palatable for the Arabs.[8] The British hoped for a
period of peace along Israel's borders in order to create a climate
conducive to negotiations. But the basic Arab demand, which
Nasser presented at the end of October, was to eliminate the
geographical division in the Arab world by creating a common
border between Egypt and Jordan. Nasser proposed that the
Israelis cede part of the southern portion of the Negev Desert,
thereby creating a "little smaller Israel, with which the Arabs
could reconcile her existence."[9]

On November 5, 1954, Dulles met with the British ambassador in Washington, Roger Makins. Makins conveyed Eden's
belief that the conclusion of the Suez base talks mandated the
development of a plan to improve Arab-Israeli relations. Evelyn
Shuckburgh, Britain's under secretary for Middle Eastern affairs,
was coincidentally on a fact-finding mission in the region. Eden
hoped that Dulles would send a representative to London to
discuss the results of Shuckburgh's trip. The worsening refugee
problem and the UN truce supervisory organization's inability to
prevent border incidents between Israel and her Arab neighbors, or even to cope with Arab-Israeli differences, were major
stumbling blocks for Makins. If the United States and the
United Kingdom did not develop a joint strategy to deal with
the problem, it would worsen. Dulles agreed and promised to
appoint a State Department representative to work with Shuckburgh.[10] The resulting ALPHA project was thus based on a

British initiative. But as Anglo-American planning proceeded, Dulles seized control of the project's timetable and forced the British to accept his views or be left out in the cold.

According to the secretary of state, two essential problems produced tensions between Israel and her Arab neighbors. First, Israel was unwilling to accept its status as a "finite state" and insisted on advertising itself as the center of world Jewry. Second, the Arabs viewed Israel as an expansionist state constantly needing to enlarge its borders to accommodate a growing influx of immigrants.[11] Dulles hoped that the pact between Iraq, Turkey, and Pakistan, which was about to be signed, would provide the Arabs with sufficient feelings of security to allow them to negotiate with the Israelis. He was fully aware that an agreement must be completed within two years because of the 1956 presidential election.[12]

From the outset Dulles's premises were mistaken: he used the 1956 election as a peace timetable, he totally misread the state of Arab nationalism, and he misunderstood domestic opinion in Israel.

Shuckburgh returned from the Middle East in mid-December and made the following observations. He professed that Tel Aviv must realize that its policy of reprisals and expansionism was at the core of Arab opposition to any settlement. The Arabs believed that a peace initiative would simply allow the Israelis more breathing space to continue their aggressive tactics. Since mid-1954 excessive military force had marked Israeli responses to every border incident. This strategy seemed designed to "test the strength of the Anglo-Jordanian Treaty," which required Britain to come to Jordan's defense should Amman be attacked by a foreign power. Shuckburgh, uncertain of Israeli goals, was convinced that "they [had] created an atmosphere which [was] detrimental to peace."[13]

The onus appeared to be on Israel; Tel Aviv must make territorial concessions to allow direct access between Egypt and Jordan. In return, London would supply Israel with the same amount of equipment provided the Arabs. Any settlement must also allow the repatriation of Palestinian refugees and Israeli compensation for those who chose not to return to Israel. The proposals would have to be worked out based on a preconceived plan agreeable to the United Kingdom and the United States, leaving questions of security guarantees for the future. The British viewpoint, clearly biased in favor of the Arabs, allowed that it was desirable to have Israeli support, "but from the point of view of preserving the Middle East from Soviet expansion, the friendly cooperation of the Arab world is not merely desirable, but vital."[14] With Iraq about to adhere to the Turkish-Pakistani pact, and British adherence a few months down the road, it was easy for the Foreign Office to sacrifice Tel Aviv's security interests by creating a Middle Eastern alliance which included a number of Arab states but not Israel. With the Baghdad Pact almost a reality, ALPHA would be a means to gain further Arab adherence to a British-sponsored regional defense organization, a goal unchanged since 1951.

Meeting informally in Paris in mid-December, Eden and Dulles agreed upon a joint Anglo-American group meeting in Washington in mid-January.[15] Dulles designated Francis Russell as the State Department representative. He and Shuckburgh would begin planning Project ALPHA.

At the outset, the positions adopted by the Egyptian and Israeli governments diminished prospects for peace. Cairo expected the creation of a land connection between Egypt and Jordan. This was to be accomplished by the cession of a strip of land in the southern part of the Negev Desert, thus eliminating the Israeli port of Eilat. Next, according to Cairo, a solution would have to be developed for the Gaza Strip and its Arab refugees, and a group of Palestinian leaders could be hand-picked to work out with the Israelis the details of repatriation and compensation. No matter what emerged in the negotiations, Egypt would not accept an across-the-board settlement if there was opposition from the Arab states. Finally, Cairo refused to consider face-to-face negotiations, so a mediator would have to shuttle back and forth between the participants. The best solution appeared to be separate approaches between Israel and individual Arab states. Cairo was willing to accept the first contact.[16]

The Israeli view struck at the heart of the Egyptian position.

Apart from the symbolic appeal of the Negev as the inspiration for Israeli idealism and pioneering spirit, the Israelis hoped to develop the area's mineral deposits, especially oil.[17] Eilat, Israel's only link to Africa, was regarded as the key to developing future trade in that region. It was highly unlikely, therefore, that Israel would consider ceding the southern Negev. Tel Aviv would at best permit a road to facilitate free movement across the desert. Two other stumbling blocks included Israeli insistence upon face-to-face negotiations with the Arabs and a Western security guarantee should negotiations prove successful. The Israelis were willing to offer Jordan a free port in Haifa in return for a relaxation of the Arab economic boycott. They were also willing to pay some compensation to the Palestinian refugees in return for transit of the Suez Canal.[18]

Despite differing views, the political situation in both Israel and Egypt seemed to make the ALPHA project feasible. Ben-Gurion's return to office in early 1955 signified a more aggressive Israeli security policy, but it also restored a strong government in Israel. Many State Department and Foreign Office officials believed that Israeli Prime Minister Moshe Sharett might have been willing to reach a compromise with the Arabs but that he did not have the necessary constituency to make the concessions that negotiations required. Ben-Gurion was the only leader with the personal power to lead Israel through a peace process whose price was expected to be high.

A similar situation existed in Egypt. Nasser's success at the Bandung conference rallied neutralist world opinion against the Baghdad Pact and increased his domestic popularity and regional leadership potential.[19] He was the only Arab leader whose domestic position and regional popularity could tolerate peace negotiations with Israel.

Other factors swayed the United States and the United Kingdom to develop ALPHA: increasing border tensions between the Arabs and Israelis, exemplified by the Gaza raid; reports that Nasser was considering the purchase of weapons from the communist bloc; a growing fear that the Israeli government might launch a preemptive attack against Egypt. The Anglo-Egyptian treaty had removed the tension caused by the Suez Canal base issue and would now allow the British to play a role in a mediation effort. The Baghdad Pact seemed to create an opportunity to develop a MEDO. Finally, with time running out, a peace approach was needed to prevent the Soviet Union from making further inroads in the region.

Following Shuckburgh's visit to Washington in late January, the State Department negotiator, Francis Russell, visited London for two weeks in February and returned again in late April. Almost immediately the domestic political concerns of the Eisenhower administration became apparent. As the talks began Dulles conveyed to London that he and Eisenhower had reversed the trends of the previous administration in pursuing a pro-Arab policy. But, the secretary told Roger Makins, the approaching presidential election required greater sympathy for the Israeli position. Many politicians in the United States believed that the "Republicans would have done better in the last election if they had paid more attention to Israeli claims." Dulles was also disturbed that the Foreign Office favored revising the 1949 UN-sponsored armistice agreement between the Arabs and Israelis. Politically the United States could not support any settlement unless it was a peace treaty. Anything less, Dulles felt, would allow the "state of war" to continue.[20]

The British knew that the world "peace" was unacceptable to the Arabs, and the peace initiative was therefore not as important to the Foreign Office as it was to the State Department. In light of Iraq's adherence to the Turkish-Pakistani pact, the British were more concerned with their own commitment and the creation of the Baghdad Pact. Although they knew ALPHA could be jeopardized, much to Washington's chagrin they were willing to risk it.

The first approach would be made to Egypt to ascertain its willingness to take part in the process. Only those elements of a settlement that specially concerned Egypt would be provided. If Nasser responded positively, the mediators would present a broad-based outline to the Israelis to determine Tel Aviv's willingness to make the necessary concessions for a settlement. If the Israelis rejected the proposed basis for discussion, the responsibility for failure of the talks would rest with them. Dulles stressed that American policy toward the Arabs would become less sympathetic as the 1956 election approached.[21] Meeting with Eden in Bangkok in late February, he reiterated the need for action on ALPHA within twelve months. He warned that "the Zionist voters would make it impossible for the United States to continue with a policy of strict impartiality."

Dulles added that the United States would look favorably on a guarantee of any agreements that emerged as well as providing funds for development.[22] Inducements would be required, particularly separate border guarantees and a substantial amount of money, for both parties to consider a treaty.[23] The stickiest area would involve territorial changes.

By March Shuckburgh and Russell completed their scheme for the settlement of territorial issues. These recommendations were premised on the success of the Johnston mission's creation of a Jordan Valley development plan. Such a plan would create water sources for the valley and allow the resettlement of Palestinian refugees in an economically viable area. Israel would be required to relinquish 5 percent of its territory to facilitate the resettlement of about 75,000 refugees; those who chose not to return would receive monetary compensation from the Israeli government. The city of Jerusalem would be divided between Israel and Jordan, with Mount Scopus included on the Jordanian side and equal access to the holy places guaranteed to both sides. Israel was expected to cede a small section of the Negev to allow the construction of a road to meet the Arab demand for a land link. The economic blockade against Israel would be lifted, and a series of treaties of guarantee would be provided by the United States and the United Kingdom.[24]

The Foreign Office and the State Department realized that the Israeli raid on Gaza in February 1955 had severely hampered prospects for peace. Shuckburgh argued that Nasser should not be approached for six to eight weeks, until after the British had adhered to the Baghdad Pact. London did not want Nasser to use ALPHA to drive a wedge between themselves and Iraq.[25] Russell agreed, promising that despite these delays the United States would not succumb to Israeli pressure. He favored telling the Israelis that the Arabs would be brought into a

defense organization first. Thereafter the United States would
be free to judge when the Israelis would be allowed to join. If
Israel continued with provocative actions like the Gaza raid, Tel
Aviv would lose any American security guarantees and the
United States would not be deterred from pursuing cooperation
with the Arab states. Shuckburgh agreed, except that the United
Kingdom was unwilling to enter into security guarantees for
Israel.[26]

Despite Dulles's urge to proceed with the ALPHA package,
the Atlantic allies were forced to acknowledge Egypt's unease
and to wait "until the dust raised by the Turkish-Iraqi Pact began
to settle."[27] Again, British actions to retain the empire were
blocking the peace initiative. The British ambassador to Cairo,
Ralph Stevenson, and the American ambassador to Cairo, Henry
Byroade, advised "that it would be unwise and useless to make
any such approach [to Nasser] at present."[28] At the same time
the Foreign Office was advising that "we should encourage as
many Arab states to join the Baghdad Pact no matter if it makes
it more difficult for Nasser to proceed with ALPHA."[29] Dulles
abhorred this view and wanted the northern tier confined to
northern-tier countries. He believed that Jordan, Lebanon, and
Syria were unimportant from a military perspective. If they
adhered to the Turkish-Iraqi pact "it would further isolate and
embitter Nasser and would give the Israeli government the
occasion for claiming that the United States had put its . . .
weight behind Israel's neighbors and therefore against Israel."
On March 24, 1955, Dulles confessed "that it looks as though
the UK had grabbed the ball on the northern tier policy and was
running away with it in a direction which would have . . . unfortunate consequences."[30]

Clearly the priorities of the two allies were poles apart. While
the United States was trying to create a favorable atmosphere for
launching ALPHA, the British, who were not ready to implement the project, were doing their best to prevent the United
States from proceeding. When the State Department refused to
postpone ALPHA, the British accused the United States of
weakening the mediation effort, which in reality London sought
to destroy.

On April 3, 1955, Byroade, to the dismay of the British, met with Nasser in Cairo and discussed the ALPHA project. Nasser's view was that things must calm down in the Arab world before the initiative could be carried forth. He reiterated his call for a land link between Egypt and Jordan, arguing that a road across the Negev was insufficient. Israel must cede the Negev south of Beersheba to the Arabs. He pledged to support the negotiating process and was open to discussion on all issues except Beersheba.[31]

Dulles's frustrations grew throughout April. He warned the British, following London's accession to the Baghdad Pact, that the United States wished to "avoid the question of Jordan's accession to the pact . . . at a time which might endanger the success of ALPHA" and would commit no aid to an Arab state that joined the pact.[32] With Nasser's performance at the Bandung conference, British pressure on Jordan, Israeli calls for weapons and a security guarantee, and a lack of cooperation from its Atlantic ally in the region, Dulles confided to Secretary of Defense Charles Wilson in a telephone conversation on April 24 that in regard to the Middle East the United States "had no overall policy there."[33] Almost two years after his fact-finding mission to the region, the secretary of state concluded that his policy of containing Soviet expansion and curtailing allied colonialism was at a dead end, and that a shift in the American approach to the region was needed.

Following the events of April, American policymakers decided to proceed with ALPHA by themselves. If the British chose to come along, so be it, but Washington would now take the lead. After two years of frustration, the United States began to take steps officially ending its "backseat role" to the British in the Middle East. Dulles feared that if he did not act quickly, British policy would destroy Western interests by delivering the Arab world, with its huge oil reserves, to the Soviet Union. Eisenhower and Dulles were unwilling to risk a worldwide recession because of the loss of oil sources, and a downturn in the American economy because of British tunnel vision.

Throughout May and early June the United States and the United Kingdom delayed ALPHA because of Nasser's triumph at the Bandung conference and the upcoming elections in Israel. Nasser emerged euphoric from Bandung, as it appeared he would be the main spokesman for Arab nationalism. He was moving closer to fulfilling his goal of a Saudi Arabian-Syrian-Egyptian pact. While Nasser was in Bandung, a number of rumors circulated concerning joint Anglo-American pressure to weaken Egypt and isolate her in the Arab world. Among these rumors were allegations that American officials were raising doubts about the stability of Nasser's regime; that Washington was sabotaging foreign financial support for the Aswan Dam; and that the United States intended to pressure Egypt into making peace with Israel.[34] The deteriorating border situation in Gaza, and the inability of Russell and Shuckburgh to agree on a formula linking Egypt and Jordan specifically across the Negev, prompted Byroade and Stevenson to advise their governments to wait.[35]

Israel's elections were scheduled for July 26. Dulles realized it was not a propitious time for any Israeli government to consider concessions, which ALPHA necessitated. In addition, Israeli distrust of the British was increasing. Believing that the Foreign Office's pro-Arab views should disqualify London from being an effective mediator, Sharett complained to the British ambassador that the United Kingdom was willing to sign three defense arrangements with Israel's enemies but none with Tel Aviv. The British government, Sharett concluded, was "unable to accord to Israel the same measure of friendship and support which it confers on the Arab states which insist on maintaining a state of war against Israel." Eden's position—that a treaty with Israel would come only after a general settlement—was regarded by Tel Aviv as discriminatory.[36] As these feelings became known in Washington, they reinforced Dulles's determination that the United States proceed on its own.

Throughout May, Russell and State Department planners devoted most of their energies to working out the final details for the ALPHA plan and the method of implementation.[37] By early June Dulles decided that it was a good time for a policy statement reviewing the American position on Arab-Israeli issues. Minimal prospects for successful negotiations determined his action. If the U.S. were to pursue secret talks, he feared either a long delay in waiting for the proper moment, or rejection. If success were to be achieved, it had to be this year. On June 8 Dulles asked his aides to prepare a draft of a public statement about ALPHA.[38] A few weeks earlier he had suggested to the British that he might make a public address to delineate Washington's view of an Arab-Israeli peace. The Foreign Office demurred because such a speech would publicize too much of the ALPHA plan.[39] Dulles's motive was to counter the political benefits among Jewish voters of a visit to Israel by Democratic party officials, including W. Averell Harriman, Robert Wagner, and former President Truman. Yet he maintained to the Foreign Office that his statement would not be designed to gain Republican votes but to clarify Washington's position and include an American guarantee for any settlement. Dulles believed it was sensible to commit the United States government to a policy now, so that later, as the election campaign heated up, he would not be compelled to take a stronger pro-Israel stand. In addition, the statement would alleviate Israeli government pressure for the United States to enter into a treaty guarantee. Dulles promised the British ample opportunity to comment on the speech before it was delivered.[40] The British argued that the original ALPHA process was best and that a public statement should not be made until Nasser was sufficiently informed about ALPHA. The British feared the Egyptian leader would regard a public statement as a betrayal.[41]

By mid-July the British were nonetheless resigned to Dulles's shift in tactics. After seeing a draft of the speech, Shuckburgh was mollified. It omitted no parts which might be unpalatable to Israel, making a point that Tel Aviv would not receive a treaty guarantee without a full settlement. The Foreign Office still feared the speech would damage its relations with the Arabs, possibly causing riots and demonstrations; and the British were greatly concerned that such violent reaction could lead to the overthrow of Nuri al-Said in Iraq and ruin the Baghdad Pact. But they considered it best to let Dulles proceed as soon as possible, before the "American Zionists" forced the secretary of state to yield in his views.[42]

In April 1955 Winston Churchill at last resigned and was succeeded by Anthony Eden as prime minister. Harold Macmillan, who assumed Eden's former position as foreign secretary, was unhappy with the idea of a public statement by Dulles, believing the risks involved "would fall to a large extent on Great Britain by reason of her commitments in the area." The foreign secretary called instead for a joint Anglo-American statement. He agreed with Shuckburgh that the United Kingdom had little choice but to support Dulles, but he also expected the British should receive something in return for that support. While meeting with Dulles in Paris on July 14 he asked his American counterpart to have the United States join the Baghdad Pact upon the conclusion of ALPHA.[43] Dulles responded favorably—once a full Arab-Israeli settlement was reached, the United States would be willing to inform Iraq that it would join the Baghdad Pact. Until then, Washington would support the northern tier and help defray the cost of supplying Centurion tanks to Baghdad. Macmillan accepted the American position, promising that the Foreign Office would issue its own statement of support after Dulles delivered his speech.[44] Through the remainder of July and August the British pushed for American assurances about "their ultimate adherence to the Turkish-Iraqi Pact and their readiness to make a substantial contribution towards the supply of British tanks to Iraq."[45] Again, the real motivation for British support of ALPHA was the expansion of the Baghdad Pact.

Dulles led the British to believe that his Middle East policy address would be delivered on September 8. By mid-August he shifted gears, informing the exasperated British that the date would now be August 26. Dulles advanced his schedule because of two developments. First was the major setback suffered by the Johnston mission when the Arabs decided not to negotiate bilateral treaties with Israel but to negotiate as a whole through the Arab League. Dulles regarded this event as an indefinite postponement of his plans for the Jordan Valley; he viewed the Arab League as a "morass" into which the Johnston plan would eventually "sink."[46] His second concern was developments between Egypt and the Soviet Union.

On June 9, unable to obtain American weapons, Nasser informed Byroade that "he should accept Russia's offer of military equipment" and planned to send a mission to Moscow the following week. Still, he told Byroade, he preferred American military equipment.[47] Throughout June and early July Nasser continued to try to close an arms deal with the United States, but the State Department believed he was not being candid about his discussions with the Soviets, so it stalled rather than pushing his requests. Aware of the long-range disadvantages of Soviet weapons, concerned about the weak morale in the Egyptian army and his own security needs, Nasser continued negotiations with Moscow.[48]

Serious arms talks between Cairo and Moscow resumed on July 23 with the arrival in Egypt of Dmitri Shepilov, editor of *Pravda*. Shepilov offered MIG fighter planes and other weapons to Egypt. Nasser again renewed efforts to obtain arms from the United States, but Dulles felt that Nasser was using his "Russian card" to pressure Washington. Once the CIA convinced him that Nasser was serious, the secretary of state dispatched Kermit Roosevelt to try to convince Nasser to forgo an arms deal with the Soviets; but it was too late.[49] According to Mohamed Heikal, Nasser was further persuaded to accept the Soviet offer after the Israeli general election on July 26 which confirmed Ben-Gurion in office. A few days later it was learned that the French, upset by Nasser's support for the rebels in Algeria, diverted to Israel six squadrons of Mystere IV planes which had been earmarked for NATO.[50] Then, on August 31, an Israeli raid on the Egyptian town of Khan Yunis left thirty-nine dead.[51] The official announcement of what came to be known as the Czech arms deal was made on September 27, 1955.

Dulles finally stated his Middle East policy in a speech to the Council of Foreign Relations in New York on August 26.[52] The secretary of state addressed three principal problems "that conspicuously require to be solved": "the plight of the 900,000 Arab refugees"; "the pall of fear that hangs over the Arab and Israel people alike"; and "the lack of fixed permanent boundaries between Israel and its Arab neighbors." Asserting that "compensation was due from Israel to the refugees," Dulles offered

American support for an international loan to assist the process and "facilitate the resettlement of the refugees." On the question of fear, Dulles offered to have "the United States join in formal treaty engagements to prevent or thwart any effort by either side to alter by force the boundaries between Israel and her Arab neighbors."

To resolve the third issue, unspecified "adjustments" were needed.[53] The United States had earlier devised a plan for the Negev Desert under which Israel would cede two small triangles north of Eilat, "one to Egypt with its base on the Egypt-Israel frontier, the other to Jordan with its base on the Jordan-Israel frontier." These two triangles were to meet at their corner points, and from there a road from Egypt to Jordan, under Arab sovereignty, would pass over the road from Beersheba to Eilat, which would remain under Israeli control.[54] This plan was unacceptable to both Egypt and Israel. By speaking of border "adjustments," Dulles hoped to create Egyptian interest without provoking a rejection of the entire plan.[55]

In Dulles's speech the United States for the first time came close to an offer of mediation, with Dulles suggesting American guarantees for a final treaty and the financing of refugee compensation and resettlement. Washington also offered to help solve the boundary issue.[56] It appears that Dulles wanted the Arabs to compare what the Soviet Union and the United States had to offer. Moscow could provide weapons for war, but only Washington could offer the possibility of redressing Arab grievances.

Reaction to the speech was heightened because of the escalation of violence in the Gaza Strip during the last week in August and the first week in September. The British publicly supported Dulles's remarks, calling them "an important contribution toward the solution of the most critical and outstanding problem in the Middle East." They promised to guarantee any agreements reached and "make their contribution to any loan to Israel which was designed to compensate Palestinian refugees." Eden's true feelings, however, were summarized in a comment made to the Foreign Office: "Mr. Dulles started all of this and, if he has gotten himself in trouble, it is not for us to help him out."[57] The Israeli and Egyptian responses were not optimistic.

To understand the Israeli viewpoint one must examine the major problems preoccupying the Israeli government in the summer of 1955. From the inception of the Jewish state, the integration of hundreds of thousands of immigrants had placed an enormous strain on both the economy and the security of Israel. In the early 1950s the Israeli government hoped that the future would hold peace with the Arabs. When the Arab terms for peace emerged during the ALPHA process—the acknowledgment of the right of the Palestinian refugees to return to Israel, and territorial concessions to the neighboring states— Israel's optimism faded. Based on the needs of Israeli security, Tel Aviv regarded Arab demands as intolerable. Jordan's inability to conclude a peace treaty drafted in 1949; greater nationalistic and anti-Israeli propaganda in the Arab world; and the growing number of border incidents led Israeli leaders to conclude that the time was not right for an American mediation effort. Prime Minister Ben-Gurion believed the Arabs would make peace only when they realized they could not destroy Israel.[58]

Despite objections, Israeli reaction to Dulles's speech left some openings for maneuver. Israel criticized Dulles's remarks about linking Israeli frontier adjustments with a security guarantee. Abba Eban informed Dulles on September 6 that while Israel had no intention of relinquishing the Negev, "frontier adjustments should not be made an obstacle to a security guarantee."[59] Publicly Moshe Sharett declared that Israel would make no unilateral territorial concessions, but it would consider minor border adjustments. Privately the Israelis decided not to reject Dulles's initiative until they saw how Egypt's negotiations for Soviet weapons would affect the American proposals.[60]

The Arab world's response to Dulles's speech lay with Egypt: if Cairo rejected the initiative, the other Arab states would follow. The Egyptian government's reaction coincided with its general policy toward Israel which had been pursued since Dulles's May 1953 visit to Cairo. The escalation of tensions in this period was a direct result of Nasser's belief that Egypt's claim to leadership in the Arab world would gain wider support if Cairo were seen as being in the forefront of the struggle against Israel. Nasser's conciliatory statements between May 1953 and Dulles's August 1955 speech were designed only to better relations with the United States. Throughout the period Egypt had sought economic and military aid from Washington as well as diplomatic support in its negotiations with the British over the Suez Canal base.

Egypt's primary concern in August 1955 was to defuse the expected angry American reaction to its approaching arms deal with the Soviet Union. Cairo therefore indicated readiness to consider the American proposals but expressed a desire to study them further. Despite this moderating position, Egypt reiterated that it must have the southern Negev in any peace settlement with Israel.[61]

Dulles was almost buoyant in discussing with Eisenhower the reaction to his speech. But when the Czech arms deal was announced, the secretary's confidence fell.[62]

Washington's response to the arms deal reflected the weakness in American Middle East policy. The administration had planned to use the Arabs as a bulwark against Soviet penetration of the region. Dulles now feared the arms deal would destroy the ALPHA plan.[63] If that occurred, Egypt would not join the West against the Soviets, and none of the administration's goals for the area could be achieved.

Instead of grasping the situation, Dulles expected to persuade Nasser to be more amenable toward American wishes for the area. This attitude continued to ignore the Egyptian leader's pan-Arabist, neutralist policy which was designed to elevate him to the leadership of the Arab world. Dulles was soon forced to realize that it would not be easy to alter Nasser's position, especially as the only "cards" the United States could play against the Egyptian leader were negative.[64] Therefore on October 4, at a press conference, Dulles read a prepared statement which remarked, "It is difficult to be critical of countries which, feeling themselves endangered, seek arms which they sincerely believe they need for their defense."[65]

Information that the Soviets had also offered to help finance the Aswan Dam project shelved any impulse on Dulles's part to use pressure against the Egyptians.[66] The Aswan Dam project was a plan to harness the waters of the Nile River at Aswan in order to provide 75 percent of Egypt's hydroelectric power needs. The plan was to be financed by Western support under the auspices of the World Bank, which had yet to reach agreement with Egypt. The United States favored the plan as a means of persuading Nasser to be more forthcoming in ending the Arab-Israeli conflict.

On October 6 Dulles informed the National Security Council that the Russians had now opened a new front in the Middle East and that the United States "could not fight the Soviet Union on the political front with the existing resources programmed for the Middle East." Dulles admitted that events were moving too fast in the area and that he needed greater guidance in making proper decisions. He called for a review of administration policy.[67] He admitted that the United States had not anticipated the Soviet Union making large quantities of military equipment available to the Arab states. This resulted in the West's losing exclusive control of the arms balance between the Arabs and Israelis.[68] In addition, intelligence estimates concluded that Soviet arms aid to Egypt would "complicate if not block the achievement of the two major US objectives in the Middle East: an Arab-Israeli settlement and the creation of effective regional defense arrangements against communism." Reports reiterated further the fear that Israel would now resort to a "preventive war."[69] Other reports warned of the effects of the arms deal on Saudi Arabia, raising American fears of the possible loss of a reliable oil source and the Dhahran air base. And trends in Syria created the possibility of Anglo-American intervention to overthrow a pro-communist regime.[70]

Intelligence sources argued that despite Nasser's joy over newfound prestige resulting from the arms deal, he was no more anxious to be dominated by the Soviets than he was to join a Western alliance. Nasser was convinced he could walk the middle path. With these ideas in mind, CIA director Allen Dulles warned that if the West turned its back on the Egyptian leader, Nasser would accept further Soviet aid and "probably with a good chance of success... bring Syria and Saudi Arabia along with him."[71]

The United States was not yet ready to write off Nasser; doing so would open the way for further penetration by the Soviet Union. In light of the administration's limited maneuverability, it seemed sounder to continue diplomacy, hoping that in time Nasser could be convinced to turn to the West.

The entire premise of Dulles's foreign policy, however, was mistaken. Rather than accept the fact that the administration had pursued a flawed strategy, Dulles sought to use Israel as a scapegoat. On October 21, in a conversation with Eisenhower, Dulles offered:

> We are in the present jam because past administrations always dealt with the area from a political standpoint and had tried to meet the wishes of the Zionists in the country and that had created a basic antagonism with the Arabs. That was what the Soviet Union was now capitalizing on. We must develop a national non-partisan policy or we will be apt to lose the entire area, and possibly Africa. There was a great danger, with the upcoming election, that the Israelis would make some moves at the time which for political reasons it might seem to the advantage of some to back, but with disastrous consequences.[72]

Until 1955 the Soviet Union was never the threat to American interests in the Middle East that Washington perceived. The Soviet role in the region was minimal until late 1955. Historically the Soviets found the Middle East ideologically incompatible. Traditionally the devotion of the Arab world to a fervent Islamic faith pointed to a vehement anticommunist stance. In addition, certain Arab governments wary of outside meddlesome powers were developing a strong preference toward neutralism and pan-Arabism. Why would Arab nationalists, fighting so hard to end Western colonial domination, exchange it for domination by the Soviets? Eisenhower administration policies in fact helped turn the Soviets' Middle East policy.

A December 21, 1955, National Security Council memorandum as much as suggested Soviet moves in the region had resulted from Western actions. After the creation of the state of Israel, the memo noted, the Soviet government had courted Tel

Aviv, but by the mid-1950s the Soviets concluded that nothing would be gained. Moscow now hoped to pressure pro-Western interests in the Middle East to modify their stance on European-related issues. In addition, the Soviets had a community of fate with the Egyptians in their opposition to the Baghdad Pact. Historically the Soviets were interested in a policy of neutralism, especially if it could be used against Western interests. Moscow knew that Nasser's brand of neutralism angered the West and decided to try to manipulate it for the Kremlin's own interests. The West could appeal to democratic institutions in the Arab world, but Easterners knew only despotism, so Dulles's hopes to develop a fear of communism went for naught. Because the only democratic Westerner the Arabs had ever known was the "imperialist," it was difficult for the State Department to convince them they should fear the imperialistic designs of the Soviet Union when they saw no concrete evidence for it.[73]

Instead of plotting to overthrow the government—a tactic which the Eisenhower administration had adopted when challenged in Iran and Guatemala—Dulles sent messengers to protest Nasser's decision and to persuade him to change his mind. This proved futile. With British support, Dulles then sought a rapprochement with the Egyptian leader. To offset any future Soviet proposals to build the Aswan Dam, he offered to help finance the project.[74] The offer was consistent with American avoidance of the Baghdad Pact and the sidestepping of Israel's requests for arms.

The Czech arms deal was a turning point for Ben-Gurion. The Israeli government always believed that the "human element" could overcome Arab materiel and weapons superiority. After the Czech arms deal, according to Israeli Chief of Staff Moshe Dayan, this rationalization was open to question. Weapons would begin flowing into Egypt by November 1955, and the Israeli general staff felt it would take six to eight months for Egypt to assimilate them. Dayan expected an attack in the late spring of 1956.[75]

Ben-Gurion believed that events seemed to favor the Arabs. On September 11, 1955, the Egyptians tightened their blockade in the Straits of Tiran. On October 4 and 18 Dulles refused to criticize the Czech arms deal. Israeli attempts to buy weapons from the United States were stalemated. The United States also appeared to be involved in the Aswan loan to Egypt. In addition, in October the Egyptians and Syrians had signed a defense pact, and the United States still refused to consider a security guarantee for Israel until an overall settlement with the Arabs was reached.[76] On October 23 a frustrated Ben-Gurion ordered Dayan to make military contingency plans involving the Gaza Strip and Sinai.[77]

Ben-Gurion felt that London and Washington were ganging up on Israel. Only land could provide security for the Israeli prime minister. A Western-sponsored peace meant a smaller and less secure Israel. Ben-Gurion believed it was again necessary to show the West Israel's independence and ability to resist pressure; yet he also coveted Western sympathy and support for his country's retention of the land it possessed. Emphasizing the harmful nature of the Egyptian blockade of the Straits of Tiran, Israel pressed forward with its military plans as well as its desire to show the West its resolve and autonomy.[78]

Insight into Israeli foreign policy is gained by understanding the continued psychological effects of the Holocaust on the Jewish state. For Israel the West must be given proof that any Middle Eastern peace structure which ignored Israel's security needs was unacceptable. Whether it was referred to as the Holocaust syndrome or the Masada complex, Israel's need for security often approached hysteria and permeated all of Israeli society. Ben-Gurion himself was convinced that should Israel temporarily lower its guard, first the Egyptians and then the other Arab states would attack. Israeli foreign policy was a response to this preconceived insecurity. Like any neurosis, an anxiety is not necessarily based on facts; but it is real if so perceived by the victim, in this case the Israeli government. Tel Aviv believed it had six to eight months before Egypt absorbed its new weapons. The Israeli government believed that Nasser was using the American peace initiative to stall until he was militarily capable of launching an attack.

Israeli fears increased not only because of Egypt's newfound weapons but also because of British diplomatic moves. On

conceivable that the American offer to help finance Aswan, which was substantially larger than the British offer, was partially linked to Nasser's acceptance of an American mediation effort.[89] Although the Czech arms deal made Nasser less likely to compromise his territorial aspirations, it did confront him with the need to appease Washington and avoid war with Israel until the Soviet equipment could be absorbed. Thus Nasser's acceptance of an American mediation effort allowed the Egyptian leader to reduce tension and gain time.[90]

The Israelis had always approved of negotiations with the Arabs to achieve minor territorial adjustments. Ben-Gurion had never rejected the idea of American mediation, only the transfer of large areas of Israeli territory to the Arabs. Thus when the United States broached its mediation effort in late December, and hinted at the possibility of providing American weapons, the Israeli government accepted.[91] Soviet equipment had begun arriving in Egypt in early December, so the need to start the negotiation process became paramount. By month's end the United States proposed an emissary to conduct secret talks with the leaders of Egypt and Israel to explore possibilities for reaching a settlement. The Anderson mission was born.

As 1956 dawned the United States and the United Kingdom appeared to agree on tactics and key issues in the Middle East. But an examination of documents pertaining to ALPHA and the Anderson mission reveals two parties whose goals for the region were very much in conflict. The Foreign Office used the peace process to reduce Arab-Israeli tensions as a means toward expanding the Baghdad Pact, thus hoping to preserve British economic and political interests in the region. The State Department believed the coming Anderson mission could reduce tensions in the area, blunt Jewish political pressure in the coming election at home, and eventually create support for an American-dominated defense organization to block Soviet encroachment in the Middle East.

The key issue between the two allies was their attitude toward the Arab governments. The British wished to bring pressure on the Arabs, particularly Jordan, to join the Baghdad Pact. The United States feared that pressure would rekindle charges of

Western colonialism and that the Soviets would turn Arab hostility against Western interests. The result would be economic disaster for the West because of the loss of vital oil sources and markets. The launching of the Anderson mission was an American attempt to control events so that Britain and the combatants in the Arab-Israeli conflict would not destroy Washington's realpolitik for the Middle East.

6 Two Failures: The Anderson Mission and the Aswan Loan

By January 1956 a pattern of disagreements had emerged between the United States and the United Kingdom over Middle East policies. Since 1953 Washington had clearly believed that London's desire to maintain as much as possible of its Middle Eastern empire hindered American efforts to reduce tensions in the area. State Department policy was designed to protect Western economic interests and impede Soviet advancement. British policy appeared to make the achievement of those goals as difficult as possible.

Despite their cooperation in creating the ALPHA project, as 1955 drew to a close the interests of the two countries were no longer complementary. The British continued to use ALPHA to broaden the membership of the Baghdad Pact to include Jordan and the United States. As Washington's awareness of this pattern grew, it decided in December 1955 to implement its own mediation effort in the region.

Known as the Anderson mission, the peace initiative was led by Robert Anderson, deputy secretary of defense until August 5, 1955, and a close friend of the president. It was designed to promote an Arab-Israeli settlement which would pave the way for securing Western interests in the region. Launched at the end of January 1956, the mediation effort failed by early March. The entire process proved how illusory it was to expect Egyptian Prime Minister Nasser to promote American interests in the area. The Eisenhower administration discovered that its two-and-a-half-year investment in the Egyptian leader had paid few dividends. As a result, on March 28, 1956, President Eisenhower approved Operation OMEGA, another attempt to reorient Nasser's policies while trying to create an alternative Arab leader, one who could help Washington gain the support of other Arab states to deny further Soviet influence in the region.

American distrust of British intentions reduced London's role in the intermediary effort. The State Department did not inform the Foreign Office that the Anderson mission was to take place until January 3, a full week after the Egyptian and Israeli governments had agreed to participate.[1] Throughout the process the British were left in the background: their involvement might resurrect the charge of "colonialism." In mid-March, reassessing its policy options, the United States informed the British that ALPHA had been replaced by a new strategy, designated OMEGA. While it appeared that the two allies were in general agreement on this new policy orientation, in fact major differences existed. These differences clouded discussions between Washington and London and set a pattern in Anglo-American relations which culminated during the Suez crisis. Exploring why the Anderson mission failed, and examining the new OMEGA strategy concerning the Aswan Dam loan, provides insight into why Nasser's nationalization of the Suez Canal in July 1956 resulted in an American declaration of independence from the British in the Middle East.

The success or failure of the Anderson mission rested with the responses of two men, Egyptian Prime Minister Nasser and Israeli Prime Minister Ben-Gurion. From the outset their positions appeared unbridgeable; Anderson faced an almost impossible task in trying to close the gap.

On November 17, 1955, Egyptian Foreign Minister Mohammad Fawzi, speaking for Nasser, informed American Ambassador Henry Byroade that Egypt was prepared to work toward a settlement of Arab-Israeli issues at the earliest practical date. The process was to be highly secret, and "if matters could be moved to where Egypt believed there was a 51% chance of success, Egypt would at that time take [the] lead with other Arab states even at the risk of severe opposition."[2] Until an agreement was reached, Fawzi emphasized, no other Arab state should be brought into the process.

As to substance, in determining which party should control Jerusalem, Nasser supported any solution that was acceptable to the world community. The Egyptians favored an agreement for the refugees based on a combination of repatriation and compensation by Israel. The refugees could choose which option to accept.[3] The key issue was territorial. Stressing that the "actual continuity of Arab sovereignty should be reestablished," Nasser was not satisfied with a narrow corridor between Egypt and Jordan through Israel. He demanded a sizable amount of territory, the specifics to be determined later. Once all issues were resolved, the Arabs would lift their economic blockade of Israel, and Egypt would allow the transit of Israeli shipping through the Suez Canal.[4] Another point of contention which developed during the talks was Nasser's refusal to discuss issues with Ben-Gurion face to face.[5]

At the outset Nasser's approach was couched in generalities; once these generalities became clouded with details, problems ensued. The United States accepted the Egyptian viewpoints at face value but made a major error in not understanding what motivated Nasser.

From the outset the Israelis suspected they would face "intolerable pressure to achieve an intolerable settlement."[6] In a meeting with Secretary of State Dulles on November 21, 1955, Israeli Foreign Minister Moshe Sharett argued against the concept of territorial contiguity between the Arab states, since it had never previously existed. Sharett believed it was an Arab slogan for Israel "to cut itself in two." Israel would agree to exchange "territory on a small scale on the principle of mutuality," but it would not give up vital areas such as Eilat.[7] Indeed, by December 6 the Israelis had taken the "irrevocable decision not to surrender any territory," particularly in the Negev.[8] Sharett stressed Israeli acceptance of the Jordan Valley plan, which if adopted by the Arabs would contribute to the resettlement of Arab refugees. At the time the Israeli foreign minister could not see Israel undertaking the settlement of tens of thousands of Arab families in Israel in addition to all "her burdens and contributions."[9] Ben-Gurion's insistence upon a face-to-face meeting with Nasser at some point during negotiations illustrated the disparity between Egyptian and Israeli positions. Lying beneath the surface was Israel's strong belief that Egypt was getting "the best of both worlds: arms from Russia, loans from the United States and United Kingdom, and support for concessions from Israel." Ben-Gurion suspected that Nasser had agreed to the Anderson mission only to gain time for the Egyptian army to absorb Soviet weapons. The Israeli government expected an Egyptian attack sometime during the summer of 1956.[10]

The American position aimed at reversing Soviet penetration of the region.[11] Dulles wanted Israel to go a long way to meet the needs of the Arabs, including "concessions in the Negev to provide an Arab area joining Egypt with the rest of the Arab world."[12] The remainder of Dulles's views, outlined in his August 26 speech, had changed little by January 1956. To implement his vision, America would pressure Israel by withholding a decision on Israeli arms requests for as long as possible. In addition, the United States would extend the hope of a bilateral security arrangement once a settlement was reached.[13] As an inducement to Egypt, Washington would use its December 16 offer to help finance the Aswan Dam project.[14]

From the beginning of the Anderson mission, the British simply were not a major factor. Both the Egyptians and the Israelis distrusted London—and so did Washington. The Israelis believed that Eden sought to reimpose the 1947 United Nations Partition Plan. Egypt was convinced that the British wished to isolate Cairo in the Arab world in order to expand the Baghdad Pact and maintain its colonial presence. Eisenhower's attitude toward the British is most interesting. On January 10 the president wrote in his diary that existing problems had been aggravated "by the fact that Britain and ourselves have not seen eye to eye in a number of instances...." Eisenhower listed British pressure on Jordan to adhere to the Baghdad Pact and the resulting domestic unrest in Amman as examples of London's foolishness in the region.[15] On the eve of the Anderson mission, it was clear that London was to be excluded.

According to William Ewald, an aide to President Eisenhower, the mission, code-named GAMMA, was put together in the utmost secrecy by Dulles and his brother, CIA chief Allen Dulles. Travel took place on disguised flights by a small plane that shuttled from Cairo to Jerusalem by way of Rome and Athens. Progress on negotiations was reported to Eisenhower by Anderson using a cable network developed by the CIA, not the State Department. The entire mission was anchored by two of the agency's most capable officers, Kermit Roosevelt in Egypt and James Angleton in Tel Aviv. They reported directly to the "case officer," Allen Dulles.[16]

Anderson, Secretary of State Dulles, and Eisenhower met in the White House on January 11 to discuss strategy for the upcoming mission. Eisenhower realized he could no longer control the arms buildup in the Middle East with the emergence of the Soviets as a major arms supplier for the Arabs. Having lost its role as the sole distributor of weapons in the region, the United States must arrange an accommodation between the Arabs and the Israelis in order to avert a war that would be a political and economic disaster for the West.[17] Eisenhower gave Anderson letters to Nasser and Ben-Gurion establishing Anderson's credentials to speak for the president. He authorized Anderson to offer both sides virtually any material aid in return for concessions to achieve peace. "Eisenhower," Anderson later recalled, "just about gave me carte blanche."[18]

Anderson arrived in Cairo on January 17 and met with Nasser that evening. Immediately Nasser attacked the Baghdad Pact as representing the West's attempt to isolate him in the Arab world, leaving him to fight Israel by himself. He was angry with the British also because of London's pressure on the Jordanian government to adhere to the pact.[19]

Nasser's outburst stemmed from a single-minded desire to maintain his special position in the Arab world. Elaborating on a theme that characterized all his meetings with Anderson, Nasser argued that a settlement with Israel would be highly unpopular in the Arab world. He feared he would appear as "having sold out to the western powers." If an agreement were reached, the Egyptian leader said, it could not be made public until Arab feelings toward Israel could be soothed.[20] Nasser called for a six-month period following an agreement to prepare the Arab world. But this was unacceptable to the United States because it would coincide with the presidential campaign, and to the Israelis because it would allow time for the Egyptian military to absorb its Soviet weapons.[21]

Two evenings later Nasser stated again that a "quick settlement was impossible" and that an atmosphere for Arab acceptance must be created. On other points, he believed that while few Arab refugees would choose to return to Israel, they must be allowed to select either repatriation or compensation. A formula calling for 20 percent of the refugee population per year to be allowed to return over a five-year period was acceptable, with financial compensation for those who chose not to be repatriated. To ensure his position in Egypt and in the Arab world, the Egyptian leader reiterated the need for a large territorial cession in the Negev linking Egypt and Jordan, and insisted that a face-to-face meeting with Ben-Gurion was "impossible."[22]

Throughout the talks Nasser often alluded to his fear that if he made peace with Israel he "would be regarded as a traitor and would face the loss of power or the threat of assassination." Nasser told Anderson on January 21 that he wanted the Arabs to believe they had received a substantial part of the territory "which they felt was unjustly taken from them." But any agreement would take time, and the process could not be rushed.[23] Nasser's main goal was to preserve his standing in the Arab world. After Anderson's departure for Israel, Nasser confided to Kermit Roosevelt that if he went along with Anderson's suggestions he would "give Nuri Said a weapon with which to destroy him."[24]

Anderson proceeded to Tel Aviv and began a series of meetings with Ben-Gurion and Sharett on January 23. Ben-Gurion emphasized Nasser's lack of sincerity. After hearing Anderson's summary of his Cairo talks, the Israeli prime minister expressed concern that the longer the settlement process, the more time Egypt had to digest Soviet weapons.[25] Ben-Gurion feared Egyptian warplanes because he lacked the defensive weapons to protect Israeli cities. A United States sale of necessary equipment to Israel would, he argued, deter an Egyptian attack. The prime minister also feared the Arabs would use the refugee issue as a "fifth column" against Israel. And he rejected Nasser's territorial demand, refusing to allow Israel to be dislodged from the Red Sea and Eilat.[26] Ben-Gurion's chief concern was to crush the idea that "Israel should be sacrificed in order to achieve Arab alliances."[27]

On January 24 Sharett stated that Nasser could easily assuage Israeli suspicions by agreeing to face-to-face talks. Why, Sharett asked, was Israel expected to make concessions for peace, but not the Arabs? While the West refused to sell weapons to Israel, the Soviets made unlimited quantities available to the Arabs.[28] Anderson's first round of talks revealed an Egyptian leader obsessed with his stature in the Arab world and an Israeli prime minister who wanted direct talks as a show of faith.

Dulles was convinced, nevertheless, that it was a propitious time for Nasser to make peace. Egypt was receiving weapons from the Soviet Union. Nasser could obtain the Aswan Dam loan if he accepted the offer of the World Bank. The West was not selling weapons to Israel, and the Israelis were willing to negotiate. Finally, the British were about to complete their withdrawal from the Suez Canal base. If Nasser did not respond quickly enough, Dulles's greatest fear was that the Israeli military would sway the cabinet into launching a preemptive strike against Egypt. What's more, if progress in the talks was not made by March 1 the Israeli government planned to construct a hydroelectric power plant at the Banat Ya'cub bridge, just north of Lake Galilee. This would create a water diversion canal in the demilitarized zone between Israel and Syria and affect the flow of the Jordan River in Syrian territory. If the Israelis resumed

digging the canal, the Syrians would certainly attack and precipitate a full-scale war.[29]

When Anderson returned to Cairo on January 26 he again
faced Nasser's anger over Iraqi membership in the Baghdad
Pact. The Egyptian leader also told Anderson that if Israel
resumed work at Banat Ya'cub, he would provide military support for Syria.[30]

Allen Dulles warned his brother that the status quo could not
be maintained for three to six months. The American public
would not accept an arms embargo on Israel at a time when
Soviet arms were pouring into Egypt and Syria. Allen Dulles
was also concerned that the "British will not stand still long in
getting into [the] act and in other area operations."[31]

Before Anderson's return to Tel Aviv, Nasser told Roosevelt
that the major issues involved in a settlement were the Negev
and the question of timing. He thought the other issues were
minor and of no consequence without agreement on the major
issues.[32] Upon arriving in Tel Aviv, Anderson encountered Ben-
Gurion's renewed call for direct meetings: "I am willing to
concede things that Nasser never dreamed of but only if we can
discuss matters with him personally. . . . If we could meet, I
know there would be peace in ten days." Ben-Gurion agreed to
border adjustments linking Palestinian villages to farms, but he
was predictably adamant about concessions in the Negev.[33]
Upon completion of his talks with the Israelis, Anderson had
accomplished little in bridging the gap between the two sides.

The prevailing atmosphere in the region seriously limited
both Egyptian and Israeli freedom of action. Military raids,
border infiltration, and abusive propaganda made it politically
impossible for either leader to budge. Despite the dismal outcome of his talks, Anderson returned to Washington believing he
had laid the groundwork for future discussions.[34] In addition, he
delivered a letter from Ben-Gurion to President Eisenhower
expressing disappointment with Nasser's attitude and again asking for defensive weapons.[35] Before Anderson returned to the
region in early March, a number of related issues began to
crystallize.

In late 1955, despite State Department opposition, Arabists in the British Foreign Office had begun to pressure Jordan to adhere to the Baghdad Pact. The pressure manifested itself in a gift to Jordan of ten jet fighters and an offer of economic aid and $11 million for the Arab Legion.[36] On December 6 General Sir Gerald Templer, chief of the British imperial general staff, had gone to Amman for discussions with Jordanian officials. It was readily understood that he aimed to convince King Hussein to adhere to the Baghdad Pact. On December 14 Prime Minister Said al-Mufti and four members of the Jordanian cabinet resigned. Hussein asked Haza al-Majali, a proponent of the Baghdad Pact, to form a new government. At once demonstrations against the new government and the pact broke out in Amman and throughout the West Bank, forcing al-Majali to resign. The demonstrations continued until December 20.[37]

In early January the British Foreign Office concluded that "His Majesty's Government's essential interests in the area can hardly be secured without a reasonable degree of Egyptian cooperation." With Nasser's domestic position secure and his neutralist stance gaining in popularity, British policymakers realized that Egyptian cooperation would evolve only if Nasser achieved economic and political advantage in the region. On January 7 the Foreign Office discussed the possible removal of Nasser but concluded that *no* Egyptian regime would relinquish a leading role in the Arab world. As long as the Arab-Israeli conflict continued, the Soviet threat would remain. Nasser was the best bet to secure peace over the "Palestine" issue; if he failed, the Foreign Office believed "we should probably be better off with a government of politicians."[38]

As Anthony Eden prepared to visit Washington at the end of January, Anglo-American differences over Middle East strategy were clear. The State Department still favored a long-term policy of encouraging Arab unity under Egyptian leadership, arguing this was the only way to forestall the Soviet Union from acting as the champion of the Arabs. Conversely, the Foreign Office had difficulty reconciling Egyptian leadership aspirations with London's need to promote loyalty to the Baghdad Pact. The United States did not favor involvement in inter-Arab politics, particularly with Egypt, which would only increase Israeli pressures for an American security guarantee.[39] These views, and American pressure on the British to settle the Buraimi dispute with Saudi Arabia, had underlined policy disagreements between London and Washington even before Eden arrived in the United States.

Eden visited Washington from January 30 through February 1. Three issues were uppermost in his mind: how to put "teeth" in the Tripartite Declaration of 1950; how to preserve and expand the Baghdad Pact; and how to win American support for his dispute with Saudi Arabia. On all these counts, his meetings with American officials were deeply disappointing.[40]

The British prime minister needed more than another declaration of Anglo-American determination to prevent hostilities between the Arabs and Israel. He wished to develop preparatory military moves to convince the Middle Eastern states of Anglo-American seriousness.[41] Although Dulles appeared sympathetic, he sidestepped Eden's request by pointing out constitutional difficulties with Congress in making such moves. Dulles's major concern was to avoid appearing to act in concert with the British in the region. For the immediate strategy of coping with Nasser, both sides appeared to be in agreement. Both realized that their future status in the region depended upon Nasser. Hoping his response to the Aswan Dam loan would be an indication of Nasser's sincerity, Eden warned the Eisenhower administration that "he did not know how long we could go along with Nasser" if he continued his attitude toward Nuri and his attempts to destroy the Baghdad Pact. Eden reluctantly agreed that no further efforts would be made to bring other states into the arrangement.[42]

The remaining issue was Buraimi. Eden wanted American pressure on King Saud to produce concessions in favor of the British position. Eisenhower felt the British should offer the Saudi government more than "minor" frontier modifications. Washington's view was colored by the interests of American oil companies, the hope of reorienting King Saud to a stronger pro-Western position, and the desire for British support in U.S. negotiations with the Saudis over the Dhahran air base.[43]

Dulles briefed Eden on the ongoing Anderson mission and

told Sir Anthony that "the initial reactions of Israel and Egypt were worse than expected." Dulles believed that Nasser "would follow dilatory tactics as long as he could get what he wanted."[44] As his visit drew to a close, Eden realized it would not be the success he had hoped. Washington had refused to offer anything of substance. The Declaration of Washington, issued at the trip's conclusion, resounded with empty words. Eisenhower's aide, Sherman Adams, has written, "Eden's visit to Washington did not resolve one serious difference between the American and British positions on the Middle East question."[45] In addition to these disappointments in Washington, developments in Jordan pointed to a further erosion of British power in the Middle East.

Egyptian propaganda against the British in Jordan continued until March 1, when King Hussein announced the dismissal of General John Glubb Pasha, the British officer in command of the Arab Legion. Glubb's dismissal was a turning point for Eden, who blamed the entire episode on Nasser. Although Egyptian propaganda created an anti-British atmosphere in Jordan, King Hussein's dismissal of Glubb was motivated by domestic politics and his desire to command his own army, the most powerful force in the country. Explaining the move to Paul Duke, the British ambassador, Hussein claimed that Glubb's administration had permitted grave deficiencies in equipment and stores in the Arab Legion and provoked discontent among Arab officers. Hussein also resented the generally accepted belief that Glubb was the most important figure in Jordan. Failing to act, Hussein said, would have resulted in a coup against his government.[46]

Whether or not Hussein's explanation was sincere, Eden's reaction was clouded by British politics and his own developing hatred for Nasser. In the 1956 parliamentary elections the Conservatives had suffered substantial losses to the Labor party. In addition, differences over economic matters between Harold Macmillan, the former foreign minister and current chancellor of the exchequer, and Eden were becoming daily more pronounced. Many of Eden's advisers suspected Macmillan of working within the party to replace Eden as prime minister. With British troops about to complete their withdrawal from the Suez Canal base, Eden could little afford another major setback.[47]

For Eden the Glubb firing was a major blow to Britain's waning prestige as an imperial power. It could not go unpunished. According to Anthony Nutting, the minister of state for foreign affairs, Eden placed "the entire blame on Nasser and brushed aside every argument that more personal considerations had in fact influenced Hussein." The British prime minister decided the world was not big enough for himself and Nasser. The Egyptian dictator must be eliminated before he destroyed Britain's position in the Middle East and Eden's position as prime minister.[48] To Eden, Nasser had become another scapegoat for Britain's decline and his own personal political problems.

Despite Anderson's initial lack of success, the ongoing Arab-Israeli conflict convinced Eisenhower administration officials to continue the mediation effort. On the eve of Anderson's return to the Middle East, a number of related problems required solutions. Israel continued to pressure Washington for weapons; Eric Johnston's efforts to work out an Arab-Israeli agreement over water development projects in the area remained in limbo; and Nasser had yet to accept the Aswan Dam loan proposal.

Perhaps the stickiest of these problems was the Israeli arms request. The unofficial American policy was to drag its feet as a means of persuading the Israeli government to reach a settlement with Egypt. Abba Eban met with Dulles on February 10 and again pushed for a decision on Israel's November 16, 1955, request for forty-eight F-86 fighter planes. Dulles responded that whatever progress the Anderson mission had achieved was due to the American policy of not supplying weapons to Israel. Dulles feared that providing arms would further hinder efforts to reach a settlement.[49] Nonetheless, motivated by congressional pressure and his own concern that the Israelis in desperation might resort to offensive action against the Arabs,[50] Dulles began to explore ways to give the Israelis a minimal number of defensive weapons without destroying the Anderson mission. On February 21 Kermit Roosevelt discussed Dulles's idea with Nasser. With a predictably hostile reaction Nasser warned it would not only "put an end to the Anderson Mission, but to everything."[51] Roosevelt advised Allen Dulles that a United

States weapons sale to Israel would terminate the Anderson mission and that Nasser would reject the Aswan Loan and seek further aid from the Soviet Union.[52] Dulles realized, after his appearance before the Senate Foreign Relations Committee on February 24, that he could not indefinitely refuse Israeli purchases of any type of weapons.[53] American intelligence reports predicted a summertime Israeli preemptive strike once Tel Aviv lost all hope of obtaining Western arms.[54] This information intensified Dulles's desire for Anderson's return to the region.

Anderson met new resistance upon his return to the Middle East on March 3. Asking for a meeting with Nasser, he was told that the Egyptian leader was unavailable until March 9 due to meetings with Syrian and Saudi leaders.[55] Nasser finally agreed to see Anderson on March 4.

The two met on the evenings of March 4 and 5. The Egyptian leader's positions had changed. The American emissary learned that Syria, the last stumbling block in gaining acceptance of the Jordan Valley plan, had refused to cooperate, and Nasser would not pressure Damascus to change its mind. Nasser blamed the Baghdad Pact for Egypt's viewpoint. Even if an agreement could be reached with the Israelis, he warned, he did not speak for all the Arabs, nor would he present a settlement to the other Arab states as his own idea.[56] A third party would have to submit a formal agreement, and Egypt and the other Arab leaders would negotiate the acceptability of the terms. Anderson responded that Nasser had altered his position and must realize that this new obstacle destroyed any chance of success for his mission. Nasser's refusal to sponsor an agreement led Anderson to conclude that "at this time it appears that what we can most realistically hope and work for is not a settlement of the dispute but the avoidance of war."[57]

Nasser altered his position in part because of his meetings with King Saud of Saudi Arabia and President Sheikri al-Quwwatli of Syria. The talks, which took place from March 6 through 11, were designed to coordinate plans for peace and war in the Middle East. Possibly these talks did not go well for Nasser, so that he refused to risk his own prestige by sponsoring a peace settlement.[58]

Anderson visited Ben-Gurion on March 9 and summarized his talks with Nasser. Ben-Gurion called a "mockery" Nasser's suggestion that the talks continue. Israel, he said, must assure "our own defenses." The Israeli prime minister argued that Anderson's mission hurt Israel because it allowed the Egyptians time to absorb their Soviet weapons. Sharett reiterated Ben-Gurion's arguments and asked the United States to make a decision on Israeli arms requests.[59] Anderson could not bridge the gap between the Egyptian and Israeli positions.

The Anderson mission failed in the face of heavy odds against its success. Fear of alienating the United States coerced Egypt and Israel to agree to the mediation effort, but both knew the process would quickly become a futile proposition.

As the self-professed leader of Arab nationalism, Nasser could not act as a sponsor for a treaty with Israel and hold on to the vast majority of Arab support. He feared that Nuri al-Said would usurp his position by using an expanded Baghdad Pact, thus allowing the British to retain power in the region. Nasser also feared for his own life and did not wish to risk a repetition of what happened in 1951 to the Jordanian monarch, King Abdullah—he had advocated a settlement with Israel and was assassinated by Arab extremists. With Russian weapons pouring into Egypt, and possible Soviet financing of the Aswan Dam, Nasser could take his time and not jeopardize his plans.

The peace initiative provided time for Egypt to absorb Soviet weaponry while denying American arms to Israel. Ben-Gurion was correct. Further, the Israeli prime minister regarded Nasser's territorial demand for a substantial segment of the Negev as destroying Israel's future economic development. Given the chance to place the onus for the failure of the mission on Nasser, Ben-Gurion was happy to see the mediation end.

Finally, the failure of the peace initiative can also be attributed to a decline in American interest. It was part of a comprehensive effort to limit Soviet influence in the region and test Nasser's reliability. The Egyptian prime minister proved uncooperative in arranging the Aswan Dam loan, and he continued to stir up trouble in Syria and Saudi Arabia.[60] For these reasons, and the flow of Soviet weapons into Egypt, American willingness to mediate a solution to the Arab-Israeli conflict dissipated.

The failure of the Anderson mission and the dismissal of John Glubb Pasha made the first week of March 1956 the great turning point on the road to Suez. The United States and the United Kingdom realized that relying on Nasser was fruitless. During the next three weeks State Department planners worked on a major American policy change. The British went along with whatever suited their needs, but they remained an obstacle to Washington's goals.

Eden wrote Eisenhower in early March, expressing the familiar view that "the Russians [were] resolved to liquidate the Baghdad Pact" and that events in Jordan reflected Egyptian chicanery. Eden again called for United States adherence to the Baghdad Pact and tank sales to Iraq. The prime minister warned "that a policy of appeasement will bring us nothing in Egypt."[61] The president's response agreed with Eden's assessment of Soviet policy but refused to "close the door on Nasser" and join the Baghdad Pact.[62]

The collapse of the Anderson mission led Eisenhower to develop a new course of action which would neither upset Israel and the European allies nor cause him political difficulties in the coming election. The president's March 8, 1956, diary entry provides insights into his plans.

> . . . We have reached the point where it looks as if Egypt, under Nasser, is going to make no move whatsoever to meet the Israelites in an effort to settle outstanding differences. Moreover, the Arabs, absorbing major consignments of arms from the Soviets, are daily growing more arrogant and disregarding the interests of Western Europe and of the United States in the Middle East region. It would appear that our efforts should be directed toward separating Saudi Arabians from the Egyptians and concentrating, for the moment at least, in making the former see that their best interests lie with us, not with the Egyptians and with the Russians.[63]

The new strategy of reinforcing the Saudis was reflected in a memo written by Dulles for Under Secretary of State Herbert Hoover, Jr. The memo stressed the importance of a settlement between the United Kingdom and Saudi Arabia over Buraimi, and increasing United States military aid to the Saudis.[64]

In mid-March State Department planners blamed Nasser for the shortcomings of American policy.[65] This view was reinforced by a letter from Eden to Eisenhower on March 15 based on British intelligence sources at the Conference of Egyptian Ambassadors and Ministers to the Arab states, held in Cairo at the end of January. Egyptian policy was to be designed, among other things, to unseat Nuri al-Said and frustrate the Baghdad Pact, "overthrow the Hashemite families of Iraq and Jordan," and eventually "isolate Saudi Arabia . . . then remove King Saud."[66] It is doubtful that Eisenhower needed further evidence against Nasser, but this letter certainly reaffirmed his convictions.

At Eisenhower's request, Dulles prepared a memorandum, dated March 28, which became the basis of the new American policy in the Middle East, code-named OMEGA. Dulles's statement reflected the failure of bringing Egypt into a regional defense organization as the focal point of an anti-Soviet alliance. The new policy was designed to notify Nasser that he "could not cooperate as he is doing with the Soviet Union and at the same time enjoy most-favored-nation treatment from the United States." But Dulles wished to avoid an open break with Nasser which might throw the Egyptian leader "irrevocably into a Soviet satellite status."

Dulles proposed, first, to deny export licenses covering government or commercial arms shipments to Egypt. In addition, he recommended that the United States and the United Kingdom "continue to delay the conclusion of current negotiations on the High Aswan Dam," and delay "pending Egyptian requests for grain and aid and suspend CARE Package shipments" to Egypt. The memo also called for greater U.S. support for the Baghdad Pact "without actually adhering" to it, and speedy negotiations with the Saudis, assuring King Saud "that some of his military needs will immediately be met and others provided for subsequently."[67]

On March 28 Eisenhower commented on Dulles's memorandum, noting in his diary that the fundamental

factor in the problem is the growing ambition of Nasser. . . . I suggested to the State Department that we begin to build up some
other individual as a prospective leader of the Arab world. . . . My
own choice of such a rival is King Saud . . . possibly as a spiritual
leader. Once this was accomplished we might begin to urge his right
to political leadership.[68]

The new plan, entitled OMEGA, was designed to replace the
failed ALPHA mission.

Dulles's March 28 memo concluded that "planning should be
undertaken at once with a view to possibly more drastic action in
the event that the above courses of action do not have the
desired effect."[69] This covert action would be coordinated with
the British government, which was still reeling from King Hussein's dismissal of John Glubb Pasha. It is not clear from
available documents that Nasser was to be eliminated, but in
light of Eden's references to Nasser following Glubb's dismissal—
"I want him destroyed . . . I want him removed"—it is logical to
conclude that Nasser was to be killed. It is interesting that
Dulles's own views on the matter were moving closer to Eden's.
In Karachi on March 7 Dulles reportedly told the British high
commissioner in Pakistan that unless Nasser did something
definite soon, "we would have to ditch him."

This covert planning with the British in no way halted the
divergence of the two allies' policies. The British wished to
isolate Egypt and strengthen their own position in the Arab
world. Fearing that Nasser would try to overthrow Hussein and
assassinate Nuri, Eden favored withholding military supplies
from Egypt, withdrawing the Aswan Dam loan, and eliminating
Nasser.[70]

On April 1 Dulles met with Ambassador Makins to update the
British government on the reassessment of American policy. The
major area of disagreement was the role of Saudi Arabia. For
Dulles it was essential to win King Saud away from Nasser. This
depended upon British concessions in reaching an agreement
over the Buraimi dispute. The British agenda was quite different. Although they agreed with Washington's analysis of Nasser,
Makins stressed that the most urgent matter was the upcoming
meeting of the Baghdad Pact which called for the utmost Ameri-

can cooperation. Makins, reflecting Eden's views, thought "the situation in Saudi Arabia was less immediate, but over a period of time we should try and work that out."[71] For Britain, Iraq and Jordan were still paramount.

Concerned about British policy, Dulles told Eisenhower on March 27 that the British were doing a number of things hurriedly and without prior consultation. Lester Pearson, the Canadian secretary of state who was present at the meeting, questioned Eden's mental stability, pointing out that the British prime minister was not reacting well to the strains and pressures of the present situation. Pearson, as aware as Dulles and Eisenhower of Eden's medical history, alluded to the eccentricities of Eden's father. He noted that Eden, for the first time in his career, no longer had Churchill to shield him from the full brunt of responsibility for British policies.[72] Dulles agreed and over the next few months worked to persuade British intelligence against trying to overthrow Nasser.[73]

Over the next four months the Aswan Dam loan became the focal point of Anglo-American strategy in the aftermath of the Anderson mission. Major questions surrounding the period have arisen among historians: When did the United States decide to withdraw the loan? What was the British role in reaching that conclusion? And when did Nasser realize that the loan was not forthcoming? Because the withdrawal of the Western offer to finance the Aswan project led directly to Nasser's nationalization of the Suez Canal and hence to the Israeli, British, and French conspiracy to topple the Egyptian leader, it is important to answer these questions.

Throughout the planning of ALPHA, the United States and the United Kingdom had recognized that economic inducements would be needed to gain Egyptian cooperation. Washington and London had agreed that "one of the most effective forms which this could take would be assistance in financing the construction of the High Aswan Dam."[74] The Czech arms deal had added a new sense of urgency to the idea of financing the dam. With evidence of a Soviet offer of technical and financial assistance to

Egypt in the construction of the dam, the State Department and the Foreign Office had agreed that if the Soviets were to fund the Aswan project in addition to supplying Egypt with weapons, Western prestige and influence in the Middle East would suffer greatly. A successful Soviet program could influence the political and economic policies of a region which was strategically and economically vital to the West.[75]

On October 20, 1955, Chancellor of the Exchequer Macmillan informed the State Department that he was anxious to work out Western financing for the dam. The Foreign Office was afraid that protracted negotiations with the World Bank would allow the Russians to gain a head start. At the Paris foreign ministers meeting during the last week of October, the United States and Britain agreed that the International Bank for Reconstruction and Development (IBRD) would be the best source of funds for the project, and that Washington and London would facilitate negotiations between Egypt and the bank. In addition, if Cairo exhibited "a constructive attitude towards Middle Eastern problems," both the United States and the United Kingdom would continue "substantial grant economic aid over the next ten years."[76] The Foreign Office and State Department concurred that a package deal should be presented to Nasser. The West would agree to make military equipment available to Egypt; pressure Israel to conclude a favorable peace with the Arabs; finance the cost of the Aswan Dam; and influence Iraq and the Sudan to put their relations with Egypt on a sound footing. In return, Nasser would "turn away from Russia on the completion [of the] present arms deal" and "agree to open negotiations with Israel for a settlement."[77]

On November 15 American, British, and IBRD officials began exploratory discussions on the financing of the dam.[78] After meeting with Egyptian officials at the end of November, and after repeated warnings from the British that if the Soviets outbid the West "the future of Africa" would be at stake, on December 1 the United States decided to "contribute substantially to the financing of the . . . High Aswan Dam."[79] American officials presented a formal proposal to finance the dam to Egyptian officials on December 16.[80]

During the course of the Anderson mission, negotiations proceeded between World Bank officials and the Egyptian government. Major problems centered on assurances which the bank requested of the Egyptian government pertaining to the soundness of its economy over the time of the project.[81] In addition, the bank would not proceed with the loan unless an agreement was reached with the Sudan over division of the Nile waters.[82] Affecting the discussions was Nasser's distaste for Eugene Black, president of the IBRD. The State Department asked Black not to give Nasser "a take it or leave it proposition."[83] Throughout the talks Nasser was extremely sensitive about Egyptian sovereignty and the appearance of begging "the British and American governments for money."[84]

On February 24, 1956, a firm Anglo-American offer was finally presented to the Egyptian government. It called for an American contribution of $54.6 million, a British offer of 5.5 million pounds sterling, and a World Bank loan of $200 million for the initial stage of construction.[85] Despite these positive developments as the Anderson mission was drawing to a close, Nasser refused to make a decision on the offer and hinted at Soviet participation in the project.[86] The collapse of the Anderson mission then ended the American attempt to use the Aswan loan as a quid pro quo for an Arab-Israeli peace.

The United States and the United Kingdom, as part of the new Operation OMEGA, delayed a decision for the Egyptians on the Aswan loan until it was finally withdrawn in July. According to Mohamed Heikal, Nasser knew in April that the United States would not fund its share of the project. The Egyptian government had obtained this information from top-secret minutes of the meeting of foreign ministers of the Baghdad Pact in mid-March.[87] Typical of American policy during the period, the State Department did not inform the Egyptians that the loan offer was to be withdrawn. Instead it stalled and kept Cairo in the dark. American officials instructed Byroade to stress Egypt's difficulties in its negotiations with the Sudan and to inform Nasser that his latest counterproposal was under consideration.[88]

The foreign ministers meeting in Paris in early May 1956 left no doubt that Western policy had turned against Nasser. Discussing the status of the Aswan loan, Dulles cited growing congressional opposition and the need to convince the Egyptians that we had not changed our minds.[89] The meeting ended with British Foreign Secretary Selwyn Lloyd and Dulles concluding "that the Aswan project should languish."[90] In addition, the foreign ministers agreed on a plan to make jet aircraft available to Israel. Conscious of the approaching election, Dulles wanted Israel to resort to its traditional European source for weapons. The secretary told French Foreign Minister Christian Pineau that he wished to avoid the appearance that the United States was giving in to Zionist pressure; that would greatly hinder American efforts to resolve Middle Eastern problems. Dulles approved the sale of another twelve French Mystere IV and twelve Mystere II fighters to Israel, and also called for Canada to sell twenty-four F-86s to Tel Aviv.[91]

Following the foreign ministers meeting, Nasser did not endear himself to the United States by recognizing the People's Republic of China. His decision in part arose from reports of Western approval of arms shipments to Israel, and from Soviet leader Nikita Khrushchev's April 27 statement in London that the Soviet Union would agree to a four-power arms embargo for the Middle East. Nasser believed that by recognizing China he would ensure a reliable backup source of weapons for Egypt.[92] Dulles told Ahmed Hussein, the Egyptian ambassador in Washington, that the action had "brought about an almost impossible situation" and that Nasser "could hardly have found anything that would make it harder for us to continue good relations with Egypt."[93]

State Department planners began to call for a reorientation of policy toward Egypt. Congressional reaction to Nasser's anti-Western actions and increasing opposition from cotton-growing states made it unlikely that the administration would gain legislative approval for the Aswan loan, even if Dulles had wanted to proceed with it. Under Secretary of State William Rountree suggested that the "relatively soft attitude toward Nasser" be replaced by much stronger measures.[94]

Throughout, the British took a firm stand toward Soviet actions in the Middle East and encouraged the United States to continue its pressure on Egypt. During the visit of Soviet Prime Minister Nikolai Bulganin and First Secretary Nikita Khrushchev to London on April 20, Eden had informed the Russian leaders that, with regard to the Middle East, "we have to have our oil and we are prepared to fight for it."[95] In May and June the British worked behind the scenes to detach other Arab states from Egypt, using covert means to weaken Nasser's ability to disrupt British goals in the region.[96] The Foreign Office concluded that it was too late to forestall Soviet penetration of the area and that it should no longer keep the Aswan project alive.[97] By early June the State Department and the Foreign Office were moving in the same direction.

On June 17, while Soviet Foreign Minister Dmitri Shepilov visited Egypt, the Russian official offered "a Soviet plan to finance the Aswan High Dam over a ten-year period. The USSR offered [a] $400,000,000, interest-free loan . . . with repayment to be spread over 60 years." Moreover, the Soviets agreed to buy all of Egypt's cotton and pay for it in sterling, to accept no further Egyptian payments for arms already received, and to build a new steel factory in Egypt and construct other factories on highly favorable terms.[98]

During Shepilov's visit Eugene Black also met with Nasser to try to break the World Bank's impasse with the Egyptians. During their meeting Nasser made no mention of Shepilov, nor did he hint that he was considering a Soviet offer for the dam. Returning to the United States, Black informed Dulles that the Egyptian economic situation was similar to that of December 1955 and that the loan could proceed because Egypt had reached agreement with the Sudan over the Nile waters. Dulles, who already seems to have decided to withdraw the loan, pointed to his "knotty difficulties with Congress over the project."[99] By the end of June Dulles knew that Nasser had dropped the objections he had raised to the loan in February. And Washington officials were aware of the Soviet offer to finance the dam—and that the Egyptians had not yet accepted it.[100] Despite this information, Dulles's ire was such that he was set on teaching Nasser a lesson for playing off both sides in order to achieve the best deal.

At the June 28 meeting of the National Security Council,

Dulles stated that if the United States withdrew the loan offer, it would eventually change Egypt's attitude toward American plans.[101] On July 10 Byroade informed Dulles that Nasser had dropped all objections to the December 1955 proposal and was returning Ambassador Hussein to Washington to conclude an agreement for the financing of the Aswan loan.[102] Three days later, meeting with the president at his Gettysburg farm, Dulles suggested that Hussein be told that the United States was not in a position to deal with the Aswan matter because of the situation with Congress, and that the American view had been "somewhat altered."[103]

Despite having made up his mind to withdraw the loan offer, Dulles did not immediately inform the British. In fact, on July 10, in a meeting with State Department officials, the British expressed their desire "to await developments before doing anything further in respect to the Aswan High Dam."[104] On July 13 Dulles told Makins he agreed, and that the United States was hardening its view toward proceeding with the loan.[105]

Four days later, on July 17, State Department planners recommended that Dulles "clearly withdraw the December offer on the Aswan Dam" when he met with Hussein.[106] In London that same day Foreign Secretary Lloyd told the British cabinet that "the offer of financial aid for the building of the High Dam at Aswan should now be withdrawn."[107] The next day, when British officials informed William Rountree of Lloyd's viewpoint, they were told that no official American decision had been made.[108] British representatives at the meeting assumed there would be further talks between London and Washington before "anything was actually said to the Egyptians."[109]

The following morning, July 19, Dulles met with Eisenhower, and they agreed to rescind the loan offer.[110] An hour and half later Dulles met with Makins and informed the British ambassador that later that day the Aswan loan offer would be withdrawn. Dulles rationalized that if he failed to act, the Senate during its debate on the 1957 foreign aid bill would kill the loan offer. The very next day Makins responded that his government had not yet reached a definitive decision and requested a further exchange of views.[111] That afternoon, receiving no further com-

munications from the British, Dulles met with Hussein and
withdrew the offer.[112] In a speech in Alexandria on July 26,
Nasser responded by nationalizing the Suez Canal.[113]

Plainly, Dulles, acting with Eisenhower's approval, had made
up his mind to withdraw the Aswan loan at least three weeks
before he actually did so. The British were essentially kept
informed of Dulles's attitude and ostensibly agreed with the
American action. Eden's later comments that he "was informed,
but not consulted"[114] are incorrect. Dulles informed the British
on July 13 that the American position on the loan had hardened.
He offered to wait before withdrawal, but on July 17 Foreign
Secretary Lloyd informed the British cabinet that the loan would
now be withdrawn. Informed by Makins on the morning of the
19th that the British had not made a final decision, Dulles
waited five hours before acting. Having not heard from the
British during that period, Dulles assumed that London did not
object and proceeded to withdraw the loan.

Nasser was not surprised by the withdrawal. His anger stemmed from Dulles's suggestion that he had withdrawn the offer
because the Egyptian economy was not sound enough to undertake the Aswan project. Nasser saw this as a deliberate attempt
to humiliate him as well as his country.

The evidence suggests that Dulles withdrew the loan not out
of any calculated plan in cooperation with his British allies to
implement a more workable policy toward the Middle East, but
because of his personal pique toward Nasser. This anger had
been spawned by Nasser's neutralist policies; by July 1956 they
had totally frustrated American efforts to keep the Russians out
of the region. By July the British had already agreed that
something must be done about Nasser. Although London and
Washington talked throughout June and early July about the
possibility of withdrawing the loan, no joint Anglo-American
decision was made. When Dulles finally withdrew the offer on
July 19, his action was inevitable given Nasser's stalling tactics in
the peace process, the Egyptian recognition of Communist
China in May, and the Soviet offer to finance the dam in June.
Dulles believed that in the long run the withdrawal of the loan
offer would benefit the United States. Instead it precipitated the

Suez crisis and pushed the United States to replace the British as the most important Western power in the region.

The secretary of state had demonstrated a basic lack of understanding of nationalist forces in the Arab world as he tried to punish Nasser for his transgressions. He intended to warn the rest of the undeveloped world as well. But instead of destroying Nasser's neutralism, which Dulles found so distasteful, he elevated the Egyptian president's position in the Arab world to new heights. Over the next few months Dulles pursued a policy with dual aims: to punish Nasser, and further to erode Britain's position in the Middle East.

7 *Conspiracy at Suez*

Trying to design a strategy to deal with Nasser's nationalization of the Suez Canal placed the British government
in a precarious position. It could continue the policy of retrench-
ment in the Middle East, begun in 1947 in Palestine and most
recently exemplified by a withdrawal from the Suez Canal base;
or Britain could try to reverse its decline in the area. Prime
Minister Eden blamed Nasser for the depletion of British power
in the region. The Egyptian leader's machinations in Syria,
Saudi Arabia, and Jordan; his opposition to the Baghdad Pact;
and now the seizure of Britain's oil lifeline, the Suez Canal, was
too much to bear. Rather than gracefully accepting the weakening of the empire, the British prime minister chose to exacerbate an already existing crisis. As a consequence, he destroyed
his country's position in the region and ended his political
career.

Eden's chosen path presented the United States with an
opportunity to replace the British as the dominant power in the
Middle East. Cognizant of the significance of Nasser's actions,
the United States decided to proceed cautiously because of the
coming presidential election and possible worldwide economic
repercussions. In these early stages of the Suez crisis, the
Eisenhower administration did not actively seek to dislodge the
British from the Middle East. It chose to delay any confrontation
with Egypt until after the 1956 presidential election. But the
British and French invasion of Egypt changed the direction of

American policy, and the crisis was used to remove British influence from the region. The larger picture of Anglo-American relations in the Middle East during the period shows that Washington pursued consistent policies from May 1953. Eden's tactics and blindness toward Eisenhower's repeated warnings against the use of force facilitated the American ascendancy. By November 1956 the United States believed the United Kingdom could no longer be relied upon to thwart Soviet penetration in the area. Washington was tired of walking a tightrope between British colonialism and the friendship and understanding of the Arab world.

The crisis was aggravated by the inability of Eisenhower, Dulles, and Eden to evaluate and understand one another's positions. Eisenhower, in total control of America's Middle East policy, was adamant against the use of force. Running for reelection as a peace candidate, the president firmly believed the age of colonial wars was past. Dulles, who sympathized with Britain's plight, was Eisenhower's lawyer. In defending his client, the secretary of state pursued a purposefully ambiguous policy— and in many instances a duplicitous one—by delaying the crisis as long as possible, hoping it would solve itself or at least not result in war until after the American election.[1]

Eden, for his part, chose either to ignore Eisenhower's messages or read into them false hopes. His habit was to latch onto statements made by Dulles and Eisenhower and rationalize them into United States support for his actions. Eden failed to realize that Eisenhower's domineering personality required that he be in control of all aspects of American Middle East policy. Nor did the prime minister understand that Washington's policy toward the region was both anticolonialist—geared against Britain and France, as well as anticommunist—designed to contain the Soviet Union. For Eden, American policy was thus confusing and difficult to predict. Rather than accept Britain's satellite status vis-à-vis the United States, Eden tried to act as the great power Britain no longer was.

*   *   *

The British reaction to nationalization of the canal was predictable. After meeting with American and French officials, Eden immediately summoned his cabinet. They characterized Nasser's act as a callous betrayal of the Suez Canal base treaty and an intolerable threat to Western economic interests. Eden immediately began comparing Nasser with Mussolini.

Warning his ministers of the seriousness of the situation, Eden suggested that if the Western powers did not "take the necessary steps to regain control over the canal [it] would have disastrous consequences for the economic life of the Western powers and for their standing and influence in the Middle East."[2] The prime minister called for a "common understanding" between the United Kingdom, France, and the United States. The cabinet could not rest its position on the legalities of Nasser's action, for the Egyptian leader had promised to compensate shareholders of the Suez Canal Company at ruling market rates. In effect, Nasser's nationalization was a decision to buy out the canal.[3]

But the cabinet emphasized that the canal "was not a piece of Egyptian property but an international asset of the highest importance and should be managed by an international trust." It was not an object for Cairo to exploit for purely internal purposes.[4] The British position was clear and remained so throughout the crisis. Political pressure must be brought to bear on Nasser because economic pressure would not work. If political pressure with the threat of force behind it proved unsuccessful, the British would resort to military action. The cabinet concluded that "if it failed to hold the Suez Canal [it] would lead inevitably to the loss one by one of all our interests and assets in the Middle East."[5]

The British were operating on two false assumptions: first, that the Egyptians were without the technical ability to operate the canal efficiently; second, that the British had the military readiness to support their threats. They believed that military preparations would require several weeks; in reality they would take several months. Indeed, Nasser had suspected that British preparedness was weak, and it was one reason why he decided to nationalize the canal.[6]

Nasser had received reports on July 25 that the British had

only "one old aircraft carrier in Malta, one destroyer in patrol in the area between Cyprus, Haifa and Alexandria, with another destroyer in the Red Sea on its way from Port Sudan to Aden." According to Mohamed Heikal, Nasser concluded that the British could not mount a military threat for at least two months. He believed that if he had one month to show the world Egypt's good intentions, the crisis would blow over.[7]

Winthrop Aldrich, the American ambassador to London, attended the British cabinet meeting of July 27 and later warned Dulles that the British would use military force, if necessary, to reestablish Western control over the canal.[8] The afternoon of the 27th Eden informed Eisenhower of London's position. Eden wrote, "We cannot afford to allow Nasser to seize control of the canal in this way." He warned that if a firm stand were not taken, "our influence and yours throughout the Middle East will, we are convinced, be finally destroyed." The British position was clear: "we must be ready in the last resort, to use force to bring Nasser to his senses." In closing, Eden called for a tripartite meeting "at the highest level."[9] Eisenhower's response arrived July 28, informing Eden that he was sending Under Secretary of State Robert Murphy to London for consultations and calling a meeting of the "maximum number of maritime nations affected by the Nasser action."[10] From the onset of the crisis, Eisenhower wished to avoid acting through the "big three club," fearing association with British and French colonialism.

In a meeting on July 28, before dispatching Murphy to London, Eisenhower stressed that from the start the United States government should stay clear of any precipitate action with the British and French "which could tie our hands later."[11] Later in the day, Ambassador Roger Makins met with Under Secretary of State Herbert Hoover, Jr., and informed him that the canal was too valuable to be entrusted to Egypt. Hoover's response was that only an overt act by Egypt could justify military action. The American government, Hoover said, was acutely aware of the domestic repercussions should the administration be forced to ration oil. After this talk Makins advised Eden that the State Department did not see itself as a principal in the dispute. Success for the British hinged on making a forceful impression on Murphy during his visit.[12]

Arriving in London late in the evening of July 28, Murphy witnessed the belligerence of the British position firsthand. Macmillan told Murphy that "if Britain did not accept Egypt's challenge, Britain would become another Netherlands."[13] Murphy presented Eisenhower's position, suggesting there was a distinction between the British, French, and American interests in the Suez Canal Company. Although the United States hoped to be closely affiliated with its allies, "the question of eventual military intervention . . . would depend on developments." The president believed the use of force "should be delegated to the background."[14] Meeting next with Foreign Minister Pineau and Foreign Minister Lloyd, Murphy listened to Pineau's comparison of Nasser and Hitler and Lloyd's call for military precautions. Then he pointed out that American public opinion was not prepared for the idea of using force. Pineau was even more adamant about Nasser than Lloyd. Angered over Nasser's increasing presence in North Africa, particularly in Algeria, the French saw the nationalization of the canal as an opportunity to destroy the Egyptian leader once and for all.[15]

The next day Murphy met Eden and became convinced that the British would use force. He concluded that the prime minister "was laboring under the impression that a common identity existed among the allies." The under secretary quickly informed Eden that this was not the American view.[16] After Murphy cabled Eisenhower recounting British intentions, the president became alarmed and immediately dispatched Dulles, just recalled from Peru, to London.

Before leaving for Britain Dulles told Makins that "the United States government would not be in sympathy with any attempt to make the Egyptian government rescind their nationalization decrees, or to regard them as inoperative, under the threat of force." Dulles continued, "There was no American treaty obligation at stake and no legal basis for intervention." The president's authority must come from Congress, and as long as Egypt limited its action to nationalization, no case could be put before Congress. With the election around the corner, furthermore, the recall of an adjourned Congress was impractical. Makins correctly concluded that Britain should not expect much help from the United States. Considering the American political situation, Nasser had chosen his time wisely.[17]

Rationale for American policy was simple. Eisenhower believed the use of force was out of date, especially without offering a counterproposal to Egypt. He also thought there was too much emphasis on Nasser. On July 31 Eisenhower remarked to Hoover and Dulles, "Nasser embodies the emotional demand of the people of the area for independence and for slapping the white man down." Eisenhower sought a peaceful resolution of the crisis to prevent Nasser from successfully nationalizing the canal. Concerned about possible implications for the Panama Canal, the president favored basing America's position on the Constantinople Convention of 1888, an international agreement which respected the free navigation of the Suez Canal.[18]

Dulles shared the president's viewpoint and believed Nasser had to be made to "disgorge" the canal—but only through international means, not force. His concern was that if Middle East oil were lost to the West, gasoline rationing would result, "with the curtailment of automobile production, and a severe blow to the United States economy."[19] But if the United Kingdom resorted to war, it would generate economic disaster for the United States because of the loss of markets abroad and jobs at home. In the end the Soviet Union would pick up the pieces. Dulles's strategy was apparent when he left for London: he would try to "dissuade [the British], perhaps a bit at a time, gradually deflecting their course of action."[20] This is the strategy the United States relied upon until the Israeli invasion of Egypt.

Any doubt about the American position was clarified in a letter from Eisenhower which Dulles presented to Eden upon his arrival. He recognized the importance of the canal, the president wrote, and the possibility that force might be necessary. But he wanted an international conference to pressure the Egyptian government to assure the "efficient operation of the canal." The president concluded that American and world reaction would not support the use of force.[21] It should have been obvious to Eden that Eisenhower did not think the nationalization of the canal was worth a war.

The British were not overjoyed by the prospect of an international conference, but they agreed to it if it was confined to considering a plan for the future internationalization of the waterway. Two other reasons affected the British decision: first, "it would occupy time until [they were] in a position to take other action,"[22] and, second, to mollify the United States.

Meanwhile, Dulles was surprised by the depth of British feeling. On August 1 Eden told him that the moment of decision had arrived and that

> if Nasser were to get away with his action, we should lose the pipelines and our oil supplies. Our economy would then be slowly strangled. . . . Nasser was a paranoiac and had the same type of mind as Hitler. . . . Our object was to achieve a reasonable settlement, by peaceful persuasion if this were possible. If not . . . we would have to assert the right of free passage through the Canal by force if necessary.[23]

Dulles's reaction was typical of the "dual-bind" responses he would make throughout the crisis. The secretary stated that "it was unacceptable to have one nation control the canal, and that it was even more unacceptable because the nation was Egypt. A way had to be found to make Nasser disgorge what he was to swallow."[24] For Dulles, "disgorging" would have to be accomplished by international means; for Eden, this type of statement was interpreted as support for the use of force.

During the same meeting with Eden, Dulles provided another dual-bind message, arguing that the use of force would have to be supported by world opinion. The secretary doubted that the United States government would associate itself with military action unless it was "preceded by genuine efforts to reach a satisfactory solution by negotiation."[25] The problem was the definition of the term "genuine." For Dulles the process could go on interminably; for Eden it could not. While the United States regarded negotiations as a satisfactory solution, the British saw them as a stalling tactic until force could be used.

On August 2 Dulles, Pineau, and Eden agreed to convene an

international conference in London on August 16. It would endorse the principle of international control but would not discuss a detailed program to implement it.[26] By accepting the idea of a conference, both Eden and Pineau provided Dulles with an opportunity to divert his Atlantic allies from using force. This was the first in a series of delaying tactics used by Dulles during the next two months.

After Dulles's visit, Eden still maintained that Eisenhower "did not rule out the use of force."[27] The problem, as Chester Cooper, the CIA representative in London, pointed out, was that by the end of July the British and French had already lost the game. Whether Eden or Foreign Minister Guy Mollet realized it or not, "the world had already accepted the nationalization of the canal as a fait accompli." When Nasser proved that Egyptian pilots could operate the canal as efficiently as those they replaced, a major pretext for intervention was lost. As time went on, more and more people began to accept the legality of the Egyptian action; support for the use of force was fading.[28] This attitude was reflected in a television address by Eisenhower and Dulles on August 3, which stressed that the use of force would be contrary to the principles of the United Nations charter and praised the benefits of the upcoming London Conference.[29]

Eden chose to ignore the obvious. In an August 5 letter to Eisenhower, the prime minister wrote:

> I do not think we disagree about the primary objective: to undo what Nasser has done and to set up an international regime for the Canal. But this is not all. Nasser has embarked on a course unpleasantly familiar. . . . The removal of Nasser and the installation in Egypt of a regime less hostile to the West must therefore rank high among our objectives. It is possible that Nasser may refuse to accept the outcome of the conference or seek to divide us. We and the French could not possibly acquiesce in such a situation.[30]

As the United States proceeded with plans for the London Conference to approve international operation of the canal, the British and French moved ahead with military planning.[31] Dulles was fully aware of the difficult task he faced in London. On

August 8 he advised the National Security Council that if the conference failed, or if Nasser rejected its work, the British and French "will be disposed to take forceful action." Dulles appreciated the Anglo-French predicament. He pointed to Nasser's ambition to build an Arab power bloc and reduce Western power. He saw the canal seizure not as an isolated action but as a step toward reaching these goals.[32]

Before Dulles departed for London, he and Eisenhower met with congressional leaders on August 12. Dulles reiterated his view that despite all efforts to work with Nasser, "we finally became convinced that he [was] an extremely dangerous fanatic." If a solution was not found based on the 1888 treaty, the British and French would resort to force. "The United States could not be unsympathetic to the British and French in light of Nasser's ambitions," the secretary concluded, warning that "fulfillment of Nasser's ambitions would result in reducing Western Europe literally to a state of dependency."[33] It is interesting that during the meeting Eisenhower appeared to contradict his secretary of state. The president cautioned that any attempt to capture the canal would "get to be a long and tedious one . . . [and] we can't resign ourselves to underwriting the European economy permanently."[34]

Thus Dulles appeared actually to agree with the British and French that Nasser could not be allowed to be successful. The distinction was that Dulles did not believe force, in this instance, could be used. Dulles reasoned that the use of force, instead of destroying Nasser, would either reinforce his position or create an opportunity for further Soviet inroads. In either case, force would weaken American economic and political interests in the Arab world. But the British and French were more concerned with matters of pride and prestige in seeking to maintain a dying colonial empire. Thus Anglo-French and American goals, as Dulles perceived them, were the same; the problem was that the Anglo-French strategy for achieving them was self-defeating. The president was aware of his secretary's rationale, but he was concerned with two primary objectives. The first was not to allow the Suez situation to cause difficulties for the United States in maintaining its control over the Panama

Canal.[35] The second was not to lose his cherished anticolonialist image, for it allowed Eisenhower to present himself to the American electorate and to the Third World as the peace candidate.

In London Dulles set out to prolong the crisis, hoping that force would diminish as a viable option. When he arrived he found the British and French alarmed by reports that at the August 12 meeting with congressional leaders Dulles had spoken of an international body for the canal in a mere advisory capacity. Unlike the United States, the British and French also believed that economic pressure could create difficulties for Nasser. American shipping provided the Egyptian government with 30 to 35 percent of its canal revenues. Washington nonetheless refused to pressure American shipping companies to pay tolls into a blocked account.[36]

On August 15, in a luncheon meeting with Lloyd, Dulles learned how strongly the British and French felt about the creation of an international authority that was more than just an advisory body.[37] As a result, in his opening remarks to the conference Dulles accused Nasser of acting for "Egyptian national purposes." He proposed that the canal be operated by an international body established by a treaty and associated with the United Nations. This, he argued, would restore "confidence to those who normally wish to use the Canal." The secretary emphasized that the principles set forth by the Suez Canal Convention of 1888 had been "grievously assaulted." As Robert Rhodes James points out, "The British and French were delighted, but Eisenhower was not."[38]

With the support of France and Britain, the United States proposed a public authority to operate the canal. The plan accorded equal recognition to the sovereign rights of Egypt and the safety of the canal as an international waterway. It called for the creation of international agreements under which all parties would participate in a Suez Canal board responsible for operating the canal.[39] On August 19 Eisenhower wired his approval of the American declaration.[40]

Eden supported the American proposal and the idea of creating a small committee for subsequent negotiations with Nasser.

If Nasser rejected the conference's proposals, world opinion would support the participants' pursuit of further action. Eden informed the Egypt Committee (an "inner cabinet" appointed to formulate policy) on August 20 that Dulles recognized the value of military preparations to show Britain's determination to reach a satisfactory settlement, "but he was not in favor of provoking Nasser into any further action which would justify the use of force." Dulles had informed Eden that the United States could not justify going to war over oil in the Middle East because of the oil surplus in the United States.[41] Eden could not have been satisfied with Dulles's statement when he formally presented his proposal to the conference: "There are some things that this conference is not, it is not a conference to make decisions binding on those who do not agree."[42]

The Indian delegation, headed by V. K. Krishna Menon, proposed an alternative calling for "consideration . . . without prejudice to Egyptian ownership and operation, to the association of international user interests with the Egyptian Corporation for the Suez Canal."[43] Dulles refused to amend his proposal to accept the Indian ideas because it would have given Nasser control of the canal. When Dulles's proposal was put to a vote, it passed 18 to 4, with only the Soviet Union, India, Ceylon, and Indonesia in opposition.[44] On August 22 Eden requested that Dulles present the eighteen-power proposals to Nasser, but the secretary refused. Later in the day Lloyd requested that the United States refuse to pay canal tolls to Nasser if the Egyptian leader refused to negotiate. Dulles responded ambiguously, saying he favored pressure on Nasser but not the type that would result "in forcing us into going around the Cape."[45] At the same time Lloyd was meeting with Dulles, Eden postponed "D-Day" for military action against Egypt until the London proposals could be presented to Nasser.[46] After Macmillan and Lloyd failed to convince Dulles to head the mission to present the proposals, the eighteen nations appointed Australian Prime Minister Robert Menzies to head a delegation to do so.[47]

With the end of the conference, Eden wrote to Eisenhower expressing a familiar theme:

I have no doubt that the Bear is using Nasser, with or without his knowledge, to further his immediate aims. These are, I think, first to dislodge the West from the Middle East, and second to get a foothold in Africa so as to dominate that continent in turn. . . . All this makes me more than ever sure that Nasser must not be allowed to get away with it.[48]

At this juncture the British position was clear: if a favorable settlement was not reached by September 10, Eden's self-imposed deadline for military planning, the United Kingdom and France would shortly thereafter resort to war.[49] Eisenhower's position was also unambiguous: he prohibited American participation in the Menzies mission, and on August 30 he wrote that he realized it was "tough for the British and French but this was not the issue upon which to try and downgrade Nasser. Every reasonable effort should be made to get an acceptable practical solution of the Suez dispute."[50] As the Menzies mission left for Cairo, the United States did its best to forestall any British or French attempt to present the conference proposals as the final offer to Nasser.

Few diplomats expected Nasser to accept the eighteen-power proposals. The Indian Foreign Ministry informed Washington and London that Nasser was totally opposed to the creation of an international organization to supervise the canal. For the British and French the Menzies mission was a formality to promote a peaceful solution while military preparations continued. Once Nasser rejected the London proposals, they believed they would be justified in resorting to force.[51]

The British faced a dilemma. Using force risked devastating economic consequences. In a treasury report on the consequences of military action, presented to the Egypt Committee by Macmillan on August 27, the chancellor of the exchequer reported that disruption of the canal would bring a three-month delay in oil shipments—rerouting them around the Cape of Good Hope and obtaining oil from the Western Hemisphere. If the canal were closed and pipelines from the Levant cut by other Arab states in sympathy with Egypt, the "United Kingdom and Western Europe [were] lost." Macmillan argued that should Nasser get away with nationalization, and Nuri fall, most Middle

Eastern oil sources might be nationalized. Macmillan concluded that "if the threat of Egypt was not met our economy would be slowly strangled."[52]

By the end of August Eden and Lloyd sought alternatives should Nasser, as expected, reject the proposals. On August 28 Eden suggested to the Egypt Committee that Britain reconsider presenting its case before the UN Security Council.[53] The Foreign Office viewed a Security Council resolution as a means to strengthen the case against Nasser should the use of force become a reality. Lloyd wrote Dulles on August 28 to request American support and reaffirmed British strategy. The use of the Security Council was "an exercise . . . to put us in the best possible posture internationally in relation to the acts we may be obliged to take."[54] At a press conference later that day Dulles responded that "the United States was not dependent to any appreciable degree at all upon the Suez Canal. . . . [It was] primarily of concern to the many countries—about 20—whose economies are virtually dependent upon the Canal."[55] Although Dulles told Lloyd he could count on American support at the United Nations, the secretary did not favor such a move because of Soviet interference and his own inability to control debate in the Security Council.[56]

Events in Egypt soon counteracted British hopes. British Ambassador Sir Humphrey Trevelyan repeatedly warned the Foreign Office that the Egyptian cabinet was unified and that the armed forces and police remained loyal to Nasser. The facts, as Trevelyan presented them, strongly suggested that any efforts to produce "a successor government" would fail. Although Nasser seriously underestimated the strength of Western reaction, he successfully presented himself as a reasonable leader able to keep the canal operating. The fact that the canal was functioning efficiently justified his view that if he continued to drag out negotiations, he would succeed.[57] He effectively manipulated the situation to make it appear a question of Egyptian sovereignty versus Anglo-French colonial demands. It was a strategy designed to appeal to Eisenhower's sensitivity on the issue.[58]

Dulles was fully aware that the British and French had gone along with the Menzies mission only in "the obvious hope that

Nasser would not accept the plan." The secretary knew the two
allies were "extremely serious in their intention to resort to
military force if no other acceptable solution is found."[59]

On September 2 Eisenhower again wrote Eden to make sure
there was no doubt where the United States stood. After accepting Eden's arguments about the Soviet threat, the president
cautioned

> there should be no thought of military action before the influences of
> the United Nations are fully explored. . . . I continue to feel . . . it is
> indispensable that, if we are to proceed solidly together to a solu-
> tion, public opinion in our several countries must be overwhelming
> in its support. I must tell you frankly that American public opinion
> flatly rejects the use of force. I really do not see how a successful
> result could be achieved by forcible means.[60]

Here Eisenhower's concern about his political standing for the
coming election is apparent, along with his firm anticolonial
stance. Eden's belief at this juncture, that the United States
would acquiesce in the use of force, was the ultimate act of
self-delusion.

On September 6, to Eisenhower's chagrin, Eden responded,
harping on the same tiresome themes.

> . . . The seizure of the Canal, we are convinced, [is] the opening
> gambit in a planned campaign designed by Nasser to expel all
> Western influence and interests from Arab countries. . . . If our as-
> sessment is correct, and if the only alternative is to allow Nasser's
> plans quietly to develop until this country and Western Europe are
> held to ransom by Egypt acting at Russia's behest it seems to us that
> our duty is plain. . . . We have many times led Europe in the fight for
> freedom. It would be an ignoble end to our long history if we tamely
> accepted perish by degrees.[61]

Eden's response was a weak attempt to rekindle the World War
II Anglo-American alliance. Eisenhower's response on September 8 should have alerted the prime minister to his failure: Eden
was "making of Nasser a much more important figure than he
[was]. . . ." Eisenhower warned Eden again that "the use of
military force against Egypt under present circumstances might
have consequences even more serious than causing the Arabs to

support Nasser. It might cause a serious misunderstanding between our two countries."[62]

While Eden and Eisenhower were attempting to communi-
cate, the Menzies mission arrived in Cairo on September 4.
Nasser and Menzies at once developed a distaste for each other.
Nasser, daily growing in self-confidence, was predictably uncooperative. Menzies, with his close links to British imperial
policies, warned Nasser that though he might believe that
Anglo-French military planning was a bluff, both London and
Paris were quite serious. Nasser rejected the eighteen-power
proposals but did accept a suggestion that an independent body
be created to consider the various views.[63]

Dulles, seeing that the Menzies mission had failed, now
floated a new idea to try to dissuade an Anglo-French use of
force. The suggestion became known as the Suez Canal Users'
Association.

Dulles concocted the Suez Canal Users' Association (SCUA) to
forestall the British and French from taking their case to the
United Nations.[64] The British favored going to the Security
Council to prevent a Soviet resolution favorable to the Egyptians. Dulles informed Ambassador Makins that he opposed the
move at the time and would refuse to co-sponsor a resolution
with the British. Nor would he support any initiative in the
Security Council. Instead he argued in favor of exercising canal
user rights based on the 1888 convention. "If Egypt then
resisted we should then have a clear case to take to the Security
Council."[65] Dulles's vague remarks concerning user "rights"
were in reality just another delaying tactic. For Makins the
American position was clear; he advised London "that we have a
long way to go before we can count on United States support in
making our next move an appeal to the Security Council."[66]

Dulles's SCUA scheme would use the rights guaranteed to the
maritime powers by the 1888 convention to force Nasser to alter
his tactics. SCUA's chief purpose would be to operate the canal,
including the coordination of ship traffic and the collection of
tolls. Egypt's share of the revenues was to be determined. For
Dulles SCUA was "a provisional arrangement and not a substitute ... for another arrangement which would involve Egyptian

participation."[67] Townsend Hoopes later characterized SCUA as having a "transparently grotesque, unreal quality." The association repudiated the basis of the eighteen-power proposal and rejected key political issues in favor of technical ones.[68]

The Foreign Office was disappointed in America's attitude toward the link it saw between the canal stalemate and "deflating Nasser." For the British these issues were interrelated, something Washington refused to accept. On September 8 Lloyd wrote Makins that "there appears to be little common ground between us at the moment as to how to achieve either of these objectives." Moreover, the British were upset because Dulles had reversed his position on the payment of transit dues.

When he first introduced SCUA, Dulles noted that transit dues could be used as a means of "deflating Nasser." Later the secretary changed his mind, suggesting that SCUA had no power to refuse the payment of dues to the Egyptian government.[69] Makins complained to the State Department that Dulles was "pouring cold water" on his own proposals.[70] The British had agreed to support SCUA because it offered the prospect of implicating the United States in organizing the denial of dues to Egypt. Altering course once again, Dulles angered the Foreign Office.

Eisenhower himself questioned whether SCUA was feasible. Dulles told the president that he had no other alternative to prevent the British from resorting to force.[71] Amazingly, to this point the British had made no contingency plans should they fail to win American support.

Despite vehement French opposition, Eden agreed to go along with Dulles's SCUA scheme. First, British dollar reserves were declining, and should the need arise he wanted to assure himself of American financial aid. Second, if Nasser accepted the plan, it would make a mockery of nationalization.[72] Finally, if the British later resorted to force, they had a better chance of gaining American support. SCUA ignored the issues of sovereignty and jurisdiction; the plan represented for Dulles an attempt to cooperate with Nasser. If noncooperation persisted, Dulles would have gained more time.

By accepting SCUA Eden made a great sacrifice for the

Anglo-American alliance. The prime minister was under increasing pressure from the French, from members of Parliament who had opposed the Suez base agreement in 1954, and from the financial cost of military preparations. Realizing it would be dangerous to go to the Security Council without American support, Eden decided to appease Washington. If the British supported SCUA and it failed, Eden reasoned that the United States would then feel obligated to support the British initiative in the United Nations.[73]

On September 11 Eden discussed SCUA with Mollet and Pineau and convinced them to support the concept on the basis of American participation and payment of dues to the organization. They also agreed "for the moment" not to present the matter formally to the Security Council.[74]

Later that evening the British and French were stunned when Eisenhower, responding to a press conference question about possible American support for allied military action, stated that "this country will not go to war while I am occupying my present post unless... Congress declares such a war.... We established the United Nations to abolish aggression and I am not going to be a party to aggression."[75] These remarks made Britain and France potential aggressors. Egypt's seizure of the canal, on the other hand, was no longer considered an aggressive act. At his own press conference two days later, Dulles contributed further to allied discomfort. Responding to a question about the possibility of using force to move a convoy through the canal, Dulles offered, "I know nothing about a plan to shoot our way through.... We certainly have no intention of doing so. It may be that we have the right to do it, but we don't intend to do it as far as the United States is concerned."[76] Dulles pontificated further on the possible use of force, and as a result undercut the British and French who had agreed to back SCUA in the hope of gaining future American support for whatever action they chose to take.

Dulles's performance at the Second London Conference, convened to work out details for SCUA, convinced many diplomats that the secretary did not believe in his own idea. Through a series of contradictory statements on the use of force and how

SCUA would operate, Dulles confused and angered his allies.[77] The British wished to deprive Egypt of transit dues; but Dulles insisted that membership in SCUA "would not involve the assumption by any member of any obligation."[78] While the British and French were questioning his remarks, the secretary was writing Eisenhower that "considerable progress" was taking place and that Eden had expressed great appreciation for his efforts.[79] On September 21 SCUA was declared established.

At the conclusion of the conference Foreign Secretary Lloyd questioned Dulles about introducing a resolution dealing with the Suez Canal situation in the Security Council. Dulles approved, but he wanted to wait at least ten days to allow the eighteen powers to join SCUA. Dulles also refused to compel American shippers to pay dues to SCUA, since he viewed it as a voluntary organization.[80] The next day Eden and Lloyd decided to call for a meeting of the Security Council on September 26. Dulles's efforts had failed to change the mind of the British government.[81]

By the end of September the British were fed up with the secretary's machinations. SCUA was a perfect example of Dulles's foreign policy by improvisation. It was developed to satisfy the British demand that economic pressure be brought to bear on Nasser. But, as in most diplomatic situations, Dulles provided an escape clause; he never allowed himself to be pinned down on exactly what the United States would support. He totally frustrated the British and French. Aside from their distrust of Dulles, the British decision to take their case to the Security Council was based on a number of factors: fear that the Soviet Union was about to introduce a resolution of its own, French disillusionment with the results of the Second London Conference, and the Foreign Office need to appear decisive during the crisis.[82]

After his performance in London the secretary of state again reversed himself. In meetings with Macmillan, who was then visiting the United States, Dulles supposedly spoke of six ways of "getting rid" of Nasser over a six-month period. He wanted the British to wait until after the November 6 presidential election, but Macmillan chose to disregard the significance of the date and reported to Eden that both Dulles and Eisenhower, with whom he also met, were "determined to bring Nasser down."[83] Macmillan's reports to Eden upon his return to London further confused the prime minister about Washington's policy.

On September 26, answering a question about transit around the Cape, Dulles suggested, ". . . In view of the decision of the United States, at least, as I put it, not to shoot our way through the canal, that [the British] in fact would have to go around the Cape."[84] Eden scarcely knew what to expect next from the secretary. Later that evening, despite American opposition, the British decided to introduce the matter in the Security Council.

By the beginning of October Eden had reached his physical breaking point. After two years of intense pressure from a myriad of crisis situations, the Suez problem may have put him over the edge. Until then Eden had handled the crisis in a relatively calm manner. As the Security Council debate was about to begin, however, he fell seriously ill and was briefly hospitalized with a fever of 106 degrees. According to Chester Cooper and others, at this point Eden underwent a serious personality change. Following his bout with the high fever, probably exacerbated by his "tortuous liver and jaundice," he seemed to alternate between phases of confidence and doubt. He became unusually sensitive to all events and obsessed with the consequences of every move.[85]

On October 2, at a press conference, Dulles's remarks led the Foreign Office to believe that achieving any Anglo-American understanding was lost. For Eden it was the final letdown, as Dulles stated in reference to SCUA:

> There is talk about "teeth" being pulled out of it. There was never "teeth" in it, if that means the use of force.
> Now there has been some difference in our approach to this problem of the Suez Canal. This is not an area where we are bound together by treaty. Certain areas we are by treaty bound to protect, such as the North Atlantic Treaty area, and there we stand absolutely together. There is also other problems where our approach is not always identical. For example, there is Asia and Africa the so-called problem of colonialism. Now there the United States plays a somewhat independent role.[86]

Aside from reinforcing Nasser's view that Anglo-French military preparations were a bluff, these remarks revealed the depth of Anglo-American differences in dealing with the Suez crisis. They warned the British that American interests could not always be expected to coincide with the interests of the Western allies worldwide. The threat posed by Nasser also split the allies. Eden now saw any chance of an honorable settlement disappear. On October 3 he met with *London Times* reporter Iverach McDonald who described the prime minister as being "shocked that Dulles should completely misunderstand this determination to have the canal internationally controlled as to think he was reverting to colonialism." Eden ended the conversation by remarking that "it leaves us in a quite impossible situation. We can't go on like this." Anthony Nutting corroborates McDonald's description, adding that for Eden "this was the final letdown. We had reached the breaking point."[87]

For Eisenhower it was a long-range problem; for Eden the threat was more immediate. Eden's obsession with Nasser and World War II appeasement was evident in his October 1 letter to Eisenhower.

> There is no doubt in our minds that Nasser, whether he likes it or not, is now effectively in Russian hands, just as Mussolini was in Hitler's. . . . No doubt your people have been told of the accumulating evidence of Egyptian pilots in Libya, Saudi Arabia and Iraq. At any moment any one of these may be touched off unless we can prove to the Middle East that Nasser is losing.[88]

Dulles, fully aware of how greatly American relations with the Atlantic allies had deteriorated, told the president that the British and French believe "we are not backing them sufficiently and . . . are blaming their failure to get results on the fact that we are holding them back."[89] After discussing possible American support for the British in the Security Council, Eisenhower brought up the subject of covert operations against Nasser. He concluded, upon reviewing British policy, that "we should have nothing to do with any project for a covert operation against Nasser personally." The president believed the canal issue was not the one to pursue in order to undermine Nasser. He thought the Egyptian leader had "dangerous tendencies that needed to be curbed." There was promise in "developing Arab leadership elsewhere" which "offered greater hope than a frontal attack on the Canal issue."[90] Eisenhower was referring either to plans to support King Saud as an Arab leader, or to a possible coup being planned for Syria.

On October 8 the matter of covert action was again raised in a meeting with Hoover and General Andrew J. Goodpaster, Eisenhower's staff secretary. Referring to Hoover's comment on the possibility of overthrowing Nasser, the president felt the time was not right for a coup in Egypt—there was "so much hostility at present." It would inflame the Arab world. According to Eisenhower, "a time free from heated stress holding the world's attention would have to be chosen," and he refused to approve any action until after he was reelected.[91] The British and the French, with cold weather approaching, felt they did not have the luxury of time for a military solution.

In early October, as Anglo-French military planning continued, Lloyd presented to the Security Council the British case for using the eighteen-power proposals as a basis for negotiation. Lloyd did not favor an open-ended discussion of issues; he wanted urgent action. After private talks with Egyptian Foreign Minister Fawzi between October 10 and 13, the Egyptian government accepted the idea that the canal should be insulated from the politics of any one country. The upshot was a possible agreement on what became known as the Six Principles.[92]

While talks proceeded at the United Nations, distrust between the United States and its allies grew. Dulles, in a message to Douglas Dillon, the American ambassador in Paris, complained that the British and French want us to "stand with them" but they refused to consult with Washington about their United Nations plans. Dulles resented charges that Washington did not support its allies. Characterizing allied policy, the secretary said, "Their positions so far [as] we are aware are vague to the point of non-existence. We do not know and we cannot find out whether they want war or peace."[93] British feelings were fully reciprocated, as Eden commented to Lloyd about Dulles's suggestion that another committee be set up to negotiate with Egypt.

> We have been misled so often by Dulles' ideas that we cannot afford to risk another misunderstanding. That is why a negotiating committee would be so dangerous. We should lose control of the situation and justifiably be accused by the French of betraying them.[94]

In meetings with Pineau and Lloyd on October 5, Dulles tried to smooth relations by remarking that "he fully agreed that the potential use of force must be kept in existence." But "we must make it clear in the Security Council that a real effort to get a peaceful settlement [was] made and [if] it failed it would then be permissible to consider force as an alternative."[95]

Tensions remained high as Lloyd met with Dulles on October 8. Lloyd asked the secretary where he stood and wanted to know if he was preparing something behind Britain's back. Dulles denied any such notion and insisted that he fully agreed with the British on every point except the wisdom of the ultimate use of force. Again he noted that the British had been absolutely right to make preparations to maintain the military threat.[96] Despite protestations to the contrary, Dulles still refused to support mandatory payment of transit fees to SCUA. Frustrated, Lloyd remarked, "With regard to payment of dues, I have never seen anyone so anxious to denigrate his own child as Dulles with SCUA."[97]

Meanwhile, the secretary of state falsely reported to the National Security Council that SCUA was developing into an important mechanism and that the United Kingdom had moderated its viewpoint.[98] Dulles sought to defuse the crisis by giving the impression that he was in control of events, hoping that the longer he dragged out the process the better the chance to mitigate the stalemate. In reality, he was not only misinforming his allies through his improvisational diplomacy, he was misleading members of his own government.

Throughout the entire Suez crisis the French insisted that Nasser must be replaced. Early in September, Paris began seriously to consider joining Israel in a military venture against Egypt. On September 18 Shimon Peres, a member of the Israeli Defense Ministry, traveled to Paris primarily to discuss arms purchases. Peres remained four days, and after meeting with French Defense Minister Maurice Bourges-Maunoury, agreed in principle to join the French in a military operation against Nasser.[99] At the end of September another Israeli delegation visited Paris. During meetings with Pineau, the French foreign minister, the Israelis voiced concerns about the reliability of the British. Fearing London might withdraw its support for military action, Pineau was pleased when Israeli Foreign Minister Golda Meir agreed to pursue joint action with the French even if the British should refuse to take part. The projected date for an attack was October 20, but the French could not finalize plans until discussing them with Britain following the Security Council session.[100]

On October 14, at Mollet's request, Eden met with acting French Foreign Minister Albert Grazier and Deputy Chief of Staff General Maurice Challe at Chequers. Eden and Anthony Nutting, a British under secretary of state, were given an outline of Franco-Israeli plans to gain control of the Suez Canal. Israel would attack Egypt across the Sinai; France and Britain, having given Israel sufficient time to seize most of the desert, would then order both sides to withdraw their forces from the Suez Canal area. Thereby an Anglo-French force would "intervene and occupy the canal on the pretext of saving it from damage by fighting."[101] Thus began the process of collusion between France, Israel, and the United Kingdom.

Following the October 14 meeting with the French, Eden ordered Lloyd to return immediately from New York. On October 16 Lloyd accompanied Eden to Paris for meetings with Mollet and Pineau. They all agreed that Dulles had "double-crossed" them with SCUA, which they believed was designed to block them from going to the Security Council.[102] When the talks turned to the Franco-Israeli plan, Mollet asked the British what their response would be if Israel attacked Egypt. Would they feel bound under the Tripartite Declaration? Eden replied that his government believed that, due to Nasser's attitude, the declaration no longer applied to Egypt. As for the canal itself, Eden expressed no qualms about British military intervention to protect the vital waterway. The French ministers believed that Israel was becoming desperate, that if a canal agreement was not reached with Nasser in a few days there would be trouble. They also decided that the United States would side with Nasser and "allow the annihilation of Israel." Eden accepted this assessment, but he was concerned about a possible Israeli attack against Jordan. The French and the British "considered prior consultation with the U.S." but decided "it would serve no useful purpose." Following his return to London on the 17th, Eden wired Mollet confirmation that should the canal be threatened, British forces would intervene.[103]

The plan presented to the Israelis included a written declaration of London's approval in order to overcome Israeli distrust of the British. Israel's concern about London focused on the Anglo-Jordanian defense treaty. Eden made it clear that should Israel attack Jordan, Britain would honor its treaty commitment to Jordan. Because of increasing border incidents between Israel and Jordan, Tel Aviv was worried that the Israelis might find themselves fighting British troops.[104] Ben-Gurion rejected the United Kingdom's declaration as a basis for proceeding. He refused to allow Israel to mount "the rostrum of shame so that Britain and France could have their hands in the waters of purity."[105] Ben-Gurion did not trust Eden, whom he regarded as a weak leader. He feared Eden would cancel any commitment at the last minute because of Britain's relationship with the Arab world. Both Dayan and Peres had to convince the Israeli prime minister not to forgo the opportunity, for Israel would have to confront Nasser eventually, with or without French or British aid. After an appeal from Mollet, Ben-Gurion agreed to meet with British officials.[106]

On October 18 Eden met with his cabinet and hinted at what had transpired in Paris. He informed his ministers that they should

> . . . be aware that, while we continue to seek an agreed settlement of the Suez dispute in pursuance of the resolution of the Security

Council, it was possible that the issue might be brought to a head as a result of military action by Israel against Egypt.[107]

October 22 became the most important date in the developing conspiracy. Ben-Gurion and his advisers arrived at Sevres, outside Paris, in the early afternoon. After three hours of discussion about Ben-Gurion's hope to achieve a comprehensive agreement for the Middle East, Foreign Secretary Lloyd arrived at 7 p.m. Once Lloyd was settled, Dayan presented his plan, based on previous agreements with the French. The foreign secretary was not enthusiastic. He warned the Israelis that "their military must not be a small scale encounter, but a real act of war, otherwise there would be no justification for the British ultimatum and Britain would appear in the eyes of the world as an aggressor."[108]

The initial meeting with the British did not go well. The next day, however, the French and Israelis worked out their remaining difficulties. Pineau went to London to report to Eden who provided final approval for the plan. Lloyd and Pineau agreed not to discuss the matter with the United States because of "their unsatisfactory attitude." On October 24 Pineau returned to Paris and met with the Israelis. Despite severe doubts about the operation, Ben-Gurion gave his approval.[109] Later that afternoon British representatives arrived to conclude the agreement. After a long meeting, during which tension between the Israelis and British was evident, a written agreement was drawn up. The British insisted that the "Protocol of Sevres" remain secret while all the participants were alive. The pledge was kept for more than thirty years.[110]

Later on the 24th Eden presented the most important aspects of the plan to his cabinet without exposing what was agreed to at Sevres. The following day Eden finally provided his ministers the full details. He explained that the Israelis intended to attack Egypt because they believed Nasser's ambitions threatened their continued existence as an independent state, and "they could not afford to wait for others to curb his expansionist policies." The French believed that Anglo-French intervention was necessary to prevent hostilities from spreading. If the

United Kingdom had declined to join, Paris could be expected to act unilaterally or in conjunction with the Israelis. The prime minister continued:

> In these circumstances . . . if Israel launched a full-scale military operation against Egypt, the governments of the United Kingdom and France should at once call on all parties to stop hostilities and to withdraw their forces to a distance of ten miles from the Canal; and that it should at the same time be made clear that, if one or both Governments failed to undertake within twelve hours to comply with these requirements, British and French forces would intervene in order to enforce compliance.[111]

Eden believed that Israel would comply. If Egypt cooperated, Nasser would be "fatally undermined." If Egypt did not, it would provide ample justification for military action to safeguard the canal. There were risks of being charged with collusion with Israel, but if Israel attacked, Britain would be faced with the same charges whether or not it acted. At the conclusion of discussion, the cabinet approved Eden's plans.[112]

The question remains, why did Eden go along with the Sevres conspiracy, an action so contradictory to British interests in Iraq and Jordan and to the overall Baghdad Pact strategy he had pursued for more than five years? Clearly he worried about the growing Soviet relationship with Nasser. Further, documents constantly refer to the low morale and boredom of British troops who had been on standby alert at Suez for almost three months. Eden must have believed he had exhausted all diplomatic avenues for a settlement. The Sevres plan created an option to remove Nasser with the possibility of retaining world opinion. Despite his unrealistic evaluation of potential American and Labor party opposition, Eden strongly believed that his countrymen supported his obsession to destroy Nasser and halt Britain's slide to the rank of a second-rate power. He calculated the political ramifications of his actions, but he overlooked the economic consequences which would end the British reign in the Middle East.[113]

While the conspiracy was unfolding, American intelligence analysts were not able to predict developments. Washington clung to the view that "if the United States could just keep the lid on a little longer, some kind of compromise plan would be worked out."[114] During the two weeks preceding the Israeli invasion of the Sinai, a virtual blackout of communication existed between the United States and its Atlantic allies. Aware of increased radio traffic between London and Paris, American intelligence was unable to break the codes.[115]

Eisenhower's main fear was an outbreak of hostilities between Israel and Jordan, which could activate the Anglo-Jordanian treaty. On October 15 Dulles informed the president that the Jordanian situation was deteriorating, in part due to massive Israeli border raids. Both Dulles and Eisenhower feared that Israel might make a major move against Jordan because of Western preoccupation with Suez and the upcoming presidential election. Eisenhower's anger with the French rose when American spy planes spotted sixty French Mystere jet fighters on Israeli airfields.[116] By the 18th Dulles told his brother Allen that he was worried about events in the Middle East because he believed the British and French were "deliberately keeping [us] in the dark."[117] On October 21 Dulles, still baffled about Anglo-French intentions, told Eisenhower they would not resort to military action until after the election.[118]

Israeli mobilization was designed to appear directed against Jordan. The military buildup which began on October 25 was 80 percent completed by the 28th. American intelligence sources advised on October 26 that Israeli mobilization was "not a full mobilization, and therefore Israel did not intend [to launch] general hostilities."[119] By the 28th United States intelligence sources altered their reports to indicate that the Israeli mobilization was designed to exploit any situation for war against Egypt. The intelligence community grew concerned with the "close collaboration between the French and Israeli governments," especially the dispatch of Mystere aircraft to Israel.[120]

Eisenhower administration officials were well aware that something serious was about to occur, for the president was informed of Anglo-French preparations on Cyprus. The weekend before the attack, reports from Douglas Dillon in Paris, based on his contacts with the minister of state in the French government, said that France, Britain, and Israel planned to attack Egypt soon after the American elections. Upon receiving this information, Allen Dulles, like everyone else, found it difficult to believe that the three countries would embark on such a self-defeating venture.[121] American intelligence officials were preoccupied with the developing revolt in Hungary and unable to deal effectively with the allied deception. Eisenhower wrote Ben-Gurion on the 28th expressing his concern about Israeli military preparations and urging restraint.[122] The morning of the 29th Secretary of State Dulles strongly suspected that the French had "concerted with [the] Israelis to provide action which would lead to [an] Israeli war against Egypt with the probable participation by [the] French and British."[123] Israel's attack later that day confirmed Eisenhower's suspicions of Eden's and Pineau's actions over the previous two weeks. When the Anglo-French ultimatum was delivered a short time later, everything fell into place.

Eisenhower and Dulles considered the Anglo-French ultimatum excessive and unacceptable. Confronted with the first hard evidence of allied collusion, an angry Eisenhower cabled stern warnings to Eden and Mollet. Clearly the British and French were about to make a grave error in the Middle East which could cost the West dearly. Eisenhower decided on a "damage-control" operation. Its outcome was a final split between the United States and its allies over Middle East policy, the watershed for Britain as it was replaced by the United States as the major Western power in the region.

8 *American Ascendancy*

Israeli collusion with Britain and France, leading to the allied invasion of Egypt, irrevocably changed Anglo-American relations. Occurring on the eve of the United States presidential election, and in the face of repeated warnings by Eisenhower administration officials against the use of force, the attack culminated a series of events which ushered in a new power in the Middle East.

The British and French had presented Washington with a fait accompli; it infuriated Eisenhower. Three years of trying to turn American policy away from allied colonialism and partiality toward Israel had brought a measure of success in relations with the Arab world. The Suez attack destroyed those efforts.

After two weeks of Israeli military actions designed to suggest an imminent attack against Jordan, on October 29, 1956, Israeli paratroopers were dropped deep into the Sinai Desert. The Egyptians were caught completely by surprise. Nasser thought the Israelis had simply launched a retaliatory strike against a border raid by Egyptian *Fedayeen* (terrorists). For their part, the Israelis calculated that if Anglo-French forces did not uphold their end of the Sevres agreement, they could still withdraw. The Egyptians met the Israeli attackers and full-scale war ensued. The British reminded the Egyptian government that according to the 1954 Suez Canal base agreement they had the right to intervene if Egypt was attacked. Accordingly, on October 30 Britain and France delivered an ultimatum calling for an end to the fighting and warning Egypt to withdraw to a position ten miles from the canal.[1] Nasser refused, informing the British ambassador, Sir Humphrey Trevelyan, that "since the Israelis were the aggressors... the British and French stand, consisting of the ultimatum and imminent occupation, was an act of aggression against Egyptian rights and dignity and against the Charter of the United Nations."[2]

At dusk on October 31 British and French planes began bombing Egyptian positions. The allied task force was supposed to land on Egyptian soil on November 1, but because of poor planning, American opposition in the United Nations, and weakening support in Parliament, Eden hesitated. After vetoing a UN Security Council resolution calling for a cease-fire, the Anglo-French force finally went ashore at Port Said on November 5. The French wished to advance their forces, but Eden, whose spirit had been broken by political opposition and Britain's weakening economic situation, late in the evening of November 6 agreed to a cease-fire. Despite arguing vehemently against stopping the invasion, the French reluctantly agreed to end the fighting. As these events unfolded, the Israeli army had conquered the entire Sinai from the Suez Canal to Sharm el-Sheikh before complying with the UN-sponsored cease-fire on November 3.

Eisenhower believed the British and French had made a grave error which also provided the Soviets a cover for their actions in suppressing the Hungarian revolt. He realized too that the attack on Egypt provided the means for Moscow further to penetrate the Middle East.[3] What's more, on October 29, the same day as the Israeli invasion, an American-sponsored anti-leftist coup was scheduled to take place in Syria. According to Wilbur Crane Eveland, the CIA's Syrian operative, Washington canceled the coup immediately upon learning of the Israeli attack.[4] Finally, Eisenhower was angry because the peace-candidate image he had sought to project during the 1956 election campaign was now tarnished.

The president's strategy was to reduce the damage caused by the allied action. Concluding that the British could no longer be relied upon as the dominant Western power in the region,

Eisenhower quickly turned to a policy designed to gain British withdrawal and indirectly to influence the choice of Eden's replacement as prime minister. The president wished to teach his ally a lesson, not destroy her. He wished to preserve the Anglo-American relationship yet make London a junior partner to Washington in the Middle East. The end result was the Eisenhower Doctrine—concrete proof of the American desire to take the lead in the region and break from British colonial interests.

Upon learning of the Israeli attack Eisenhower was firm in his belief that American and British prestige were at stake. He considered it imperative for both nations to honor their pledge given to Israel and the Arab states in the spring: Western support against outside aggression. Should Washington and London not keep their word, "Russia [would] likely enter the situation in the Middle East."[5]

Both Eisenhower and Dulles suspected that the continued advance of the Israeli military would disrupt the canal and allow British and French intervention. With no word from the British for ten days preceding the Israeli attack, Eisenhower concluded that London assumed the United States would support Her Majesty's Government no matter what action it took. The president was sympathetic to Britain's predicament, but he wanted London to be aware that "nothing justified double-crossing the United States." Unhappy about appearing to help Egypt in the circumstances, Eisenhower nonetheless "felt our word must be made good."[6]

On October 30 the United Nations Security Council convened to consider an American resolution calling upon Israel to withdraw from Egyptian territory and asking all UN members to refrain from using force in the Middle East. Before the second session of the Security Council, the British and French informed the General Assembly that they had already delivered an ultimatum—secretly agreed upon at Sevres in mid-October—to Egypt and Israel to withdraw. As expected, the United Kingdom and France vetoed the American resolution as well as a similar one sponsored by the Soviet Union to substitute a United Nations force for the proposed Anglo-French expeditionary force.[7]

Dulles summed up the American reaction to the ultimatum by characterizing it as "about as crude and brutal as anything he had ever seen." Eisenhower wanted Eden made aware "that we are a government of honor, and we will stick by it."[8] October 30 brought a series of communications between the president and the prime minister. The British position, Eden said, "rested on the idea that Israel [had] a case for arguing that she [was] acting in self-defense under increasing pressure of certain Arab states led by Egypt. . . ." Eden went on to mollify any American charge of acting in imperialist fashion, stating "that I can assure you that any action which we may have to take . . . is not part of a harking back to the old colonial and occupational concepts. . . . The key is to strengthen the weakest point in the war against communism."[9]

Eisenhower, livid because he was not forewarned about the ultimatum, rebuked Eden, writing:

> I have just learned from the press of the 12-hour ultimatum which you . . . have delivered to the Egyptian government. . . . It is my sincere belief that peaceful processes can and should prevail to secure a solution which will restore the armistice condition as between Israel and Egypt.[10]

Dulles correctly appraised the situation, remarking to Eisenhower that the events were "not a question of Suez, but Algeria for the French and the Persian Gulf for the British."[11] For the president it was "the damnedest business I ever saw supposedly intelligent governments get themselves into."[12]

Eden met with his cabinet the morning of the 30th amidst concern about the dangerous rate of decline of the British dollar and gold reserves. The costs of military mobilization in the midst of recession were telling. Government ministers were therefore afraid to alienate the United States, fearing they might soon be forced to turn to Washington for financial aid should an oil crisis develop.[13]

Blame for the dollar and gold reserve crisis fell directly on Harold Macmillan, the British chancellor of the exchequer.

ing. If the canal and oil pipelines were closed, the United Kingdom would face a 25 percent drop in oil supplies, even if the United States provided financial aid and oil resources. Any additional supplies would cost between $500 and $700 million per year. Under normal circumstances the British could automatically draw a maximum of $235 million in gold from the IMF, but American opposition now made this uncertain. The Bank of England refused to go to the IMF, hoping that a delay would give "tempers a chance to cool down."[20]

Despite the November 2 UN resolution, some vehicle was needed to maintain peace in the Middle East. Lester Pearson, the Canadian representative at the United Nations, proposed the creation of an international United Nations emergency force (UNEF) which "would be empowered to enter Egyptian territory with Cairo's consent in order to secure compliance with . . . the resolution adopted by the General Assembly on November 2, 1956."[21]

For the British the weekend of November 3 and 4 was terribly disheartening. On November 3 they decided to accept the concept of a UNEF but refused to commit themselves to a specific withdrawal date in order to allow their invading force to arrive from Malta.[22] Meanwhile, Dulles, suffering from cancer, entered the hospital for abdominal surgery and Herbert Hoover, Jr., openly known as anti-British, took over as acting secretary in Dulles's absence. The weekend concluded with reports that the Syrians, supporting Egypt, had blown up the oil pipelines which linked Iraqi oil to the Mediterranean.

At the United Nations the secretary-general adamantly opposed the Anglo-French request for inclusion in the UNEF. This refusal caused difficulties for Eden who had used the idea to justify British military action against Egypt. The British landing was to be an advance force for the United Nations, and any territory under its control would be turned over to the UNEF upon its arrival. At the November 4 meeting of the Egypt Committee, Foreign Secretary Selwyn Lloyd warned that if the United Kingdom insisted on a role in the UNEF, it could result in the imposition of economic and other sanctions making London's position untenable. Despite these warnings the committee decided to proceed with the invasion.[23]

Eden's ministers were most concerned about the effects of their actions on the United States. The prime minister had already apologized to Eisenhower after the president had learned of the ultimatum through the press. On November 4 he sent the president another message which recapitulated his views.[24] In Washington, British fears were about to become reality. During a morning meeting on November 5 Hoover informed Eisenhower that oil supplies from the Middle East were largely cut off except for the TAPLINE from Saudi Arabia. (The Trans Arabian Pipeline Company controlled the flow of oil from the Saudi Arabian fields on the Persian Gulf, across the desert and through Jordan to the Mediterranean Sea.) Referring to Anglo-French oil problems, the president decided that "the purpose of peace and stability would be served by not being too quick in attempting to render extraordinary assistance."[25]

Contacting Eden about the British landing at Port Said, Eisenhower requested a few days of relative calm in order to seek a solution, subtly warning Eden that he was aware of "Harold's financial problems" and he favored a less provocative policy. Eisenhower reassured the prime minister that cooperation between the United States and United Kingdom would be restored "just as quickly as it can be done."[26]

The next day a run on the pound developed, and the British situation grew increasingly critical. During the first week of November, 15 percent of Great Britain's gold and dollar reserves evaporated. Macmillan envisioned dreary prospects for the next six months with a shortfall of three to four million tons of oil for Europe and the United Kingdom. If consumption rates remained unchanged, it would cost the Treasury $800 million annually to bring oil around the Cape of Good Hope. British gold and dollar reserves had already dropped $141 million in September and October; by November these losses could double to $279 million.[27] On the morning of the 6th Macmillan telephoned U.S. Secretary of the Treasury George Humphrey seeking assistance. He was bluntly told that it would be available only if a cease-fire were arranged by midnight. According to Sir

Harold Caccia, the newly appointed British ambassador to the United States, "we meet a brick wall at every turn with the administration."[28] The British were now faced with the U.S. Federal Reserve Board selling British currency, Washington's refusal to advance a temporary loan, and American obstruction to withdraw money from the IMF. Macmillan had little choice but to urge acceptance of the cease-fire.[29]

In addition, cabinet members' concerns about possible Soviet intervention in Egypt[30] spread opposition throughout the House of Commons. Eden accepted the cease-fire that evening.[31]

On November 6 Americans went to the polls and reelected Eisenhower by nearly ten million votes. Telephoning the president to congratulate him on his victory, Eden proposed an immediate meeting between himself, Mollet, and Eisenhower to discuss procedures to follow the cease-fire.[32] Eden was ecstatic when the president responded positively. After conferring with Hoover, however, Eisenhower decided to reject the meeting. There would be no summit with the Atlantic allies until they had carried out the United Nations resolution. Were a meeting to occur before this was accomplished, the State Department feared the Arab states would interpret it as American cooperation with its colonialist allies.[33] Eisenhower wired Eden two days later and canceled any meeting for the near future.

Following this disappointing message from Eisenhower, Eden was presented with still more bad news: dollar reserves were drying up, and cash reserves were barely able to keep up with the rate of loss. In addition, on December 31 the British would need $180 million to meet their debt service on outstanding loans. The Treasury anticipated no improvement in the sterling exchange situation until political tensions subsided. Macmillan's advisers feared that the dollar balance would fall under $2 billion by January 1, 1957, unless there was a strong movement in favor of sterling. Treasury Department officials recommended drawing on the IMF for $1 billion and mobilizing $750 million in dollar securities. Clearly the British economy was plunging in the wake of Suez.[34]

On November 8 Harold Caccia wired the Foreign Office and reported on his meeting with Secretary of the Treasury Humphrey. Quite pessimistic, Caccia wrote that "there is no possibility of aid . . . as it would be very difficult to persuade the United States . . . to grant us a long-term loan for the purchase of oil . . . in light of our actions the last ten days."[35]

Later that day Eisenhower presided over the meeting of the National Security Council. Robert Anderson reported that the only remaining source of Middle East oil was the TAPLINE in Saudi Arabia, and the duration of its operation was "touch and go." Anderson argued against emergency plans to help Britain and France because the Arabs would regard the actions as American participation in aggression directed against them.[36] Humphrey warned that if the United Kingdom pulled its gold and dollars out of the IMF, the British could be heading toward bankruptcy.

Based on this information, Eisenhower decided that when the cease-fire was fully arranged and the UNEF in place, the United States would consider activating the plan of the Middle East Emergency Committee. This group of oil industry personnel, established under the Office of Defense Mobilization, was to plan for oil shipment from the Gulf Coast to Europe in the event that normal supplies of Middle Eastern oil were disrupted.[37] Aside from the oil issue, there was concern about a Soviet coup in Syria, but all at the NSC meeting agreed that the key to the American position in the Middle East was to get the Anglo-French force out of Egypt and replace it with the UNEF.[38]

Britain's economic plight made London extremely vulnerable to American pressure. On November 8 the British cabinet met to deal with a blocked canal, dwindling oil supplies, the absence of aid from Washington with which to purchase oil from the Western Hemisphere, and a president who refused to discuss long-term issues until after Anglo-French forces were withdrawn from the Suez Canal.[39] As a result the cabinet agreed to open negotiations with the United Nations commander to transfer British-occupied areas to his control.[40] The British succumbed to American coercion.

Throughout November Eisenhower promoted a bipartisan approach at home to gain approval for his actions in the Middle East. On November 8 and 9 he briefed congressional leaders on the state of the Suez war and explored with them ways to fill the political vacuum created by the British in the region. Eisenhower sought approval of a program which granted him power to act swiftly in the Middle East to thwart the Soviet Union and allow the United States to lead in formulating allied policy in the area. He wanted to propose real peace to Arab governments and ensure that every weak country understood the ramifications of Soviet domination. The president believed the Suez crisis revealed a great need for a policy that would strengthen U.S. economic and political ties to each of the states in the region.[41] Since Anglo-French policy had allowed further Soviet penetration in the Middle East, Eisenhower felt compelled to develop a new policy which would secure American interests throughout the area.

While Eisenhower lobbied for a new Middle East policy in Washington, the British government faced a number of crucial domestic and foreign policy decisions. For the duration of the crisis, two issues dominated British policy: the mechanics of British withdrawal, and the clearing of the canal to permit the resumption of oil shipments. The first problem was easily settled at a meeting of the Egypt Committee on November 12. The committee agreed that a phased troop withdrawal would take place with the arrival of the UNEF. Once the UNEF was "effective and in place," all British troops would leave.[42] The second issue was not as clear-cut. Owing to the weakened state of the British economy and its shrinking oil supplies, London wanted the canal cleared at the earliest moment.

The British government could see no chance of improving its dismal situation. Foreign Secretary Lloyd feared that the United States would force the British out of Port Said even before the UNEF arrived.[43] United Nations Secretary-General Dag Hammarskjöld was seeking Nasser's cooperation, and the Foreign Office believed he was biased against Britain.[44] When the Egypt Committee met on November 15, Egypt had no incentive to clear the canal, and it was feared that Hammarskjöld would agree that Anglo-French forces had to withdraw *before* the UNEF landed. Oil shortages, rising unemployment, and dwindling dollar reserves caught the committee in a vise. Despite the

United States having dropped its demands that Anglo-French forces be withdrawn prior to American cooperation, the British economic outlook was not likely to improve. Washington was now willing to accept at "least a start . . . on the withdrawal of [British] forces in return for their support."[45] Since the United States position was considered vital to the British economy, and with a growing fear of further Soviet penetration in Syria and Egypt, Eden agreed to a phased withdrawal coinciding with the arrival of the UNEF.[46]

Washington was fully aware of Britain's disintegrating economic position. On November 17 Macmillan discussed with American Ambassador Winthrop Aldrich the possibility of borrowing from the Federal Reserve Bank on British-owned American securities valued at $900 million. Macmillan hoped to borrow $600 million from the Federal Reserve and another $500 million from the International Monetary Fund "to tide Great Britain over the difficult period ahead."[47] Two days later Macmillan sent Humphrey a message once again pleading London's case.

> Our policy is to do everything in our power to maintain the current parity of sterling. . . . Failure to maintain existing parity of sterling— either by devaluation to a fixed rate or by allowing the rate to float—coming so soon after the devaluation of 1949 would, I am convinced, lead to a breakup of the sterling area. . . . We would have difficulty in getting our essential imports, and we would not be able to maintain a major role in the political, military and economic problems of the free world. . . . Effects would be worldwide . . . [and] would disrupt world trade and give the Communist world a victory.[48]

Macmillan reported to the cabinet later that day that reserve losses would be $250 million or more in November, a 10 to 15 percent decline in British dollar reserves since the Suez invasion just three weeks earlier. It was apparent to him that Washington would offer no substantial help until the political situation was clarified, and not before the monthly announcement of reserve losses on December 4. He recommended that the Treasury Department do everything possible to maintain the existing exchange value of sterling and try to obtain a loan through the IMF, and as a last resort borrow against dollar securities.[49] Macmillan also recommended a 25 percent reduction in oil consumption, requiring "petrol rationing" by December 17. If the United States would not provide additional oil, the chancellor of the exchequer concluded that more drastic cuts would be necessary.[50]

A Foreign Office Minute prepared on November 15 provides an insight into British anxiety over the American attitude. The minute describes a meeting with Shell Oil Company directors wherein the Foreign Office's worst fears were affirmed. After conversations with Humphrey and Hoover in the United States, Shell directors concluded that Washington had decided to disassociate itself from the British and French. This conclusion was based upon the Americans' expressed fear of a violent Arab reaction against the United States and consequent concern for the TAPLINE and Aramco oil sources. The State Department still regarded Britain as America's "best friend," who in the future would not let Washington down. But there were bitter feelings in the U.S. administration against the prime minister personally.[51] The Foreign Office failed to recognize the depth of anger over events surrounding the Suez crisis, or that members of Eisenhower's administration were convinced they could no longer work effectively with Eden.

Eisenhower's opinion of Eden declined further—if that was possible—as the crisis worsened. During a hospital visit with a convalescing Dulles on November 17 the president confessed he had started "with an exceedingly high opinion of [Eden] . . . and then [had] continually to downgrade this estimate [after] succeeding contacts with him."[52] Eisenhower's anger was not with the United Kingdom, toward which he retained warm feelings, but with the prime minister.

Unexpected changes in the British government now offered a glimmer of hope for an improvement in Anglo-American relations. By November 19 the crisis had left Eden either ill or in a state of exhaustion, and his doctors insisted that he have complete rest in a warm climate. On November 20 the cabinet learned that Eden would shortly leave for Jamaica to recuperate.

Convinced that something must be done to repair Anglo-American relations if the British economy were to survive, Macmillan on November 19 arranged a meeting with Aldrich. Lloyd and most of the cabinet were unaware of this. Although the documentary evidence is not conclusive, it appears that at this meeting Macmillan hinted that if United States oil and financial aid were forthcoming, he could gain the support of "a sufficient number of Conservative backbenchers to insure a majority for the government in favor of withdrawal from Egypt."[53] Aldrich telephoned Hoover later that day to say that if the United States could provide assurances of future support, "the Cabinet is completely to be reshuffled." With Eden resting in Jamaica and "Macmillan . . . terribly anxious to see the President," Aldrich continued, a prime minister more conducive to American views might succeed Eden at Number 10 Downing Street.[54]

Aldrich reported to Washington that Macmillan was "putting a proposition to us. They will either have to withdraw from Egypt, and have their Cabinet fall, or else they will have to renew hostilities, taking over the entire Canal."[55] Later that evening Aldrich advised that Eden "has had a physical breakdown" which "will lead to his retirement." Macmillan, faced with London's precarious economic situation, asked, "if you can give us a fig leaf to cover our nakedness," he would arrange the withdrawal of British troops from Egypt and the replacement of Eden.[56]

Eisenhower, apprised of the situation by Humphrey, was concerned that "a lot of [the] conditions . . . cannot possibly be met."[57] The president feared that supporting the British so soon after withdrawal from Egypt would extract a very high political price among the Arab states. Nevertheless Eisenhower worried that if the Conservative government fell, the socialists, as he characterized the Labor party, would replace the government. The president preferred a continued Conservative rule which deep down favored cooperation with Washington.[58]

Hoover and Humphrey met with the president at 5:30 p.m. on November 20 to discuss how to keep the Conservatives in office. Humphrey supported Rab Butler to replace Eden, but the president favored Macmillan, characterizing him as the "outstanding one of the British he served with during the war."[59] All agreed something would have to be done to keep the Conservatives in power when Britain withdrew from Port Said. Humphrey offered to arrange a $560 million loan from the World

Bank and suggested that the Export-Import Bank could establish a credit of $600 million with which the British could pay for U.S. exports to Britain.[60] Humphrey believed the United Kingdom sought only financial help; Hoover suggested that London would still pressure the United States to join the Baghdad Pact.

Eisenhower wanted Butler and Macmillan informed that once Britain announced its immediate withdrawal, "they can be assured of our sympathetic consultation and help." The president would be willing to meet with them. Humphrey pointed out that the United States would work to obtain Arab support for the reopening of oil markets to the Atlantic allies. But this could only be achieved if Anglo-French forces were withdrawn from Suez.[61] The next day the president suggested that as part of an agreement with the British, the United States should encourage them "to express their readiness to leave Buraimi." Eisenhower still hoped to develop King Saud as a force in the Arab world. The king was due to visit Washington in the near future, and with discussions proceeding on the Dhahran air base, Eisenhower believed it would be useful to get the British to cooperate in the Persian Gulf.

Humphrey agreed that more than oil was involved. He told the president:

> The British are facing a financial crisis within ten days. He thought the sequence of events was this: the British will start out of Suez in a few days; the British will want to come over here a few days later, and this will be the time when we must bargain hard with them; between these dates we must let King Saud, and even Nasser, know that, in starting talks with the British, we have not reversed our stand toward them, and that we want an understanding with them prior to the British talks; by December 3rd our arrangements must be in hand, since this is the date of the British financial announcement.[62]

Eden, unaware of what was transpiring, on November 20 departed for Jamaica. Butler, leader of the House of Commons, took charge of the cabinet, and Macmillan took control of the government. From this point on, Eden was not consulted in advance of decisions made about Suez. The British cabinet was operating with a December 4 deadline because of the pending announcement of dollar and gold reserves. With the Treasury threatening devaluation of the pound, Macmillan warned government ministers that sterling might no longer be an international currency.[63]

As Macmillan worked behind the scenes to convince his colleagues that the United Kingdom should withdraw from Port Said, the United States continued to pressure the British government. The State Department informed the Foreign Office that the "introduction of a United Nations force and a phased withdrawal of Anglo-French troops should take place without delay, and once that this was well under way [the U.S.] would enter into consultation on basic issues."[64]

When Ambassador Caccia met with Humphrey on November 27, the secretary of the treasury left no doubt about America's position: ". . . At the right time the United States would be prepared to do everything possible to help the United Kingdom, particularly regarding sterling. But this time had not yet arrived." It was important, Humphrey continued, that the United States not appear to be running out on the United Nations. It was equally important that it not appear to be openly siding with London. Washington refused to risk losing its new Arab friends by appearing to sanction British actions. The secretary of the treasury agreed that specific financial aid would be drawn from the IMF and dollar loans from the Export-Import Bank. The key, however, was British cooperation in withdrawing from Port Said.[65]

On November 28 the British cabinet met to review its limited options. Facing continued economic pressure from Washington, Macmillan reminded the members that next week's announcement of gold and dollar reserves would reveal a serious drain. It would shock public opinion and undermine international confidence in sterling. Therefore it was important to announce coincidentally Treasury Department actions to reinforce reserves. These actions—an IMF loan and an Export-Import arrangement— all depended on the approval of the United States and British withdrawal from Port Said. Macmillan stressed that since "our original objectives" had been met in Suez, he could recommend the immediate announcement of Britain's intention of removing its troops from Port Said.[66]

The cabinet reconvened the next day and received additional disheartening economic news. A Treasury Minute released on December 1 stated that at the end of November British gold and dollar reserves would be $1.965 billion. By the end of the year the predicted figure would be $1.34 billion, the lowest in the postwar era.[67] Later that day the cabinet met to consider a draft statement for the House of Commons announcing British withdrawal. On December 3 Foreign Minister Lloyd announced to the House of Commons that the United Kingdom would withdraw from the Canal Zone.[68]

On December 12, having recovered from cancer surgery, Dulles visited London with Humphrey. During their discussions Macmillan expressed a degree of bitterness at America's role in the crisis, but he was clearly happy that progress had been made toward dispelling Eisenhower's complaints about the lack of candor in Anglo-American relations. Macmillan promptly reported to Butler his private conversations with Humphrey.

> He said it was like a business deal. They were putting a lot of money into the reorganization of Britain and they would hope very much that the business would be successful. But, of course, when you were reconstructing a business that was in difficulties, the personal problems could not be ruled out.
>
> I said: "Don't you trust the board?" and he said: "Well, since you ask me, I think it would be as well if we could deal as much as possible with the directors." This rather cryptic observation he enlarged on to say that he would like to feel that he could always be on terms of private, and, where necessary, telephonic communication with you and me.[69]

When Eden returned from Jamaica on December 14 his removal from power was assured. During the prime minister's absence, Butler and Macmillan had worked with the Eisenhower administration to improve Anglo-American relations. The financial aid which the British required was granted as well as a new loan with satisfactory terms for repayment.[70] The United States made it clear that it had lost confidence in Eden because of the way he had conducted the entire Suez affair. Having established a new relationship with Butler and Macmillan, Washington expected Eden to be forced into retirement.[71]

After two weeks of further diplomatic haggling, Anglo-French forces finally withdrew from Port Said on December 22. On January 9 Eden formally tendered his resignation. Macmillan was chosen by his party over Butler to form a new government because, during Eden's absence, it was Butler who was placed in the unenviable position of having to answer to all the pent-up anger within the Conservative party. While Macmillan tended to economic problems, Butler was left to deal with the political fallout from the invasion. What's more, in the post-Suez period Conservatives wanted a man of action, not an intellectual. They wanted someone who had a personal relationship with Eisenhower and who could help restore Anglo-American relations.[72]

Initially the Suez crisis produced a number of setbacks for American policy in the Middle East. For a brief period Washington's standing in the Arab world rose, but its allies in the region were embittered, the NATO alliance weakened, and Nasser's position enhanced. Further, the Arabs learned how to manipulate a new weapon—oil, and the Soviets' position in the region was strengthened. One fact encompassed all of these problems in the minds of State Department planners: with the British no longer a power broker in the area, a major vacuum existed. If Washington did not fill it, Moscow would.[73]

Plans to develop a new U.S. approach toward the Middle East were well under way in early November 1956 when it became obvious that British influence would not survive the Suez debacle.[74] Despite American pressure on its allies during the crisis, Washington's distrust for Nasser mounted throughout November and December. Eisenhower had always opposed the use of force to overthrow the Egyptian leader, believing it would only inflame Arab passions. But by mid-December Eisenhower was seeking an alternative to dealing with Nasser and the Arab world in general. On December 12 the president wired Dulles, who was attending a NATO meeting in Paris, to be sure that the NATO allies know that we regard Nasser as an evil influence. . . . We have made it . . . clear while we share in general the British and French opinions of Nasser, we insisted that they chose a bad time . . . in which to launch corrective measures. [75]

Eisenhower wanted to deal with the Egyptian leader by "build-[ing] up an Arab rival for Nasser. . . . If we could build him up as the individual to capture the imagination of the Arab world, Nasser would not last long." The president wanted to reactivate Project OMEGA, which in part had helped to create the Suez crisis by seeking an Arab alternative to Nasser. [76]

Besides developing an alternative to Nasser, Eisenhower hoped to repair the damage to allied relations. He wanted British support to stop the Soviets from further expansion in the Middle East. Despite all the lessons the Eisenhower administration should have learned from dealing with the Arab world in the previous three years, it still viewed the region through Cold War glasses. Dismissing a rapprochement with Nasser, the United States began to consider policy options which ultimately exacerbated Arab nationalism.

On December 8 Dulles telephoned the president and presented three policy options: "(1) that the United States join the Baghdad Pact; (2) try to create a new grouping . . . ; (3) to deal on a nation to nation basis under authority that would be granted." [77] Both men rejected the second option and discussed the merits of the other two. Dulles favored dealing on a "nation to nation basis to avoid getting into trouble with the troublemakers," a clear reference to Nasser. Eisenhower agreed but held out the hope that Saudi Arabia and Lebanon might adhere to the Baghdad Pact, "then we would want to go in with them." After Dulles pointed out the problem of Jewish influence in Congress, both agreed to the third option. [78]

On January 1, 1957, Eisenhower chaired a meeting of bipartisan congressional leaders to lobby for his new policy: military and economic aid to those Middle Eastern countries under the greatest pressure from the Soviet Union. He argued that the growing Soviet threat in the region demanded an American move to fill the power vacuum now left by the Anglo-French action against Egypt. Citing Syria as a target for Soviet expansion—especially because Damascus controlled the pipeline that connected Iraqi oil to the Mediterranean—the president emphasized "the need to put the world on notice that we were ready to act instantly, if necessary." To mollify congressional leaders, Eisenhower reaffirmed his regard for constitutional procedures.

Dulles then reiterated the president's arguments, assuring the legislators that the United States would act militarily only in response to a request from a country being invaded. Dulles's Cold War antenna was evident: he wished to put the world on notice that the United States intended to act as a deterrent to Soviet aggression.[79] Throughout the meeting Dulles and Eisenhower never really explained, only alluded to, Soviet capabilities or the threat they posed.[80] The "communist menace" which had helped create the Truman Doctrine in 1947 ten years later produced a similar proposal, this time named after a different president.

On January 5 Eisenhower delivered a speech to a joint session of the 85th Congress to gain support for the new Eisenhower Doctrine. The president requested authorization to provide Middle Eastern nations with military and economic aid designed to help them maintain their national independence. Assistance and cooperation also included the use of American armed forces "to secure and protect the territorial integrity and political independence of such nations, requesting such aid, against overt armed aggression from any nation controlled by international communism." Lastly, Eisenhower called for the approval of $200 million for fiscal 1958 and 1959 for discretionary use toward these ends.[81] Congress was not totally convinced, and debate continued for two months among different factions. Many were pro-Israel; some did not wish to surrender their constitutional prerogatives in advance; others felt U.S. assistance on such a basis would weaken NATO. Whatever opposition the Eisenhower Doctrine produced, the message was clear. The United States had taken the final step in reversing its relationship with the United Kingdom in the Middle East by replacing it as the dominant power in the region.

The other chief aspect of Eisenhower's policy involved King

Saud. The Saudi monarch had revitalized his American connection as a means of security against Nasser.[82] The Saudi government, nervous about the growing Egyptian-Soviet relationship, worried where Cairo might strike next. On January 30 King Saud began a state visit to the United States, during which Eisenhower sought to convince him to support the Eisenhower Doctrine in the Arab world. The king expressed his bitterness toward the United Kingdom because of the continuing problem over Buraimi, and tried to persuade the president that reports of Egyptian and Syrian leanings toward the Soviet Union were exaggerated. Saud still hoped to promote peaceful intra-Arab relations; he did not wish to see Egypt and Syria isolated. After prodding Eisenhower to invite Nasser and Syrian officials to Washington, Saud agreed to support the doctrine and promote it in the Arab world. He also agreed to a five-year renewal of the lease on the United States air force base at Dhahran in exchange for an American commitment to provide economic and military aid.[83] The president admitted, however, that "no political advances were realized in the talks" concerning the situation in the Middle East.[84]

Debate in Congress continued throughout February on the proposed Eisenhower Doctrine. A major roadblock to passage was Israel's refusal to withdraw completely from Egyptian territory. Immediately after accepting a cease-fire in early November, Tel Aviv had begun its fight to retain as much of the conquered territory as possible.

Ben-Gurion's refusal to cooperate with American demands for withdrawal aggravated Eisenhower because it rallied pro-Israel forces in Congress and delayed final approval of the Eisenhower Doctrine.[85] On February 2 the United Nations passed two resolutions: Israel was to withdraw behind the 1949 armistice line, and Egypt and Israel were to observe the provisions of the 1949 agreement. The secretary-general was directed to place the UNEF on the 1949 demarcation line to maintain peace in the area.[86] On February 3 Eisenhower wrote Ben-Gurion, warning him that if withdrawal was not "completed without further delay" it would "lead to the invoking of further UN procedures which would seriously disturb the relations between Israel and

other member nations including the United States."[87] Ben-
Gurion's reply, received a few days later, reaffirmed that Israel
would not evacuate Gaza unless Israel retained civil administration and police power, and had assurances of freedom of navigation through the Gulf of Aqaba.[88]

Eisenhower felt Israel could thwart any chance for the United
States to gain influence with the Arab countries. To win Israeli
cooperation, Washington offered Tel Aviv an aide-memoire in
which the United States called for the withdrawal from Gaza but
accepted the Israeli claim that the Gulf of Aqaba "constitutes
international waters and that no nation has the right to forcibly
prevent free and innocent passage." The United States was
"prepared to exercise the right of free and innocent passage and
to join with others to secure general recognition of this right."[89]
When Dulles refused to formalize these pledges, Israel rejected
them.

This was as far as Eisenhower was willing to go. If Israel
would not withdraw, he would support "a resolution which
would call on UN members to suspend not just governmental
but private assistance to Israel." The president's anger stemmed
from his belief, as he told Dulles, that Israel's delay would
further jeopardize Western influence in the Middle East and
convince the Arabs that Jewish pressure controlled American
policy. The Arabs would conclude that their only hope was to
ally with the Soviet Union, thus spelling disaster for the Eisenhower Doctrine.[90]

After a series of meetings between Abba Eban, Israel's ambassador to the United States, and Dulles, along with British and
French assurances of Israeli rights in the region, Tel Aviv finally
agreed to withdraw on February 28.[91] On March 1 Israeli
Foreign Minister Golda Meir addressed the UN General Assembly and announced Israel's decision, cautioning that the UNEF
not leave "precipitously from the Gulf of Aqaba area."[92] On
March 9, with the Israeli withdrawal issue finally settled, Congress approved the Joint Congressional Resolution to "Promote
Peace and Stability in the Middle East," or what came to be
known as the Eisenhower Doctrine.

By the spring of 1957 the United States had successfully

reversed its position with Her Majesty's Government in the region. Events in Syria, Jordan, and Iraq during the late 1950s demonstrated that Washington did not seek to exclude London from the Middle East. Eisenhower saw Britain playing a key, if subordinate, role in American plans to defend the area. The United States had become the senior partner in this new relationship.

Despite the emphasis which the Eisenhower administration placed on its "new doctrine," the policy was based on the same tired assumptions of the Cold War. The failure of the Anderson mission had weakened United States efforts to solve the major cause of Arab-Israeli hostility, the Palestinian refugee problem. Instead of trying to take advantage of its recently earned goodwill in the Arab world to promote peace in the area, the Eisenhower administration returned to the same neo-colonialist methods employed earlier by the British. Rather than pursuing a more enlightened policy, Washington continued to implement an outdated policy of containment. Ultimately, indigenous forces in the Middle East came to regard the Eisenhower Doctrine as just another imperialist tool.

Epilogue

When the Eisenhower administration took office, it seemed open to a fresh approach to the problems of the Middle East. After Dulles's fact-finding mission to the region in May 1953, the State Department concluded it was unwise to try to pressure the Arabs into a regional alliance. In a new departure, the United States chose to distance itself from its colonialist allies and develop a new policy of impartiality toward Israel and the Arabs to help resolve their nagging conflict.

The Eisenhower-Dulles strategies were designed to improve American standing in the region and create mutual trust between the Arab world and the United States. American pressure on the British to withdraw from the Suez Canal base would lessen Egyptian hostility toward Western colonialism. Peace initiatives to resolve the Arab-Israeli conflict would reduce regional tensions and allow the pursuit of American goals. Washington worked to implement its program amidst growing fears that the Soviet Union would gain a foothold in the Middle East, threatening Western oil sources and the stability of Western economies.

A study of the period from 1953 to 1957 shows clearly that the Soviet Union was grappling with domestic and foreign problems of its own; a major Soviet move in the Middle East was unlikely. At home Soviet leaders were caught up in the succession crisis of the post-Stalin era; in 1956 the power struggle between Nikolai Bulganin and Nikita Khrushchev still raged. Abroad the Soviets were trying to deal with their Eastern European allies, particularly Poland and Hungary, who sought to loosen Moscow's control over their economies and political systems.

Despite these concerns, the Soviets were able to take advantage of poor judgment on the part of the United States and its allies, and penetrate the Middle East. While Anglo-American policy was based on the "communist menace" to the region (of which there is little hard evidence), the indigenous forces of Arab nationalism did not recognize that threat. For the Arabs, the main enemies were Israel and Western imperialism. No matter how vigorously the United States and the United Kingdom emphasized the Soviet threat, the Arabs refused to support Western schemes. Strategies such as the Baghdad Pact and the "northern tier" held no attraction for most Arab leaders.

Nationalist forces in the region regarded these strategies as little more than Western tools to reaffirm British colonial rule. The United States was right to pressure the British into withdrawing from the Suez Canal base, oppose American or British membership in the Baghdad Pact, and force the withdrawal of Anglo-French forces from Suez in 1956. But instead of building upon the goodwill these actions created in the Arab world, the United States adopted the Eisenhower Doctrine, which most of the Arab world interpreted as an American version of British colonialism.

Why didn't Washington learn? For three years it had questioned the goals of the United Kingdom in the Middle East— goals tolerated as long as London retained a sufficient power base. When the British became a major obstacle during the Suez crisis, the irritations of British policy could no longer be accepted. Yet Eisenhower believed he still needed London to implement his new policy to contain the Soviets in the region. Hence while the U.S. worked to force British troops out of Port Said, the president worked behind the scenes to remove Eden from power and place the pro-American Harold Macmillan in the prime minister's office.

The Eisenhower Doctrine emerged from the 1956 Suez crisis as a camouflage for Washington's failed policy. Modest American successes between 1953 and 1955 began to unravel by March

1956. Project ALPHA had been a worthwhile effort to reduce tensions in the region by pursuing a negotiated settlement of the Arab-Israeli conflict, particularly the Palestinian issue. When the policy collapsed in the wake of the Anderson mission, the United States lost interest in continuing a dialogue with Egypt's Nasser. Instead of pursuing further peace initiatives, Washington chose Nasser as a scapegoat for its failures. The National Security Council responded with Project OMEGA, an attempt to punish Nasser for his alleged Soviet leanings by isolating him in the Arab world. On its heels followed the withdrawal of the Aswan Dam loan, the nationalization of the Suez Canal, and the eventual Israeli-British-French collusion over Suez.

The United States could not see Nasser as an Arab nationalist; Washington believed he was either a Soviet tool or an anti-Western demagogue bent on frustrating American goals in the region. In fact, the Soviet Union and Nasser were not ideological soulmates, for theirs was a marriage of convenience growing out of Anglo-American policy errors. Moscow and Cairo forged a relationship based upon their mutual hostility toward Western attempts to develop a Middle East Defense Organization, which each regarded as dangerous to its interests.

Eisenhower and Dulles understood that the Western world needed Middle East oil to support the economic growth of the 1950s. Their Cold War approach was designed to contain both the Soviet Union and Nasser. It was articulated in the Eisenhower Doctrine which imposed on the region its own definition of cooperation. Far from stabilizing the Middle East, the resulting American military aid intensified rivalries between Washington's client states. Iraq and Turkey, for example, pressed Syria toward a stronger pro-Western stance but only succeeded in pushing Damascus further into the arms of the Soviet Union.[1]

The Eisenhower Doctrine also involved the United States in Middle Eastern problems unrelated to the communist threat. Early in 1958 Lebanon's president illegally manipulated his country's constitution to remain in power, resulting in anti-American, pro-Nasser riots in Lebanon. After that crisis subsided, an anti-Western coup led by pro-Nasser army officers took place in Iraq. Eisenhower viewed these events as a combination of Egyptian and Soviet interference, and on July 15, 1957, he dispatched American marines to protect Lebanon. Instead of engaging Arab nationalism, the Eisenhower Doctrine contested it, and confused it with communism.[2] The goal of isolating Nasser failed. Instead, American policy helped raise the Egyptian leader's prestige in the Arab world by constantly providing him with ammunition for his anticolonial propaganda.

In its aim of blocking further Soviet encroachment in the Middle East, the Eisenhower Doctrine failed because the Soviet threat was questionable to begin with. Government documents substantiating the Soviet threat during this period are vague at best. As historian Thomas Paterson points out about congressional hearings on the Eisenhower Doctrine, "No American official provided a detailed substantiated account of Soviet intentions, activities, or capabilities." Dulles and others admitted there was no Soviet threat, but Eisenhower and Dulles insisted that it was important to declare a "policy of deterrence for the Middle East . . . to issue a warning for the future."[3]

Throughout this period the major focus of Soviet foreign policy was Eastern Europe. With labor riots in Poland and East Germany in 1953, and a movement for political liberalization in Poland and Hungary in 1956, it is difficult to believe that Moscow planned a major drive to control the Middle East in the 1950s. Inside the Kremlin a political power struggle developed in March 1953 following the death of Stalin, culminating in Nikita Khrushchev's "de-Stalinization" speech before the 20th Soviet Party Congress on February 20, 1956. Not only did Soviet internal politics mitigate against action in the Middle East, but the ideological relationship between Islam and communism was also antagonistic. The two ideologies—one monotheistic, the other atheistic—had nothing in common. Nasser's consistent perception of Israel, not the Soviets, as the main enemy of Arabs was the reference point that Washington found difficult to accept. In its policy the United States created an opportunity for the Soviet penetration it sought to prevent.

In assessing American policy following the Suez invasion, the burden of responsibility falls equally on the shoulders of Eisenhower and Dulles. The secretary of state was either unable or unwilling to build upon the president's refusal to use force. Had Dulles been more forthright with the British, Eden might have realized he had no support in the use of force against Nasser. But Dulles, after all, believed in the justice of the British and French cause, and he never ruled out the possibility of using military action at Suez "as a last resort." As Townsend Hoopes argues, the secretary "never rose above the role of a lawyer to the President engaged in an adversary proceeding with suspect allies; his tactical maneuvers were designed merely to keep them off balance, postpone a showdown, and thus buy time for Eisenhower's reelection."[4]

The president himself was obsessed with his own reelection. His anger with Britain and France stemmed partly from his deep desire to be viewed as a man of peace by the American electorate. He reasoned that the Suez invasion, in the eyes of the Arab world, placed him on a level with his "colonial" allies. This he could not tolerate. Compounding his frustration was the opportunity which the situation seemed to create for Soviet expansion. Instead of trying to deal with the socioeconomic, political, and cultural issues that inspired the Arab world, he forced the implementation of the Eisenhower Doctrine, a strategy which eventually confronted Nasserism, not Soviet expansion.

In the final analysis, American goals for the Arab world, set forth in 1953, were not achieved. The United States preserved a close relationship with Saudi Arabia, but other results were disappointing. Allies learned that the United States was unreliable when Washington saw its own interests as paramount. The British realized they could never resort to military action outside British territories without American acquiescence, leading London to reassess its interests and relative position in the world. The French felt betrayed by the "Anglo-Saxons," and ultimately Charles de Gaulle developed an independent nuclear deterrent, withdrew France from NATO, and blocked British membership in the Common Market, actions based on lessons drawn from the Suez crisis. Most important, the United States failed to distinguish between the local forces of nationalism and worldwide communism. As a consequence, the United States lost an excellent opportunity to reduce intra-Arab rivalries and Arab-Israeli tensions.

Today the events of the mid-fifties are strikingly relevant. Thirty-five years later a major component of the Eisenhower administration's Middle East policy came to fruition during the Persian Gulf crisis of 1991. After years of American cajolery, the Saudi Arabian government emerged to take a more active leadership role in the Arab world and in the Middle East. The support by the Saudi royal family for operations Desert Shield and Desert Storm was built on the foundation of American policy inaugurated during the Suez crisis.

The origin of the Saudi-American relationship is also relevant to the strategy of Saddam Hussein. In many instances the Iraqi leader's approach to the Gulf conflict mirrored the actions of Egyptian President Gamal Nasser. In addition, the Iraqi leader hoped that the American response to his seizure of Kuwait would be similar to Washington's reaction to Nasser's nationalization of the Suez Canal. Much to his chagrin, Hussein found that his analogies did not rest on sound historical analysis. The two situations were quite different, for today the world balance of power has been radically altered by the decline of the Soviet Union.

The collapse of the Soviet empire has altered the role of the United Nations in the Middle East. In 1956 Moscow and Washington appeared to cooperate to end the invasion of Egypt. The Soviets used the distraction of Suez as a means of controlling events in Eastern Europe; the Americans sought to prevent a power vacuum from developing in the Middle East. Thirty-five years later Moscow supported Washington's United Nations strategy during the Persian Gulf crisis in order to obtain Western economic aid and technology to overcome seventy years of communist economic mismanagement. If the Soviets continue to need Western assistance, it is unlikely that Moscow will oppose Western interests in the United Nations. The UN as a result may be able to play a more effective role in managing world problems.

Although the end of the Cold War bodes well for the future of the Middle East, many unresolved issues from the 1950s remain. President Bush's proposed new world order faces the same problems that perplexed the Eisenhower administration. Both presidents sought to bring peace to the Middle East, but the two major components of a solution—the Arab-Israeli conflict and Palestinian nationalism—remain as intractable as ever. Bush adopted Eisenhower's strategy of using economic pressure to make the Israeli government more amenable to a Middle East peace conference. Meanwhile, Israel's policy of settling Soviet immigrants in the occupied territories raised the same Arab concerns over Israeli expansionism that were exhibited in the 1950s. The Palestinian issue remains a key element in the process, with no real solution on the horizon.

Notes

Preface

1. See Geoffrey Aronson, *From Sideshow to Center Stage: U.S. Policy Towards Egypt, 1946–1956* (Boulder, Colo., 1986); Gail Meyer, *Egypt and the United States: The Formative Years* (Madison, N.J., 1980); and Peter L. Hahn, *The United States, Great Britain, and Egypt, 1945–1956* (Chapel Hill, 1991). Hahn does an excellent job of discussing the Anglo-Egyptian negotiations that culminated in the 1954 treaty, and the importance of the Baghdad Pact, but he does not devote sufficient attention to the ALPHA project and the ultimate failure of the Anderson mission.

2. John Franklin Carter to John F. Dulles, December 3, 1956, John F. Dulles Papers, General Correspondence and Memorandum Series, Confidential Correspondence Sub-series, Box #2, Eisenhower Library, Abilene, Kans. (henceforth Eisenhower Library, John F. Dulles Papers, General Correspondence and Memorandum Series, Confidential Correspondence Sub-series).

3. See Terrence Robertson, *Crisis: The Inside Story of the Suez Conspiracy* (New York, 1965); Kennett Love, *Suez: The Twice-Fought War* (New York, 1969); Chester L. Cooper, *The Lion's Last Roar* (New York, 1978); and Hugh Thomas, *Suez* (New York, 1967). More recently, Donald Neff, *Warriors at Suez* (New York, 1981), and David Carleton, *Britain and the Suez Crisis* (New York, 1989).

4. For similar arguments see Meyer, *Egypt and the United States*, and Steven J. Spiegel, *The Other Arab-Israeli Conflict* (Chicago, 1985).

1. The Truman Background

1. Aronson, *From Sideshow to Center Stage*, p. 15.

2. U.S. Department of State, *Foreign Relations of the United States 1950*, I (Washington, D.C., 1957), National Security Council: 65, March 28, 1950, 132 (henceforth *FRUS, 1950*, I). Aronson, *From Sideshow to Center Stage*, p. 15.

3. Acheson was concerned that Congress would cut funds that were destined for the United Kingdom.

4. William Roger Louis, *The British Empire in the Middle East, 1945–1951* (New York, 1984), pp. 583–585; Terry Wilbur Lindley, "The Tag End of Diplomacy: American Policy in the Near East, 1949–1953," Ph.D. dissertation, Texas Christian University, 1985, p. 48.

5. Aronson, *From Sideshow to Center Stage*, p. 16.

6. The Tripartite Declaration between the United States, the United Kingdom, and France was signed on May 25, 1950, and stated,

"1. Three governments recognise that the Arab states and Israel all need to maintain a certain level of armed forces for the purposes of assuring their internal security and their legitimate self-defence and to permit them to play their part in the defence of the area as a whole. All applications for arms and war material for these countries will be considered in the light of these principles. In this connection the three Governments wish to recall and reaffirm the terms of the statements made by their representatives on the Security Council on the 4th of August, 1949, in which they declared their opposition to the development of an arms race between the Arab states and Israel.

"2. The three Governments declare that assurances have been received from all the States in question to which they permit arms to be supplied from their countries that the purchasing State does not intend to undertake any act of aggression against any other States. Similar assurances will be requested from any other States in the area to which they permit arms to be supplied in the future.

"3. The three Governments take this opportunity of declaring their deep interest in and their desire to promote stability in the area, and their unalterable opposition to the use of force or threat of force between any State in the area. The three Governments, should they find that any of these States was preparing to violate frontiers or armistice lines, would, consistently with their obligations as members of the United Nations, immediately take action, both within and outside the United Nations, to prevent such violation."

Text located in United States Department of State, *Foreign Relations of the United States 1952–54*, IX (Washington, D.C., 1986), 225–226 (henceforth *FRUS, 1952–54, IX*).

7. Aronson, *From Sideshow to Center Stage*, p. 17.

8. See the following works for different interpretations of Anglo-American motivations for issuing the pact: John C. Campbell, *Defense of the Middle East* (New York, 1960), pp. 85–86; Nadav Safran, *Israel: The Embattled Ally* (Cambridge, Mass., 1982), p. 343; Gaddis Smith, *Dean Acheson* (New York, 1972), p. 332; and Louis, *British Empire in the Middle East*, p. 583; Lindley, "Tag End of Diplomacy," pp. 50, 62–63.

9. Aronson, *From Sideshow to Center Stage*, p. 22.

10. Lindley, "Tag End of Diplomacy," p. 108.

11. U.S. Department of State, *Foreign Relations of the United States 1951*, V (Washington, D.C., 1957), Memorandum by the Assistant Secretary of State for Near Eastern, South Asian, and African Affairs to the Secretary of State, December 27, 1950, 6 (henceforth *FRUS, 1951, V*; Lindley, "Tag End of Diplomacy," p. 77.

12. Annex to Memorandum by the Assistant Secretary of State for Near Eastern, South Asian, and African Affairs, undated, *ibid.*, pp. 6–14; Lindley, "Tag End of Diplomacy," p. 77.

13. U.S. Department of State, *Foreign Relations of the United States 1949*, VI (Washington, D.C., 1957), Memorandum by Gordon P. Merriam of the Policy Planning Staff, June 13, 1949, 31–39 (henceforth *FRUS*), 1949, VI; Lindley, "Tag End of Diplomacy," p. 110.

14. Throughout 1949 and until October 1950 Turkey was rebuffed by the United States in its push to join NATO. The Turks felt they were not being treated fairly, particularly because of their support for the Western effort in Korea. Finally, on October 2, 1950, Turkey accepted the Western offer of an associate membership in NATO; Lindley, "Tag End of Diplomacy," p. 115.

15. Agreed Conclusion and Recommendations of Conference of Mideast Chiefs, Mission, Istanbul, February 14–21, 1951, *FRUS*, 1951, V, 58–60; Lindley, "Tag End of Diplomacy," pp. 119–120.

16. U.S. Department of State, *Foreign Relations of the United States 1951*, III (Washington, D.C., 1957), Memorandum of Conversation by the Acting Secretary of State for European Affairs, July 6, 1951, 544–545 (henceforth *FRUS*, 1951, III; Lindley, "Tag End of Diplomacy," p. 120.

17. The British Secretary of State for Foreign Affairs to the Secretary of State, August 15, 1951, *FRUS*, 1951, III, 372–376; Lindley, "Tag End of Diplomacy," p. 122.

18. Lindley, "Tag End of Diplomacy," pp. 129–130.

19. *Ibid.*, p. 134.

20. *Ibid.*

21. Dean Acheson, *Present at the Creation* (New York, 1969), p. 661.

22. As quoted in Aronson, *From Sideshow to Center Stage*, p. 32; Hahn, *The United States, Great Britain, and Egypt*, p. 3.

23. *Ibid.*, p. 33.

24. Memorandum by the Acting Planning Adviser, Harold B. Hoskins, to Henry Byroade, April 7, 1952, *FRUS*, 1952–54, IX, 204–13. Concern over the manipulation of U.S.-colonial power ties was not new in the early 1950s; it was a well-established concern by the mid-1940s. See D. Michael Shafer, *Deadly Paradigms: The Failure of U.S. Counterinsurgency Policy* (Princeton, N.J., 1988), pp. 213–217.

25. NSC 129/1: United States Objectives and Policies with Respect to the Arab States and Israel, April 24, 1952, *ibid.*, p. 223.

26. *Ibid.*

27. *Ibid.*, p. 224. American diplomats were concerned over Britain's inability to defend the area as early as 1943. This concept is developed in Shafer, *Deadly Paradigms*, pp. 174–179.

28. Memorandum prepared by the Policy Planning Staff, May 21, 1952, *ibid.*, pp. 233–234.

29. Louis, *British Empire in the Middle East*, p. 743.

30. Miles Copeland, *The Game of Nations* (New York, 1969), pp. 57–59.

31. *Ibid.*, pp. 59–61.

32. *Ibid.*, pp. 71–73; see Meyer, *Egypt and the United States*, pp. 42–43, and Mohamed Heikal, *The Cairo Documents* (New York, 1973), pp. 34–36. According to Copeland and Heikal, Nasser's friend and confidant, the new

Egyptian leader did not view himself as an Arab. In 1952 Arab nationalism and Israel had little to do with the Egyptian revolution. The key to dealing with Nasser was his intense hatred of the British. The Egyptian leader believed that London had patronized his people and had made Egyptians second-class citizens in their own country. Nasser's sensitivity to these feelings was paramount—anytime either the United States or the United Kingdom did anything to remind him of Egypt's past, he reacted negatively. Throughout the period from 1952 to 1956, both Washington and London refused to understand this in their dealings with Nasser.

33. Memorandum, Hoskins to Byroade, July 25, 1952, *FRUS*, 1952–54, IX, 257.

34. Acheson to Caffery, #515, September 8, 1952, *ibid.*, p. 1856.

35. Caffery to Acheson, #730, September 18, 1952, *ibid.*, p. 1860. On January 22, 1952, British strategists reacted to the rejection of the Middle East Command by proposing a Middle East Defense Organization (MEDO). The MEDO was a variation of the MEC, but one that would function as "a planning, coordinating, and liaison organization only." American officials responded favorably but without enthusiasm. They saw MEDO as "the second best solution" when compared to the MEC, but the only possibility in light of Cairo's attitude. For documents see *ibid.*, pp. 171–184.

36. Acheson to Caffery, #678, September 30, 1952, *ibid.*, pp. 1863–1865.

37. Anthony Nutting, *Nasser* (New York, 1972), pp. 45–46.

38. Barry Rubin, "America and the Egyptian Revolution, 1950–1957," *Political Science Quarterly* 97 (Spring 1982), 77–78.

39. Quoted in Elizabeth Monroe, *Britain's Moment in the Middle East, 1914–1971* (London, 1963), p. 173.

40. Memorandum of Conversation by the Secretary of State, January 7, 1953, *FRUS*, 1952–54, IX, 1954. The State Department believed that providing military assistance to Egypt was an essential element in negotiations for the Anglo-Egyptian dispute over the Suez Canal base and Cairo's adherence to a MEDO. If Egypt adhered to the MEDO, it was hoped, other Middle East states would follow. On November 11, 1952, Acheson argued that General Naguib indicated that once an agreement was reached with the British over the Suez base he would provide assurances that "one of our ultimate objectives . . . is participation with the US, the UK and other free world powers in planning for the common defense of the area within the framework of the UN." See Acheson to Lovett, December 12, 1952, *ibid.*, pp. 1910–1912.

41. *Ibid.*, p. 1955.

42. Acheson to London, #3860, December 9, 1952, *ibid.*, pp. 1906–1907.

43. Anthony Eden, *Full Circle* (Boston, 1960), pp. 260–261.

44. J. C. Hurewitz, *Middle East Dilemmas: The Background of United States Policy* (New York, 1953), p. 247. Between 1949 and 1952 Israel formally received from the United States $86.5 million in grants and $135 million in loans as economic and military aid. During the same period Israel received $450 million in donations from world Jewry, mostly from the United States. In 1951 alone Israel sold $52 million in bonds in the United States.

45. *Ibid.*, p. 246.

46. David Ben-Gurion, *Israel: Years of Challenge* (New York, 1963), p. 65.

47. Memorandum of Conversation between Israeli Ambassador Abba Eban

and Secretary of State Acheson, January 3, 1953, *FRUS*, 1952–54, IX, 1088–1089.

48. *Ibid.*, p. 1092.

49. Monnet B. Davis to the Department of State, #1200, January 27, 1953, *ibid.*, p. 1109.

50. *Ibid.*

51. Monnet Davis to the Department of State, #1183, January 23, 1953, *ibid.*, pp. 1102–1103.

2. The Eisenhower Initiative

1. Richard A. Melanson, "The Foundations of Eisenhower's Foreign Policy: Continuity and Consensus," in David Mayers and Richard A. Melanson, ed., *Reevaluating Eisenhower: American Foreign Policy in the 1950s* (Chicago, 1987), p. 33.

2. *Ibid.*

3. John Lewis Gaddis, *Strategies of Containment: A Critical Appraisal of Postwar American National Security* (New York, 1982), pp. 79–81.

4. See National Security Council: 68, April 1, 1950, *FRUS*, 1950, I, for the full text of the document. For the debate over the development of NSC-68, see Gaddis, *Strategies of Containment*, pp. 89–126.

5. Melanson, "Foundations," p. 37.

6. *Ibid.*, p. 40.

7. See Robert Griffith, "Dwight D. Eisenhower and the Corporate Commonwealth," *American Historical Review* 87 (February 1982), 87–122; Melanson, "Foundations," p. 42.

8. Melanson, "Foundations," p. 43.

9. *Ibid.*, p. 44.

10. *Ibid.*

11. *Ibid.*, pp. 49–50.

12. *Ibid.*, p. 50.

13. *Ibid.*, pp. 54–55.

14. William Stivers, "Eisenhower and the Middle East," in Mayers and Melanson, *Reevaluating Eisenhower*, p. 193.

15. *Ibid.*, p. 194.

16. Robert Ferrell, ed., *The Eisenhower Diaries* (New York, 1981), p. 319.

17. *Ibid.*, p. 223.

18. Department of State Press Release #299, June 1, 1953, John F. Dulles Papers, Box #71, Seely G. Mudd Library, Princeton, N.J. (henceforth Seely G. Mudd Library, John F. Dulles Papers).

19. Emmet John Hughes, *The Ordeal of Power: A Political Memoir of the Eisenhower Years* (New York, 1963), p. 205.

20. Ronald W. Pruessen, *John Foster Dulles: The Road to Power* (New York, 1982), pp. 267–268.

21. *Ibid.*, p. 270.

22. *Ibid.*, p. 272.

23. *Ibid.*, p. 276.

24. Mark G. Toulouse, *The Transformation of John F. Dulles: From Prophet of Realism to Priest of Nationalism* (Atlanta, 1985), p. 171.

25. *Ibid.*, pp. 175–176.

26. *Ibid.*, p. 192. For a characterization of Dulles as a pious moralist, see Townsend Hoopes, *The Devil and John Foster Dulles* (Boston, 1973), and John Stoessinger, *Crusaders and Pragmatists* (New York, 1979).

27. John Foster Dulles, *War or Peace* (New York, 1950), p. 2.

28. *Ibid.*, pp. 71–73. John Lewis Gaddis argues that the American position was based on power politics. For Dulles the "implication was that adversaries, like interests, were indivisible; that when any nation went communist, regardless of its geographic location or strategic potential, American security was lessened thereby." The issue was not ideological, according to Gaddis, because Dulles argued that the "Kremlin could change its ideological position whenever it found it convenient to do so." Gaddis, *Strategies of Containment*, pp. 136–138.

29. As quoted in Michael Guhin, *John Foster Dulles: A Statesman in His Times* (New York, 1972), p. 253.

30. Aronson, *From Sideshow to Center Stage*, p. 59.

31. *Ibid.*, p. 60.

32. For the theoretical underpinnings of liberal internationalism, see Lloyd C. Gardner, *Safe for Democracy* (New York, 1984); N. Gordon Levin, Jr., *Woodrow Wilson and World Politics* (New York, 1968); and Arno P. Mayer, *Wilson vs. Lenin: Political Origins of the New Diplomacy* (New York, 1959).

33. Dulles, *War or Peace*, p. 109.

34. As quoted in Pruessen, *Dulles*, p. 211.

35. Gaddis, *Strategies of Containment*, p. 129.

36. *Ibid.*

37. See Herman Finer, *Dulles Over Suez: The Theory and Practice of His Diplomacy* (Chicago, 1964), pp. 11, 90–92. For other scholars who argue that Eisenhower was in control of American foreign policy, see Herbert S. Parmet, *Eisenhower and the American Crusades* (New York, 1972); Peter Lyon, *Eisenhower: Portrait of a Hero* (Boston, 1974); Barton J. Bernstein, "Foreign Policy in the Eisenhower Administration," *Foreign Service Journal* 50 (May 1973), 17–20, 29–30, 38; Richard Immerman, "Eisenhower and Dulles: Who Made the Decisions?" *Political Psychology* 1 (Autumn 1979), 21–38; Robert A. Divine, *Eisenhower and the Cold War* (New York, 1981); Fred I. Greenstein, *The Hidden-Hand Presidency: Eisenhower as Leader* (New York, 1982); Stephen Ambrose, *Eisenhower the President* (New York, 1984); and William B. Ewald, Jr., *Eisenhower the President: The Crucial Days, 1951–1960* (Englewood Cliffs, N.J., 1981). For Eisenhower as the activist in relation to the CIA, see Blanche Wiesen Cook, *The Declassified Eisenhower* (New York, 1981); Melanson and Mayers, *Reevaluating Eisenhower*, pp. 5–9.

38. Immerman, "Eisenhower and Dulles," p. 24.

39. Bernstein, "Foreign Policy in the Eisenhower Administration," p. 20.

40. *Ibid.*

41. Robert Rhodes James, *Anthony Eden* (London, 1986), pp. 343, 345.

42. *Ibid.*, pp. 362–364. See David Carleton, *Anthony Eden* (London, 1981), which agrees with James's presentation regarding the effects of Eden's medical problem on his personality and the conduct of his diplomacy. In particular,

Carleton points to the role of Eden's liver condition in his handling of the Suez crisis, especially in October 1956. It appears that after Eden's third operation he developed a chemical imbalance due to the inability of doctors to repair the severed bile duct. As a result, Eden at times was prone to violent mood swings.

43. James, *Eden*, p. 365.

44. Evelyn Shuckburgh, *Descent to Suez: Diaries 1951–56* (London, 1986), p. 75.

45. *Ibid.*, p. 104.

46. Owen Harris, "Anthony Eden and the Decline of Britain," *Commentary* 83, No. 6, June, 1987, 37.

47. *Ibid.*, p. 40.

48. *Ibid.*

49. See Nutting, *Nasser*, pp. 60–61; Neff, *Warriors at Suez*, pp. 142–148; David Carleton, *Eden*.

50. Robert Murphy, *Diplomat Among Warriors* (New York, 1964), p. 382.

51. Shuckburgh, *Descent to Suez*, p. 23.

52. Saadia Touval, *The Peacebrokers: Mediators in the Arab-Israeli Conflict, 1948–1979* (Princeton, N.J., 1982), pp. 107–108.

53. Excerpts of Memorandum, Re: Current Conditions in the Middle East, April 9, 1953, John F. Dulles Papers, White Memorandum Series, Box #1, Eisenhower Library, Abilene, Kans. (henceforth, Eisenhower Library, John F. Dulles Papers, White House Memorandum Series).

54. *Ibid.*

55. Louis L. Gerson, *John Foster Dulles* (New York, 1957), pp. 246–247.

56. Important Points of the Trip, Seely G. Mudd Library, John F. Dulles Papers, Box #73.

57. Dulles to Eisenhower, #1373, May 17, 1953, Ann Whitman File, Dulles-Herter Series, Box #1, Eisenhower Library, Abilene, Kans. (henceforth Eisenhower Library, Ann Whitman File, Dulles-Herter Series).

58. Conclusions of the Trip, Seely G. Mudd Library, John F. Dulles Papers, Box #73.

59. *Ibid.* It is interesting that Dulles would soon move against the State Department's analysis and certain conclusions which he himself had developed.

60. Dwight D. Eisenhower, *Mandate for Change, 1953–1956* (New York, 1963), p. 156.

61. Mohamed Heikal, *Cutting the Lion's Tail: Suez Through Egyptian Eyes* (London, 1986), p. 39.

62. Hoopes, *Devil and John Foster Dulles*, p. 183; Love, *Suez*, pp. 272–273.

63. U.S. Congress, Senate Committee on Foreign Relations, Executive Sessions, V (Washington, D.C., 1977), 441.

64. Discussions at the 147th Meeting of the National Security Council, June 2, 1953, Eisenhower Library, Ann Whitman File, National Security Council Series, Box #4.

65. United States Objectives and Policies with Respect to the Near East, National Security Council: 155/1, July 14, 1953, Eisenhower Library, White House Office for the Special Assistant for National Security Council Affairs, Near East (2) Box #5. The document was originally presented on June 17,

1953, and later adopted on July 9, 1953. One year later, on July 11, 1954, a progress report was issued and combined with the original document to create NSC-5428, which was adopted as an updated version of American Middle Eastern policy on July 23, 1954. NSC-5428 retained the essential elements of NSC-155/1, and basic American policy toward the region was not changed until January 1957 with the announcement of the Eisenhower Doctrine.

66. *Ibid.* The document called for Israel to take back between fifty thousand and a hundred thousand refugees, perhaps in the Galilee. Israel was to be prepared "to make territorial concessions above the 1947 Partition Plan" and reduce immigration, because the Arabs believed Israel's underlying purpose was to "foster territorial expansion" of the Jewish state.

67. *Ibid.*

68. *Ibid.*

3. The British Withdraw from Suez

1. Louis, *British Empire in the Middle East*, p. 721; Lindley, "Tag End of Diplomacy," p. 160.

2. Lindley, "Tag End of Diplomacy," p. 161.

3. Chargé in London to the Department of State, September 13, 1950, *FRUS*, 1950, V, 295–296; Lindley, "Tag End of Diplomacy," p. 177.

4. Chargé in London, *FRUS*, 1950, V, 324–325; Lindley, "Tag End of Diplomacy," 177–178.

5. Lindley, "Tag End of Diplomacy," pp. 184–185.

6. Caffery to the Department of State, October 9, 1951, *FRUS*, 1951, V, 397; Lindley, "Tag End of Diplomacy," p. 192.

7. The United Kingdom proceeded for fear of Conservative opposition and the possibility that Iraq might follow the Egyptian example with regard to the Anglo-Iraqi treaty which was due to expire in 1955.

8. Lindley, "Tag End of Diplomacy," p. 199.

9. Meyer, *Egypt and the United States*, p. 50.

10. F. S. Northedge, *British Foreign Policy: The Process of Readjustment, 1945–1961* (London, 1962), pp. 213–214.

11. Terrence Robertson, *Crisis: The Inside Story of the Suez Conspiracy* (New York, 1965), p. 3; Selwyn Lloyd, *Suez: A Personal Account* (London, 1978), p. 21.

12. Turkey's move culminated in its defense pact with Pakistan in 1953 and in its joining with Iraq to form the Baghdad Pact in April 1955. The evolution of the Baghdad Pact is explored in the next chapter.

13. Anthony Eden, Memorandum to the Cabinet, February 17, 1953, Minutes of Cabinet Meeting, CAB 128/26, C.C. (53)12 (henceforth, CAB followed by file #, date, and meeting #, Public Records Office, London).

14. *Ibid.*

15. Chargé in Egypt to the Department of State, #1524, December 29, 1953, *FRUS*, 1952–54, IX, 1920–1923.

16. *Ibid.*

17. Perkins to Dulles, December 31, 1952, *ibid.*, pp. 1928–1934.

18. *Ibid.*

19. *Ibid.*

20. Caffery to the Department of State, #1552, January 2, 1953, *ibid.*, pp. 1937–1938.

21. For the full version of British options, see United Kingdom Memorandum on Defense Negotiations with Egypt, *ibid.*, pp. 1931–1933.

22. Gifford to the Department of State, #3635, January 3, 1953, *ibid.*, pp. 1938–1941.

23. Gifford to the Department of State, #3774, January 9, 1953, *ibid.*, pp. 1958–1959.

24. Gifford to the Department of State, #3642, January 3, 1953, *ibid.*, pp. 1946–1948.

25. Gifford to the Department of State, #3691, January 6, 1953, *ibid.*, pp. 1952–1953.

26. Public Records Office, CAB 128/26. C.C.(53)2, Anthony Eden, Memorandum to the Cabinet, January 14, 1953.

27. Caffery to the Department of State, #1703, January 22, 1953, *FRUS*, 1952–54, IX, 1969–1970.

28. Summary of Telegrams, January 21, 1953, Eisenhower Library, Ann Whitman File, Dulles-Herter Series, Box #1.

29. Discussions at the 133rd Meeting of the National Security Council, February 24, 1953, Eisenhower Library, Ann Whitman File, National Security Council Series, Box #4.

30. Eden, *Full Circle*, p. 284.

31. Dulles to London, #5957, March 7, 1953, *FRUS*, 1952–54, IX, 2009–2010; see also Public Records Office, CAB 128/26, CC.(53)17, Eden's Report from the United States, March 9, 1953.

32. Case "B" and "C" had never received British cabinet approval. Case "C" was politically impossible for the Churchill government. Eden would not consider "C" because it would mean the abandonment of the Canal Zone. The foreign secretary was even skeptical that the cabinet would accept Case "B." Dulles to London, #5957, March 7, 1953, *ibid.*, p. 2010. See also Eisenhower, *Mandate for Change*, pp. 150–152.

33. *Ibid.* Throughout these talks Ambassador Caffery continued to advise Dulles that Egypt would not possibly accept Case "A." If Eden remained adamant, the British would have to withdraw in three years anyway. Another factor was increasing opposition from Conservative backbenchers in Parliament who were highly critical of the Sudan agreement. Churchill was deeply concerned that Sudan might be seen as a "scuttle." He believed that Case "B" would also be seen as a "scuttle," therefore Eden had to push for Case "A." Chargé in the United Kingdom to Dulles, #4995, March 9, 1953, *FRUS*, 1952–54, IX, 2013–2014.

34. Eden, *Full Circle*, pp. 280–281. Dulles wired Caffery that the American role in the talks must be limited to behind-the-scenes activities. American policy was opposed to the discussion of a MEDO as part of a "package" in negotiations. It was the State Department's view that evacuation of the Canal Zone and its maintenance must be agreed upon first; then, if Egypt desired, discussions for a MEDO should take place. "The best approach is immediate talks between the UK-Egypt without US participation and for the UK to proceed without linking a MEDO in the talks." Dulles to Caffery, #1827, March 16, 1953, *FRUS*, 1952–54, IX, 2022–2023.

35. Copeland, *Game of Nations*, pp. 133–134.

36. *Ibid.*

37. Churchill to Eisenhower, March 18, 1953, *FRUS*, 1952–54, IX, 2026–2027; Churchill to Eisenhower, March 18, 1953, Eisenhower Library, Ann Whitman File, Eisenhower Diaries, December 1952–July 1953, Box #3; see Eisenhower, *Mandate for Change*, p. 152; Shuckburgh, *Descent to Suez*, p. 82.

38. Eisenhower to Churchill, March 19, 1953, *FRUS*, 1952–54, IX, 2027–2028.

39. Dulles to Eisenhower, March 19, 1953, Eisenhower Library, Ann Whitman File, International Series, Box #16.

40. Caffery to the Department of State, #2076, March 17, 1953, *FRUS*, 1952–54, IX, 2025–2026.

41. Meyer, *Egypt and the United States*, p. 59.

42. Public Records Office, CAB 128/26, C.C.(53)26, Churchill Report to the Cabinet, April 14, 1953.

43. Dulles to Caffery, #2156, May 7, 1953, *FRUS*, 1952–54, IX, 2059–2060.

44. Caffery to Dulles, #2417, May 12, 1953, *ibid.*, pp. 2065–2069. See Caffery to Dulles, #2416, May 12, 1953, Eisenhower Library, Ann Whitman File, Dulles-Herter Series, Box #1.

45. *Ibid.*

46. *Ibid.*

47. Walter B. Smith to Dulles, #1665, May 23, 1953, *FRUS*, 1952–54, IX, 2077–2078.

48. Aldrich to the Department of State, #6245, May 26, 1953, *ibid.*, pp. 2079–2081.

49. Discussions at the 147th Meeting of the National Security Council, June 11, 1953, *FRUS*, 1952–54, IX, 379–386.

50. Dulles to Caffery, #2346, June 11, 1953, *ibid.*, pp. 2093–2094.

51. Aldrich to Dulles, #6665, June 19, 1954, Eisenhower Library, Ann Whitman File, Dulles-Herter Series, Box #1.

52. Eisenhower to Churchill, July 6, 1953, *FRUS*, 1952–54, IX, 2110–2111; Dulles to Cairo, #24, July 7, 1953, *ibid.*, pp. 2111–2112.

53. Dulles to London, #203, July 12, 1953, *ibid.*, pp. 2117–2119.

54. Public Records Office, CAB 128/26, C.C.(53)42, Minister of State Report to the Cabinet, July 13, 1953. Dulles wrote Ambassador Caffery, following the Bermuda Conference, that "in certain respects we share the British position." Dulles believe that a three-year duration was too short. "In other respects we share the Egyptian position and in many respects we strongly backed the Egyptian viewpoint in our talks with the British." Dulles had emphasized to Salisbury that the Foreign Office's view on availability and duration was too restrictive, and "we doubted whether a UK formula should be insisted on." Dulles to Caffery, #96, July 22, 1953, *FRUS*, 1952–54, IX, 2124–2125.

55. *New York Times*, July 13, 1953.

56. Public Records Office, 128/26, C.C.(53)49, Lord President to the Cabinet, August 13, 1953.

57. Caffery to the Department of State, #253, August 25, 1953, *FRUS*, 1952–54, IX, 2128–2129; Dulles to Cairo, #239, August 28, 1953, *ibid.*, pp. 2129–2130; Caffery to the Department of State, #292, September 5, 1953, *ibid.*, p. 2132.

58. At this time Turkish-Pakistani negotiations to achieve a security pact were well under way. They would eventually develop into the Baghdad Pact, the United Kingdom's grand design to retain its position in the Middle East. Thus it is obvious why London kept insisting on availability for Turkey. See Public Records Office, 128/26, C.C.(53)51, Egypt: A Review of the Situation in the Canal Zone, September 8, 1953; and State of Negotiations with Egypt, September 8, 1953, Cabinet Papers, CAB 129/62, C.P.(53)249 (henceforth CAB 129/62, followed by date, and Cabinet Paper #, Public Records Office, London, United Kingdom).

59. Dulles to London, #1354, September 12, 1953, *FRUS*, 1952–54, IX, 2136.

60. Caffery to Dulles, #360, September 24, 1953, *ibid.*, p. 2140. The British cabinet was becoming extremely distrustful of the United States regarding American tactics during the negotiations. Members of the cabinet believed that the Americans were "exercising a disturbing influence on Egypt in regard... to securing Cairo's agreement for our proposals." Public Record Office, 129/69, C.(53)54, Egypt Defense Negotiations, Memorandum by the Lord Privy Seal, September 14, 1953.

61. Public Records Office, CAB 128/26, C.C.(53)54, State of Negotiations with Egypt, October 2, 1953; Public Records Office CAB 128/26, C.C.(53)58, Review of C.P.(53)281, October 15, 1953.

62. Nutting, *Nasser*, p. 58.

63. *Ibid.*, p. 59.

64. Smith to London, October 17, 1953, *FRUS*, 1952–54, IX, 2146.

65. Aldrich to the Department of State, #1830, October 28, 1953, *ibid.*, p. 2156.

66. Keith Wheelock, *Nasser's New Egypt* (New York, 1960), pp. 29–36.

67. *Ibid.*, pp. 31–34.

68. Memorandum by Henry Byroade, Economic Aid to Egypt, *FRUS*, 1952–54, IX, 2160–2161.

69. Eden to the Foreign Office, December 8, 1953, Prime Minister's File 11/699, #153 (henceforth PREM and file #, Public Records Office, London, United Kingdom).

70. *Ibid.*

71. Eisenhower to Churchill, December 20, 1953, *FRUS*, 1952–54, IX, 2178–2180; Public Records Office, PREM 11/699, #2753, Scott to Foreign Office, December 21, 1953. Churchill had become so frustrated that he alluded to a withdrawal of British support for keeping the People's Republic of China out of the United Nations if the United States did not follow London's lead in its negotiations with Cairo.

72. Public Records Office, CAB 129/65, C.P.(54)6, Middle East Policy Memorandum by Anthony Eden, January 7, 1954.

73. Public Records Office, CAB 129/65, C.P.(54)9, Mideast Defense Memorandum by the Chiefs of Staff, January 9, 1954. The Chiefs of Staff recommended approval on "current proposals" and were "even" willing to make concessions over uniforms.

74. Public Records Office, CAB 128/27, C.C.(54)2, State of Egyptian Negotiations, January 12, 1954.

75. *Ibid.* Eventually this resulted in the adherence of the United Kingdom to the Baghdad Pact in April 1955.

76. Caffery to the Department of State, January 25, 1954, *ibid.*, *FRUS*, 1952–54, IX, 2208–2209. By the end of January Eden was having doubts whether it was worth holding up the agreement for uniforms. He told Shuckburgh that perhaps the British should have "reached an agreement long ago, regardless of uniforms for technicians etc." Shuckburgh, *Descent to Suez*, pp. 130–131.

77. Public Records Office, PREM 11/701, #414, Washington to Foreign Office, March 14, 1954; #346 and #347, Stevenson to Foreign Office, March 11, 1954.

78. *Ibid.*

79. Public Records Office, CAB 129/66, C.P.(54)99, Egypt Defense Negotiations, Memorandum by Anthony Eden, March 13, 1954; CAB 128/27, C.C.(54) 18, Discussion of Eden Memorandum, March 15, 1954.

80. Caffery to the Department of State, #1258, April 5, 1954, *FRUS*, 1952–54, IX, 2258–2259.

81. Smith to London, CA-6247, April 30, 1954, *ibid.*, pp. 2268–2270.

82. Dulles to London, CA-7323, June 12, 1954, *ibid.*, pp. 2273–2274.

83. Public Records Office, CAB 129/68, C.P.(54)187, Egypt Defense Negotiations, Memorandum by Sewlyn Lloyd, June 3, 1954.

84. Public Records Office, PREM 11/702, Eden to Churchill, June 21, 1954; CAB 128/27, C.C.(54)43, Egypt Defense Negotiations, June 22, 1954.

85. Robert Ferrell, *The Diaries of James C. Hagerty: Eisenhower at Mid-Course, 1954–55* (Bloomington, Ind., 1983), p. 74.

86. Public Records Office, PREM 11/702, Record of Meeting Held at the White House, June 26, 1954.

87. Public Records Office, CAB 128/27, C.C.(54)47, Egypt Defense Negotiations, July 7, 1954.

88. Caffery to the Department of State, #40, July 11, 1954, *FRUS*, 1952–54, IX, 2279.

89. Caffery to the Department of State, #57, July 13, 1954, *ibid.*, pp. 2282.

90. Caffery to the Department of State, #113, July 27, 1954, *ibid.*, pp. 2287–2288; see Public Records Office, CAB/69, C.P.(54)248, Egypt Defense Negotiations, Memorandum by Anthony Eden, July 23, 1954. The memo reflects Eden's rationalizations in finally accepting an agreement.

91. Public Records Office, CAB 129/70, C.P.(54)299, Anglo-Egyptian Negotiations, Memorandum by the Secretary of State for Foreign Affairs, September 28, 1954.

92. Public Records Office, PREM 11/702, #1442, Stevenson to Foreign Office, October 5, 1954; CAB 128/27, C.C.(54)63, Egypt Defense Negotiations, October 5, 1954.

93. U.S. Department of State, #594, Statement by Secretary of State Dulles on the Signing of the Suez Canal Base Agreement, Seely G. Mudd Library, Dulles Papers, Box #84.

94. Public Records Office, FO 371/111075, Shuckburgh Foreign Office Minute, October 19, 1954.

95. For the full text of the speech and another which the Israelis found

objectionable on April 26, 1954, in Dayton, Ohio, see Department of State Bulletin #5469, Near and Middle Eastern Series 16.

96. See Memorandum by Henry Byroade, Representation to Israel on Arab-Israel Border Incidents, April 7, 1954, *FRUS*, 1952–54, IX, 1502–1505, for the State Department case concerning Israeli aggression against the Arabs. Dulles commented on Byroade's speech, stating that "the speech in question, while it contained certain expressions of US policy, was primarily an analysis of some of the basic problems underlying the tensions between the Arab states and Israel." This did not help the Israeli reaction. Seely G. Mudd Library, Dulles Papers, Box #82.

97. *Jerusalem Post*, August 21, 1954.

98. David Ben-Gurion, *Israel: A Personal History* (New York, 1971), p. 440.

99. Michael Bar-Zohar, *Ben-Gurion* (New York, 1977), p. 210. For the full story of the affair, see pp. 210–216; Michael Scott Bornstein, "From Revolution to Crisis: Egypt-Israel Relations, 1952–1956." Ph.D. dissertation, Princeton University, 1986, pp. 241–242.

100. Bar-Zohar, *Ben-Gurion*, p. 210; Bornstein, "Revolution to Crisis," pp. 246–250.

101. Rubin, *Arab States and the Palestine Conflict*, p. 223.

102. See William Crane Eveland, *The Ropes of Sand: America's Failure in the Middle East* (New York, 1980), pp. 97–101. In late October 1954 Nasser was told by Washington in no uncertain terms that whether it made sense or not, military planners wished to see a workable area defense plan, and that all military and economic aid to the Middle East would be proportionate to their enthusiasm for the idea. Thus the aid promised to Cairo in return for an Anglo-Egyptian Agreement now had new conditions, which Nasser found unacceptable. See Copeland, *Games of Nations*, pp. 145–148.

103. See Rubin, "America and the Egyptian Revolution, 1950–1957; Copeland, *Game of Nations*, pp. 123–131 and Eveland, *Ropes of Sand*, pp. 90–92.

104. Dulles to Byroade, August 9, 1954, Eisenhower Library, John F. Dulles Files, White House Memorandum Series, Box #1.

105. See Michael Brecher, *Decisions in Israel's Foreign Policy* (New Haven, Conn.), pp. 173–224, for a full discussion of the Johnston mission to gain a Jordanian-Israeli agreement concerning water usage in the Jordan River Valley.

106. Safran, *Israel*, p. 371.

107. Carleton, *Anthony Eden*, p. 359.

4. The Pursuit of the Baghdad Pact

1. Donald Decker, "United States Policy Regarding the Baghdad Pact," Ph.D. dissertation, American University, 1975, p. 94; Meyer, *Egypt and the United States*, p. 100; Love, *Suez*, p. 199.

2. Conclusions of the Trip, Seely G. Mudd Library, John F. Dulles Papers, Box #73.

3. Memorandum of Discussion at the 147th Meeting of the National Security Council, June 1, 1953, *FRUS*, 1952–54, IX, 379–386.

4. *Ibid.*

5. Meyer, *Egypt and the United States*, p. 88.

6. Copeland, *Game of Nations*, p. 194; see Gamal Abdel Nasser, *Philosophy of Revolution* (New York, 1959).

7. Decker, "United States Policy," p. 94.

8. *Ibid.*, pp. 89–90.

9. *Ibid.*, p. 94.

10. Memorandum of Conversation, by the Assistant Secretary for Near Eastern, South Asian, and African Affairs, June 17, 1953, *FRUS*, 1952–54, IX, 389–390.

11. Memorandum of Discussion at the 153rd Meeting of the National Security Council, July 9, 1953, *ibid.*, pp. 394–398.

12. Statement of Policy by the National Security Council, 155/1, July 14, 1954, *ibid.*, pp. 399–406. Dulles actually believed that Pakistan, because it was a Muslim nation, could be built up as a rival to Nasser's Egypt in the Arab world.

13. Warren to the Department of State, #291, September 17, 1953, *ibid.*, p. 418.

14. Memorandum by the Assistant Secretary of State for Near Eastern, South Asian, and African Affairs to the Assistant Secretary of Defense, October 15, 1953, *ibid.*, pp. 421–423. The United States was concerned about the possible reaction of India to aid to Pakistan due to its war over Kashmir. The State Department believed that if the aid were used to equip Pakistani troops being sent to Korea, it would help to mollify India's disapproval.

15. Memorandum by the Joint Chiefs of Staff to the Secretary of State, November 14, 1953, *ibid.*, pp. 430–432.

16. Jernegan to Henderson, November 9, 1953, *ibid.*, pp. 424–428.

17. Warren to the Department of State, #557, November 30, 1953, *ibid.*, pp. 433–434.

18. Public Records Office, FO 371/111002, Paul S. Falla, Foreign Office Minute, December 22, 1953.

19. Public Records Office, FO 371/111002, #723, Troutbeck to Foreign Office, December 22, 1953.

20. Public Records Office, FO 371/111002, Paul S. Falla, Foreign Office Minute, January 6, 1954.

21. Patrick Seale, *The Struggle for Syria* (New Haven, Conn., 1986), p. 195.

22. *Ibid.*

23. Dulles to the Embassy in Turkey, #686, December 24, 1953, *FRUS*, 1952–54, IX, 439–441.

24. Memorandum of Conversation, by the Secretary of State, January 5, 1954, *ibid.*, pp. 443–444.

25. Memorandum of Conversation, by the Deputy Assistant Secretary of State for Near Eastern, South Asian, and African Affairs, January 6, 1954, *ibid.*, pp. 444–446.

26. Public Records Office, CAB 128/27, C.C.(54)1, Discussion of Eden Memorandum C(54)4, January 7, 1954.

27. Warren to the Department of State, #747, January 21, 1954, *FRUS*, 1952–54, IX, 458–459.

28. Memorandum by Assistant Secretary of State Byroade, January 23, 1954, *ibid.*, pp. 460–462.

29. Warren to the Department of State, #759, January 25, 1954, *ibid.*, pp. 462–463.

30. Smith to Warren, #816, January 26, 1954, *ibid.*, pp. 463–464.

31. Excerpts of the Turkish-Pakistani pact are located in *ibid.*, p. 491. For key security provisions of the agreement, see footnote to paragraph 6(b) of NSC-5428 located in *ibid.*, pp. 527–528.

32. Public Records Office, FO 371/111002, Hooper to Falla, February 24, 1954.

33. Eden, *Full Circle*, pp. 103–104.

34. *Ibid.*, p. 110.

35. Berry to the Department of State, #590, April 5, 1954, *FRUS*, 1952–54, IX, 491–492.

36. Dulles to Berry, #566, April 8, 1954, *ibid.*, pp. 2375–2376.

37. Smith to Berry, #577, April 15, 1954, *ibid.*, pp. 2377–2378.

38. Berry to the Department of State, #624, April 18, 1954, *ibid.*, pp. 2380–2381.

39. Dulles to Berry, #588, April 19, 1954, *ibid.*, pp. 2381–2382.

40. Seale, *Struggle for Syria*, p. 196.

41. Summary of Record of Conference of Mission Chiefs in NEA Area, Istanbul, May 14, 1954, White House Office; National Security Papers, OCB Central Files, Near East (1) Box #77; Eisenhower Library, Abilene, Kans. (henceforth Eisenhower Library, White House Office, National Security Papers, OCB Central Files).

42. *Ibid.*

43. National Intelligence Estimate, Prospects for Creation of a Middle East Defense Grouping and Probable Causes of Such a Development, June 22, 1954, *FRUS*, 1952–54, IX, 516–520.

44. Statement of Policy by the National Security Council, NSC-5428, July 23, 1954, *ibid.*, pp. 525–536.

45. *Ibid.*

46. Public Records Office, FO 371/111002, C.C.(54), Future Defense Arrangements with Iraq, May 6, 1954.

47. Public Records Office, FO 371/111000, Selwyn Lloyd, Foreign Office Memorandum, July 29, 1954.

48. Public Records Office, FO 371/111003, Paul Falla Foreign Office Minute, August 10, 1954.

49. This analysis is developed by Patrick Seale in *Struggle for Syria*, pp. 199–201.

50. *Ibid.*, p. 201.

51. Bornstein, "Revolution to Crisis," pp. 155–156; Public Records Office, FO 371/108453, Makins to Foreign Office, July 3, 1954.

52. Details of Sarsank conversations appear in Seale, *Struggle for Syria*, pp. 201–206. Much of Seale's information is based on his interview with Salah Salim in April 1960. See Public Records Office, FO 371/110000, Hooper to Foreign Office, August 20, 1954; Bornstein, "Revolution to Crisis," pp. 156–157; Waldemar I. Gallman, *Iraq Under Nuri: My Recollections of Nuri al-Said, 1954–1958* (Baltimore, 1964), p. 23; Ireland to the Department of State, #105, August 22, 1954, *FRUS*, 1952–54, IX, 541–543.

53. Seale, *Struggle for Syria*, pp. 203–204. Dulles was not pleased with the

results of the Sarsank talks as it appeared Nuri was building up the Arab League against Israel. Dulles to Byroade, August 23, 1954, *FRUS*, 1952–54, IX, 545.

54. Bornstein, "Revolution to Crisis," p. 157; Cairo to the Department of State, #260, August 27, 1954, *FRUS*, 1952–54, IX, 546.

55. Seale, *Struggle for Syria*, pp. 206–208, Heikal, *Cairo Documents*, pp. 53–55; Gallman, *Iraq Under Nuri*, p. 25.

56. Public Records Office, FO 371/111000, Paul Falla Foreign Office Minute, September 20, 1954.

57. Seale, *Struggle for Syria*, p. 208.

58. Dulles to Ankara, #430, October 7, 1954, *FRUS*, 1952–54, IX, 549–550.

59. Warren to the Department of State, #441, October 23, 1954, *ibid.*, pp. 553–555; Gallman, *Iraq Under Nuri*, p. 25.

60. Public Records Office, FO 371/115484, #9, Hooper to Foreign Office, January 1, 1955.

61. Public Records Office, FO 371/115484, #31, Hooper to Foreign Office, January 13, 1955.

62. Public Records Office, FO 371/115484, #60, Stevenson to Foreign Office, January 14, 1955.

63. Public Records Office, FO 371/111485, #92, Stevenson to Foreign Office, January 20, 1955.

64. Public Records Office, FO 371/111486, #113, Stevenson to Foreign Office, January 24, 1955; see Heikal, *Cairo Documents*, pp. 54–58; Seale, *Struggle for Syria*, pp. 215–217, for the Egyptian view of the conference. For the British evaluation, see Public Records Office, FO 371/115491, Stevenson to Foreign Office, February 10, 1955.

65. Seale, *Struggle for Syria*, p. 217.

66. Dwight D. Eisenhower, *Waging Peace, 1956–61* (Garden City, N.Y., 1965), p. 26.

67. Public Records Office, FO 371/115488, E. M. Rose Foreign Office Minute, January 31, 1955.

68. Public Records Office, FO 371/115488, #530, Foreign Office to Washington, February 3, 1955.

69. Public Records Office, FO 371/115488, #332, Makins to Foreign Office, February 4, 1955.

70. Public Records Office, FO 371/115488, #387, Makins to Foreign Office, February 9, 1955.

71. For an account of both sides of the meeting, see Heikal, *Cairo Documents*, pp. 76, 82; James, *Eden*, pp. 397–398; see also Public Records Office, FO 371/115493, Discussion Between the Secretary of State and the Egyptian Leader, February 27, 1955; U.S. Department of State, *Foreign Relations of the United States 1955–57*, XIV (Washington, D.C., 1989), Dulles to the Department of State, #13, February 24, 1955, 71–72 (henceforth *FRUS*, 1955–57, XIV).

72. Ben-Zohar, *Ben-Gurion*, p. 218; Byroade to the Department of State, #1256, March 1, 1955, *FRUS*, 1955–57, XIV, 73–74; Lawson to the Department of State, #740, March 1, 1955, *ibid.*, pp. 75–76.

73. *Ibid.*

74. Love, *Suez*, p. 13.

75. Hoopes, *Devil and John Foster Dulles*, 323–324; Love, *Suez*, p. 88; Memorandum of a Meeting of the 239th Meeting of the National Security Council, March 3, 1955, *FRUS*, 1955–57, XIV, 81–82.

76. Public Records Office, FO 371/115494, #48, Nicholls to Foreign Office, February 28, 1955. The State Department strongly suspected that the raid was launched because of Israel's displeasure with the Turkish-Iraqi pact. Although Sharett strongly denied it, State Department officials were skeptical. Lawson to the Department of State, #754, March 4, 1955, *FRUS*, 1955–57, XIV, 83–86.

77. Bornstein, "Revolution to Crisis," pp. 300–301; see Dulles to Lawson, #456, February 14, 1955, *FRUS*, 1955–57, XIV, 55–56; Dulles to Lawson, #510, March 9, 1955, *ibid.*, pp. 92–93.

78. Seale, *Struggle for Syria*, p. 224; Bornstein, "Revolution to Crisis," p. 291; Public Records Office, FO 371/115495, #350, Stevenson to Foreign Office, March 5, 1955; Public Records Office, FO 371/115496, #359, Stevenson to Foreign Office, March 7, 1955.

79. See Aronson, *From Sideshow to Center Stage*, pp. 112–115 for a copy of Byroade's description of his meeting with Nasser, which was forwarded to Dulles. See also Public Records Office, FO 371/115497, #378, Stevenson to Foreign Office, March 11, 1955; Byroade to the Department of State, #1261, March 1, 1955, *FRUS*, 1955–57, XIV, 78–79.

80. Heikal, *Cutting the Lion's Tail*, p. 67; see Sylvia K. Crosbie, *A Tacit Alliance: France and Israel from Suez to the Six Day War* (Princeton, N.J., 1974), pp. 46–50. The French saw the development of a relationship with Israel as a way to reassert their influence in the Middle East and to strike at Nasser, whom the French suspected of supplying weapons to FLN rebels in Algeria. According to Paul Jabber in his book *Not by War Alone: Security and Arms Control in the Middle East* (Berkeley, Calif., 1981), pp. 159–161, the Israelis were to receive fifteen Mystere II fighters, one hundred AMX-13 tanks, 75 mm. guns, 155 mm. guns, and twelve Ouragan fighters.

81. Jabber, *Not by War Alone*, p. 159; Love, *Suez*, p. 88.

82. See Bornstein, "Revolution to Crisis," pp. 164–194, and Aronson, *From Sideshow to Center Stage*, pp. 125–149, for a complete discussion of Nasser's frustration over the inability to acquire Western weaponry and military equipment.

83. Public Records Office, FO 371/115496, #95, Duke to Foreign Office, March 7, 1955.

84. Public Records Office, FO 371/115498, #389, Stevenson to Foreign Office, March 14, 1955.

85. *Ibid.* By this time the British and Iraqi governments had reached an agreement on the revision of the Anglo-Iraqi Treaty of 1930. British accession to the Turkish-Pakistani pact was seen as capping their agreement. According to British sources, the United States fully approved of the accession of the United Kingdom; see Public Records Office, 128/28, C.C.(55)24, Middle East Defense and Revision of the Anglo-Iraqi Treaty of 1930, March 15, 1955.

86. Seale, *Struggle for Syria*, p. 228.

87. *Ibid.*

88. Public Records Office, 371/115501, #415, Stevenson to Foreign Office,

March 21, 1955. Nasser feared that if Jordan and Lebanon acceded and Syria soon followed, he would be left to face Israel alone. Public Records Office, FO 371/11505, #486, Stevenson to Foreign Office, April 6, 1955.

89. Public Records Office, CAB 128/28, C.C.(55)27, New Anglo-Iraqi Treaty, March 30, 1955.

90. Public Records Office, FO 371/115506, Nicholls to Macmillan, April 12, 1955; Lawson to the Department of State, #881, April 12, 1955, *FRUS*, 1955–57, XIV, 149–151.

91. Public Records Office, FO 371/115505: J. F. Brewis Foreign Office Minute, March 28, 1955.

92. Eden, *Full Circle*, pp. 374–375. Despite Egyptian opposition, the United States still hoped that Cairo would eventually adhere. This angered Eden who believed that if the United States favored the eventual adherence of the Egyptians, then Washington should also join. Aldrich to the Department of State, #4351, *FRUS*, 1955–57, XIV, 128–129.

93. In 1952 a dispute developed between Saudi Arabia and the British over the Buraimi Oasis. Although the disagreement centered on the border between Saudi Arabia and the Sultan of Muscat, the underlying reason was the strong possibility of oil reserves in the oasis. In 1952 the Saudi government occupied the disputed area. The British government, also concerned about oil reserves, supported the claim of the Sultan of Muscat. All attempts at negotiation to gain the withdrawal of Saudi forces failed, and the dispute festered until October 1955 when the armies of the ruler of Abu Dhabi and the Sultan of Muscat, commanded by British officers, reoccupied the oasis. Secretary of State Dulles was upset by the British action as he saw in the Buraimi dispute another obstacle for American policy. Bornstein, "Revolution to Crisis," pp. 360–361; see Memorandum of a Conversation, March 24, 1955, *FRUS*, 1955–57, XIV, 118–119.

94. Eisenhower Diary Entry, December 16, 1955, Eisenhower Library, Ann Whitman File, DDE Diaries, Box #11.

5. *The Search for Peace: The ALPHA Project*

1. Public Records Office, FO 371/115866, Beely to Shuckburgh, March 24, 1955. The British position is best summarized in a memo written by Shuckburgh: "Our declared object is to make the pact the foundation for an effective defense system for the Middle East. If this is to be achieved, Syrian, Lebanese, and Jordanian accession will eventually be necessary. We cannot afford to risk giving the impression in the Middle East that we are wavering and that our policy has changed. I fear that, if we or the United States were to discourage Jordan from joining the pact at the present moment, the fact would certainly become immediately known throughout the Middle East and would do much damage not only in Syria and Lebanon, but also Iraq and Turkey. It would, moreover, be counted by Nasser himself as a triumph for his policy of opposition to the pact, and might make him less rather than more anxious to cooperate in ALPHA." In addition, Shuckburgh did not trust Byroade and argued that the American ambassador in Cairo was turning Nasser against the British. *Ibid.*, #1349, Foreign Office to Washington, March 31, 1955.

2. The United States was involved in other peace initiatives before this, the

best known being the Johnston mission, designed to create an agreement over water usage in the Jordan River Valley. The Johnston mission, like other mediation efforts, dealt with specific issues, not a comprehensive program.

3. First Progress Report on NSC 155/1 by the Operations Coordinating Board, July 30, 1954, Eisenhower Library, White House Office for the Special Assistant for National Security Council Affairs, Near East (2), Box #5.

4. Dulles launched the Johnston mission in order to pave the way for a resolution of the Palestinian refugee problem. The State Department hoped that by developing the Jordan River Valley it would maximize the efficient use of the region's water resources—and in the end would assist in providing a large area for Palestinian refugee resettlement. *Ibid.*

5. Policy Statement by the National Security Council, NSC 5428, July 23, 1954, Eisenhower Library, White House Office for the Special Assistant for National Security Council Affairs, Near East (1), Box #12; also in *FRUS*, 1952–54, IX, 525–536.

6. *Ibid.*

7. Public Records Office, FO 371/111075, Evelyn Shuckburgh Foreign Office Minute, October 4, 1954.

8. Both Eden and Dulles believed that the Israelis could probably defeat the combined military power of the Arabs. Public Records Office, FO 371/111075, Kirkpatrick to Shuckburgh, October 2, 1954.

9. Public Records Office, FO 371/111076, Garvey to Eden, October 25, 1954.

10. Memorandum of Conversation between Roger Makins and John F. Dulles, November 5, 1954, *FRUS*, 1952–54, IX, 1683–1684. In an aide-memoire on November 17, 1954, Dulles formally accepted Eden's suggestion calling for a comprehensive discussion with the Foreign Office in January 1955. *Ibid.*, pp. 1693–1694.

11. Dulles to Certain Diplomatic Missions, November 22, 1954, *ibid.*, pp. 1695–1700.

12. *Ibid.*

13. Public Records Office, FO 371/115864, Shuckburgh's Notes Concerning his Mid East Trip, December 21, 1954.

14. *Ibid.*

15. The State Department was concerned that Anglo-American talks not interfere with the work of Eric Johnston who was returning to the Middle East on January 23, 1955. The State Department wanted assurances of British support for the Johnston mission and the willingness of the Foreign Office to pressure the Jordanian government to accept his plan. Public Records Office, FO 371/115864, Russell to Shuckburgh, December 21, 1954; Russell to Shuckburgh, December 21, 1954, *FRUS*, 1952–54, IX, 1732–1734. The State Department believed that once Johnston was successful in gaining Arab and Israeli support for his agreement, the way would be paved for a larger settlement. Public Records Office, FO 371/1115865, Shuckburgh Foreign Office Minute, January 1, 1955.

16. Caffery to the Department of State, #1145, December 11, 1954, *FRUS*, 1952–54, IX, 1715–1717.

17. Public Records Office, FO 371/111076, Nicholls to Falla, November 16, 1954; *ibid.*, J. P. Tripp Foreign Office Minute, Palestine Geography in Con-

nexion with an Arab-Israeli Settlement, December 11, 1954; *ibid.*, FO 371/115864, Nicholls to Shuckburgh, January 11, 1955.

18. Memorandum of Conversation, December 17, 1954, *FRUS*, 1952–54, IX, 1719–1724.

19. The Bandung conference, a meeting of African and Asian countries, took place in April 1955. At the conference Nasser made contacts with Indian and Communist Chinese officials and in general emerged as a new and prestigious world leader who spoke for the Afro-Asian bloc. Nasser found that the support of these nations augmented his capacity to bargain with the great powers. Public Records Office, FO 371/115865, Record of Conversation between Dulles and Makins, January 29, 1955.

20. *Ibid.*

21. Public Records Office, FO 371/115864, #311, Shuckburgh to Kirkpatrick, February 2, 1955. Throughout the process Dulles's concern with the 1956 election emerges. He told the Lebanese ambassador in February 1955 that it was to the advantage of the Arabs to move as far as possible now, in 1955, "since in 1956 the atmosphere is likely to be such that it will be difficult or impossible for the administration to act towards the Arabs in such ways as it is now in a position to do." Memorandum of Conversation, January 27, 1955, John F. Dulles Papers, General Correspondence, Memorandum Series, Box #1, Eisenhower Library, Abilene, Kans. (henceforth Eisenhower Library, John F. Dulles Papers, General Correspondence, Memorandum Series).

22. Public Records Office, FO 371/115866, #147, Bangkok to Foreign Office, February 23, 1955.

23. The American share was seen as a continuation of its current expenditure of $486 million. Additional funding was estimated at $595 million for loans to Israel to compensate Arab refugees, and increased military and economic aid to Israel and the Arab states. Russell to Dulles, February 14, 1955, Eisenhower Library, John F. Dulles Papers, White House Memorandum Series, Box #3. The British share for similar items was estimated at 30 million pounds sterling. Public Records Office, FO 371/115865, Estimate of Cost of a Palestine Settlement, February 14, 1955.

24. Memorandum from Russell to Hoover, February 2, 1955, *FRUS*, 1955–57, XIV, 34–42; Russell to the Secretary of State, February 4, 1955, *ibid.*, pp. 45–47; Points of Agreement in London, Discussions of Arab-Israeli Settlement, March 10, 1955, *ibid.*, pp. 98–107; Public Records Office, FO 371/115866, Paper on Six Main Points of the Arab-Israeli Dispute, February 26, 1955; *ibid.*: Shuckburgh to Kirkpatrick, March 8, 1955.

25. *Ibid.*; Department of State to Cairo, #1531, March 19, 1955, *FRUS*, 1955–57, XIV, 114–115.

26. Public Records Office, FO 371/115866, Shuckburgh to Kirkpatrick, March 8, 1955.

27. Public Records Office, FO 371/115866, Stevenson to Shuckburgh, March 16, 1955; *ibid.*, #600, Makins to Foreign Office, March 17, 1955.

28. Public Records Office, FO 371/115866, Shuckburgh Foreign Office Minute, March 23, 1955.

29. Public Records Office, FO 371/115866, Beely to Shuckburgh, March 24, 1955.

30. Memorandum of a Conversation, March 24, 1955, *FRUS*, 1955–57, XIV, 118–119.

31. Public Records Office, FO 371/115867, Shuckburgh to Kirkpatrick, April 6, 1955; *ibid.*, #497, Stevenson to Foreign Office, April 7, 1955; see Memorandum of a Conversation, March 26, 1955, *FRUS*, 1955–57, XIV, 122–126; Cairo to the Department of State, #1458, April 3, 1955, *ibid.*, pp. 129–133; Cairo to the Department of State, #1482, April 5, 1955, *ibid.*, p. 71.

32. Public Records Office, FO 371/115867, #779, Makins to Foreign Office, April 6, 1955; Memorandum from MacArthur to Hoover, April 7, 1955, *FRUS*, 1955–57, XIV, 146–147.

33. Dulles-Wilson Phone Conversation, April 24, 1955, Eisenhower Library, John F. Dulles Papers, Telephone Memorandum Series, Box #3.

34. Cairo to the Department of State, #1719, May 16, 1955, *FRUS*, 1955–57, XIV, 188; see footnote at the bottom of the page.

35. Public Records Office, FO 371/115868, #609: Stevenson to Foreign Office, May 10, 1955; *ibid.*, FO 371/115870, #727, Stevenson to Foreign Office, June 9, 1955; *ibid.*, FO 371/115869, #640, Stevenson to Foreign Office, May 19, 1955; London to the Department of State, #5099, May 19, 1955, *FRUS*, 1955–57, XIV, 190; Russell to Byroade, April 29, 1955; *ibid.*, pp. 166–167; Dulles to Cairo, #1906, May 3, 1955, *ibid.*, p. 169; Russell to MacArthur, May 5, 1955, *ibid.*, pp. 176–178; Dulles to the Department of State, #38, May 12, 1955, *ibid.*, pp. 185–186.

36. Public Records Office, FO 371/115868, Nicholls to Macmillan, May 10, 1955; *ibid.*

37. Murphy to Hoover, May 23, 1955, *FRUS*, 1955–57, XIV, 199–200; Russell to Dulles, May 18, 1955, *ibid.*, pp. 200–204; Russell to Dulles, May 24, 1955, *ibid.*, pp. 205–208; Russell to Dulles, June 2, 1955, *ibid.*, pp. 210–214; Dulles to Hoover, June 6, 1955, *ibid.*, pp. 222–226.

38. Dulles to Allen, June 4, 1955, Declassified Documents Reference System (Washington, D.C., 1975–89) (87) 002799 DOS; Memorandum of a Conversation, June 8, 1955, *FRUS*, 1955–57, XIV, 231–234.

39. Public Records Office, CAB 128/29, C.C.(55)15, Anglo-U.S. Plan to End the Arab-Israeli Conflict, June 16, 1955; Memorandum of a Conversation, June 8, 1955, *FRUS*, 1955–57, XIV, 231–234.

40. Public Records Office, FO 371/115870, #477, Dixon to Foreign Office, June 16, 1955; Shuckburgh, *Descent to Suez*, pp. 266–267; Public Records Office, FO 371/115871, Shuckburgh to Kirkpatrick, July 8, 1955; Dulles to Cairo, #53, July 9, 1955, *FRUS*, 1955–57, XIV, 282–283.

41. Public Records Office, FO 371/115870, #3101, Foreign Office to Washington, July 4, 1955.

42. Public Records Office, FO 371/115871, Shuckburgh to Kirkpatrick, July 8, 1955. Anthony Nutting, in a Foreign Office minute, expressed British annoyance: "It is maddening that we should be pushed around by the requirements of American politics in this way. But this is not the first time this has happened nor will it be the last." *Ibid.*

43. Memorandum of a Conversation, July 14, 1955, *FRUS*, 1955–57, XIV, 295–298; Public Records Office, FO 371/115872, Memorandum of Conversation, July 14, 1955; *ibid.*, CAB/128/29, C.M.(55)23, Discussion of Memorandum by the Secretary of State, July 14, 1955. The British had no choice but to

support Dulles's statement. If the statement were not made, Macmillan believed that American policy would surrender to Israeli demands for a security guarantee, thus destroying ALPHA. *Ibid.*, CAB 129/76, C.P.(55)87, Memorandum by the Secretary of State for Foreign Affairs, July 22, 1955.

44. *Ibid.*

45. Memorandum of a Conversation, August 3, 1955, *FRUS*, 1955–57, XIV, 335–336.

46. Public Records Office, FO 371/115873, #930 and 931, Makins to Foreign Office, August 18, 1955; Johnston-Dulles Phone Conversation, August 18, 1955, Eisenhower Library, John F. Dulles Papers, Telephone Conversation Memorandum, Box #4. Memorandum of a Conversation, August 18, 1955, *FRUS*, 1955–57, XIV, 363–364.

47. Cairo to the Department of State, #1881, June 9, 1955, *ibid.*, pp. 237–240.

48. Cairo to the Department of State, #1928, June 17, 1955, *ibid.*, pp. 255–256; Cairo to the Department of State, #10, July 2, 1955, *ibid.*, pp. 270–273. On July 11 Eisenhower said that Egyptian arms requests did not represent a potent military force and we should make a "concerted effort to woo Nasser." *Ibid.*, p. 274; Memorandum of a Conversation, July 29, 1955, *ibid.*, pp. 332–334.

49. Cairo to the Department of State, #234, August 15, 1955, *ibid.*, pp. 355–358; Eveland, *Ropes of Sand*, pp. 132–133; Heikal, *Cutting the Lion's Tail*, p. 77.

50. The United States secretly supported the transfer of the planes to Israel. Johnston-Dulles Phone Conversation, August 18, 1955, Eisenhower Library, John F. Dulles Papers, Telephone Memorandum Series, Box #4. See Bornstein, "Revolution to Crisis," pp. 422–431, for a full historiographical discussion of the origins of the Czech arms deal.

The historiography concerning the Egyptian motivation for the Czech arms deal is divided. The school of thought which argues that Nasser was motivated by the impact of the Gaza raid and the West's subsequent neglect of Egypt's arms requests is represented by Jabber, *Not by War Alone*; Love, *Suez*; Neff, *Warriors at Suez*; Seale, *Struggle for Syria*; and Heikal, *Cairo Documents* and *Cutting the Lion's Tail*. Others argue that Nasser's regional ambitions, displeasure over the Baghdad Pact, and rivalry with Iraq were the major factors, not Israeli policy. These proponents include Uri Ra'anan, *The U.S.S.R. Arms in the Third World: Case Studies in Soviet Foreign Policy* (Cambridge, Mass., 1969); Walter Laqueur, *Communism and Nationalism in the Middle East* (New York, 1956); and Michael Brecher, *Decisions in Israel's Foreign Policy* (New Haven, Conn., 1975).

51. Heikal, *Cairo Documents*, pp. 73–74.

52. On August 19, 1955, in a memo to the president, Dulles explained his rationale for the speech: "We have accelerated somewhat the program for a number of reasons. The first is that momentarily at least Colonel Nasser seems more friendly and more sympathetic to such a project. . . . The second is that Johnston's project which I have given the right of way now has taken a bad turn because the Arab states have apparently decided not to deal with him directly but through the Arab League. . . . Events could happen in terms of a Soviet-Arab rapprochement so that we would have to back Israel much more strongly

and drop our role of impartiality. . . . If ALPHA is to be done at all, it should be done while we can speak as the friend of both. . . . We need to make such an effort before the situation gets involved in 1956 politics." Dulles to Eisenhower, August 19, 1955, *FRUS*, 1955–57, XIV, 368–369; Dulles to Eisenhower, August 19, 1955, Eisenhower Library, John F. Dulles Files, White House Memorandum Series, Box #3.

53. For the full text of the speech, see Paul Zinner, ed., *Documents on American Foreign Relations, 1955* (New York, 1956), pp. 349–354.

54. Public Records Office, CAB 129/75, C.C.(55)35, Palestine Settlement, Memorandum by the Secretary of State for Foreign Affairs, June 11, 1955; The Points of Agreement in London Discussion of the Arab-Israeli Settlement, March 10, 1955, *FRUS*, 1955–57, XIV, 98–107.

55. Saadia Touval, *The Peace Brokers: Mediators in the Arab-Israeli Conflict, 1948–1979* (Princeton, N.J., 1982), p. 115; Public Records Office, FO 371/115875, Statement on the Arab-Israeli Problem, August 27, 1955.

56. Touval, p. 115.

57. Public Records Office, FO 371/115876, Foreign Office Reaction to Mr. Dulles's Statement, August 31, 1955.

58. Touval, *Peace Brokers*, p. 115. See Brecher, *Decisions*, pp. 282–290; Public Records Office, FO 371/115878, G.G. Arthur Foreign Office Minute, September 8, 1955; *ibid.*, FO 371/115875, #291, Nicholls to Foreign Office, August 28, 1955.

59. Memorandum of a Conversation, September 6, 1955, *FRUS*, 1955–57, XIV, 451–453; Lawson to the Department of State, #246, September 10, 1955, *ibid.*, pp. 457–461.

60. Touval, *Peace Brokers*, p. 118.

61. *Ibid.*, p. 120. Public Records Office, FO 371/115876, Rose to Amman, September 2, 1955; *ibid.*, FO 371/115878, #1256 and 1258, Trevelyan to Foreign Office, September 13, 1955; *ibid.*, FO 371/115879, #1286, Trevelyan to Foreign Office, September 20, 1955; Byroade to the Department of State, #461, September 14, 1955, *FRUS*, 1955–57, XIV, 468–469.

62. On September 20, 1955, the United States had evidence that the deal would take place. The initial Egyptian order called for two hundred MIG fighters, one hundred tanks, and submarines to be delivered within three months. Byroade to the Department of State, #518, September 21, 1955, *FRUS*, 1955–57, XIV, 492–493. According to State Department intelligence sources of September 23, the Egyptians had contracted for two hundred jet aircraft (including thirty-seven medium jet bombers, the rest being MIGs), six jet training planes, one hundred heavy tanks, six torpedo patrol boats, and two submarines. Intelligence sources concluded that if the Egyptian military could maintain the equipment, it would provide them with superiority over Israel since Tel Aviv had no medium jet fighters and only twenty jet fighters. In addition, the Israelis had no heavy tanks and stockpiled only three hundred medium and light tanks. Memorandum from the Secretary of State's Special Assistant for Intelligence to Dulles, September 23, 1955, *ibid.*, pp. 507–508.

63. Memorandum of a Conversation, September 26, 1955, *ibid.*, pp. 516–519.

64. Dulles-Hoover Phone Conversation, September 27, 1955, Eisenhower Library, John F. Dulles Papers, Telephone Memorandum Series, Box #4.

65. Department of State Press Releases, #588 and 589, October 4, 1955, Seely G. Mudd Library, John F. Dulles Papers, Box #95.

66. Department of State Press Release, #606, October 18, 1955, *ibid.*, Box #92; Memorandum of a Conversation, October 3, 1955, *FRUS*, 1955–57, XIV, 542–550. The Aswan project consisted of a dam to be built across the Nile about four and one-third miles south of the existing Aswan Dam. It was to consist of a powerhouse at the dam with an initial capacity of 720,000 kilowatts which could later be doubled; a transmission line to Cairo and necessary interconnections; conversion of 700,000 acres from the basin to perennial irrigation; and reclamation, irrigation, and settlement of an additional 1.3 million acres, including provisions for necessary roads and other public facilities. The dam would be 364 square feet high and 3.1 miles long across its crest. The reservoir would have storage capacity for about 45.9 million cubic feet of water, sufficient to regulate the flow throughout the year. Construction of the dam and initial power facilities were to begin in July 1957, with preparatory work to begin earlier. The first stage was to take five years to complete, with a total cost estimated at $275 million, of which the equivalent of $110 million represented expenditures in foreign currencies. The cost for the United States in the first stage was to be a $56.6 million grant, for the British 5.5 million pounds sterling. Department of State to Byroade, #1282, December 16, 1955, *ibid.*, pp. 868–870.

67. Draft Paper on Arab Countries, October 20, 1955, Seely G. Mudd Library, John F. Dulles Papers, Subject Series, Box #10; Memorandum of Discussion at the 260th Meeting of the National Security Council, October 6, 1955, *FRUS*, 1955–57, XIV, 553–558.

68. Draft Report on Deterrence of Major Armed Conflict Between Israel and Egypt or Other Arab States, October 17, 1955, Eisenhower Library, Special Assistant for National Security Affairs, Near East (2), Box #12.

69. Special Intelligence Estimate, SNIE 30-3-55, October 12, 1955, *FRUS*, 1955–57, XIV, 77–86.

70. Memorandum of Discussion of the 262nd Meeting of the National Security Council, October 6, 1955, Eisenhower Library, Ann Whitman File, National Security Council Series, Box #7. Memorandum of Discussion at the 262nd Meeting of the National Security Council, October 20, 1955, *FRUS*, 1955–57, XIV, 616–630.

71. Allen W. Dulles to John F. Dulles, October 29, 1955, *FRUS*, 1955–57, XIV, 679–680.

72. Memorandum of Conversation, October 21, 1955, Eisenhower Library, John F. Dulles Papers, Subject Series, Box #10.

73. Memorandum for Elmer Staats, Eisenhower Library, White House Office for National Security Council Affairs, OCB Papers, Central Files, Ser./091.A, Mid East (3), Box #77.

74. London to the Department of State, #1603, October 20, 1955, *FRUS*, 1955–57, XIV, 633–636; Department of State to Paris, October 25, 1955, *ibid.*, pp. 645–647; National Intelligence Estimate, NIE 36.1-55, November 15, 1955, *ibid.*, pp. 750–772.

75. Moshe Dayan, *The Story of My Life* (New York, 1976), pp. 179–180.

76. Memorandum of a Conversation, October 26, 1955, *FRUS*, 1955–57,

XIV, 650–656; Geneva to the Department of State, October 26, 1955, *ibid.*, pp. 657–659.

77. Moshe Dayan, *Diary of the Sinai Campaign* (New York, 1967), p. 12.

78. On November 2, 1955, Israeli forces attacked an Egyptian position near the El Auja demilitarized zone. The Israelis claimed to have killed fifty Egyptians and taken forty prisoners. Israel reported casualties of four killed and nineteen wounded. Memorandum of Discussion at the 264th Meeting of the National Security Council, November 3, 1955, *FRUS*, 1955–57, XIV, 696–700; Neff, *Warriors at Suez*, p. 116.

79. Public Records Office, FO 371/115880, Speech by Prime Minister Eden at the Lord Mayor's Banquet, November 9, 1955.

80. Public Records Office, FO 371/115880, #740, Foreign Office to Amman, November 9, 1955.

81. Public Records Office, CAB 128/29, C.M.(55)36, Discussion of Czech Arms Deal, October 20, 1955. Progress Report on the Near East, November 2, 1955, Eisenhower Library, White House Office for the Special Assistant for National Security Council Affairs, Near East (2), Box #12. Despite Eden's hopes, the United States again made it quite clear to the British that it had no plans of adhering to the Baghdad Pact, nor did it want any Arab states joining the pact until the ALPHA project had run its course. Dulles wrote Macmillan, "An immediate move to expand the Baghdad Pact would probably deny us Nasser's cooperation. Therefore I think we should wait a little before trying to bring in Jordan and Lebanon. If we are not successful in Egypt, we should endeavor to secure the adherence of those two states as soon as possible." Dulles to Macmillan, #3132, December 5, 1955, *FRUS*, 1955–57, XIV, 821–824; see Memorandum of a Conversation, November 9, 1955, *ibid.*, pp. 720–723.

82. Public Records Office, CAB 128/29, C.M.(55)34, Discussion of Arab-Israeli Peace, October 4, 1955.

83. Public Records Office, FO 371/115881, Text of Speech made by Ben-Gurion to the Knesset, November 15, 1955; Tel Aviv to Department of State, #515, November 17, 1955, *FRUS*, 1955–57, XIV, 784–786.

84. Public Records Office, FO 371/115883, Shuckburgh to Nicholls, December 2, 1955.

85. Public Records Office, FO 371/115880, #1693, Trevelyan to Foreign Office, November 10, 1955.

86. Public Records Office, FO 371/115885, #994, Wright to Foreign Office, December 5, 1955.

87. Public Records Office, CAB 128/29, C.M.(55)37, Discussion of Aswan Loan, October 25, 1955.

88. Dulles was concerned that the Soviet Union was doing its best "to bring off a deal with the Egyptians on the Dam." He hoped that by supporting the Aswan project it "would constitute a strong influence in keeping Egypt on the side of the free world." Memorandum of Discussion at the 268th Meeting of the National Security Council, December 1, 1955, *FRUS*, 1955–57, XIV, 812–817; Department of State to Cairo, #1230, *ibid.*, pp. 841–843; Memorandum of Conversation, December 12, 1955, *ibid.*, pp. 849–851.

89. Memorandum by the Under Secretary of State, December 2, 1955, *ibid.*, pp. 818–819.

90. Touval, *Peace Brokers*, p. 123.

91. Department of State to Cairo, #1231, December 10, 1955, *FRUS*, 1955–57, XIV, 843–844; Sharett to Dulles, December 12, 1955, *ibid.*, pp. 844–848; Memorandum of Conversation, December 30, 1955, *ibid.*, pp. 890–892; see footnote on p. 890 which describes the Israeli and Egyptian acceptance of Anderson as an intermediary.

6. Two Failures: The Anderson Mission and the Aswan Loan

1. Memorandum from Russell to Dulles, December 28, 1955, *FRUS*, 1955–57, XIV, 888–889.

2. Byroade to the Department of State, #976, November 17, 1955, *ibid.*, pp. 781–783. This position Nasser later denied when the Anderson mission was collapsing.

3. Byroade to the Department of State, #1027, November 27, 1955, *ibid.*, pp. 807–808; Public Records Office, FO 371/115885, G. G. Arthur Foreign Office Minute, November 28, 1955.

4. Public Records Office, FO 371/115882, G. G. Arthur Foreign Office Minute, November 18, 1955. The Egyptian approach was fairly close to the ALPHA plan, with the exception of the Negev, which became a major obstacle for a settlement.

5. Public Records Office, FO 371/115883, #1793, Trevelyan to Foreign Office, November 26, 1955.

6. Public Records Office, FO 371/115883, #487, Nicholls to Foreign Office, November 21, 1955.

7. Memorandum of a Conversation, November 21, 1955, *FRUS*, 1955–57, XIV, 793–796; Public Records Office, FO 371/115884, Memorandum of a Conversation Between Dulles and Sharett, November 21, 1955.

8. Aide Memoire from Israel to the Department of State, December 6, 1955, *FRUS*, 1955–57, XIV, 823–825; Memorandum of a Conversation, December 6, 1955, *ibid.*, pp. 826–832; Public Records Office, FO 371/115885, #2983, Makins to Foreign Office, December 6, 1955.

9. Letter from Sharett to Dulles, December 12, 1955, *FRUS*, 1955–57, XIV, 844–848.

10. Memorandum of a Conversation, December 6, 1955, *ibid.*, pp. 826–832, Lawson to the Department of State, #676, January 5, 1956, *FRUS*, 1955–57, XV, 12–13; Lawson to the Department of State, January 6, 1956, *ibid.*

11. Memorandum of a Conversation, December 6, 1955, *FRUS*, 1955–57, XIV, 793–796.

12. Department of State to Byroade, #1051, November 22, 1955, *ibid.*, pp. 802–803.

13. On October 31, 1955, at Geneva, Sharett broached an Israeli arms request to Dulles to bridge the gap caused by the Czech arms deal. Dulles to the Department of State, #90, October 31, 1955, *ibid.*, pp. 683–684; the request was renewed on November 16, 1955, Memorandum of a Conversation, November 16, 1955, *ibid.*, pp. 773–776.

14. Department of State to Byroade, #1282, December 16, 1955, *FRUS*, 1955–57, XIV, 868–870.

15. Diary entry by the President, January 10, 1956, Eisenhower Library,

Ann Whitman File, Eisenhower Diaries, Box #9. Eisenhower is referring to the Templer mission of December 1955, which is described in detail later in this chapter.

16. William Bragg Ewald, *Eisenhower the President* (Englewood Cliffs, N.J., 1981), p. 194.

17. Memorandum of a Conversation, January 11, 1956, *FRUS*, 1955–57, XV, 20–22. Diary Entry by the President, January 11, 1956, *ibid.*, p. 23; Memorandum of a Meeting with the President, January 11, 1956, Eisenhower Library, John F. Dulles Papers, White House Memorandum Series, Box #4.

18. Ewald, *Eisenhower*, p. 194; Stephen Ambrose, *Eisenhower the President* (New York, 1985), p. 316.

19. Nasser actually calculated how much support he would lose in the Arab world if he agreed to a settlement with Israel. He would immediately lose 60 percent of his support in Egypt and in the Arab world. Within thirty to sixty days he would recover 30 percent of his support, and within six months he would recover another 10 percent. But 10 percent would never be recovered. Message from Anderson, #2, January 19, 1956, *FRUS*, 1955–57, XV, 28–36.

20. *Ibid.*

21. Lawson to the Department of State, #693, January 10, 1956, *Ibid.*, pp. 16–19.

22. Message from Anderson, #13, January 21, 1956, *ibid.*, pp. 43–47.

23. Nasser was concerned he would end up like Jordan's King Abdullah, who had advocated coming to terms with Israel and was assassinated by Arab extremists in 1951. Message from Anderson, #16, *ibid.*, pp. 47–50.

24. Message to Washington, #22, January 24, 1956, *ibid.*, pp. 60–63. Nasser and Anderson agreed to avoid the appearance of negotiating directly with Israel. The Egyptian leader would present his views in a letter to Eisenhower, and once the United States accepted Nasser's terms they would be presented to Ben-Gurion. See *ibid.* and Heikal, *Cutting the Lion's Tail*, pp. 232–234.

25. Message from Anderson, #19, January 23, 1956, *FRUS*, 1955–57, XV, 51–56.

26. David Ben-Gurion, *My Talks with Arab Leaders* (New York, 1973), pp. 274–283; Message from Anderson, #21, January 24, 1956, *FRUS*, 1955–57, XV, 58–60. Until the spring of 1989 Ben-Gurion's account was the only accurate source for Anderson's conversations with Nasser. The release of the *Foreign Relations* volume documents Ben-Gurion's description of events.

27. Message from Anderson, #26, January 24, 1956, *ibid.*, pp. 63–66.

28. Message from Anderson, #29, January 25, 1956, *ibid.*, pp. 66–68; Lawson to the Department of State, #743, January 25, 1956, *ibid.*, pp. 72–74. Ben-Gurion, *My Talks*, pp. 287–292. The next day Dulles gave his permission for the French to sell Israel twelve Mystere IV planes; Dulles to Dillon, #2714, January 26, 1956, *FRUS*, 1955–57, XV, 78–80.

29. Dulles to Anderson, January 28, 1956, *ibid.*, pp. 91–92.

30. Message from Anderson, #33, January 28, 1956, *ibid.*, pp. 86–88.

31. Allen W. Dulles to John F. Dulles, January 29, 1956, *ibid.*, pp. 92–94.

32. Message to Robert B. Anderson at Athens, #60, February 1, 1956, *ibid.*, pp. 119–120.

33. Message from Anderson, #66, February 1, 1956, *ibid.*, pp. 122–124; Ben-Gurion, *My Talks*, pp. 296–308.

34. Memorandum to Washington, February 8, 1956, *FRUS*, 1955–57, XV, 152–156.

35. Ben-Gurion to Eisenhower, February 8, 1956, *ibid.*, pp. 185–187; Ben-Gurion, *My Talks*, pp. 309–311.

36. Humphrey Trevelyan, *The Middle East in Revolution* (New York, 1970), p. 57; Eden, *Full Circle*, p. 381.

37. Footnote, *FRUS*, 1955–57, XV, 10; Meyer, *Egypt and the United States*, p. 137.

38. Public Records Office, FO 371/121724, Brief for Shuckburgh for Official Talks with the United States, January 7, 1956.

39. Public Records Office, FO 371/1121270, Meetings Between USDS Officials on Russian Influence in the Middle East, January 20, 1956.

40. Memorandum of Conversation, January 30, 1956, *FRUS*, 1955–57, XV, 101–107.

41. Memorandum of Conversation, January 30, 1956, *ibid.*, pp. 101–107; Eden, *Full Circle*, p. 372; Public Records Office, FO 371/121759, #241, Makins to Foreign Office, January 30, 1956. Before arriving in Washington Eden's true feelings were apparent. As Shuckburgh wrote in his diary, "A.E. threw a tantrum because according to the programme just received from Washington he is not going to see Ike as much as he would like. 'I am not going to be treated like this. I will take the next boat home. We shall achieve nothing. It is no use talking to Dulles and the State Department, though you will do it very well, Sewlyn dear; they cannot treat the British Prime Minister like this....' " Shuckburgh, *Descent to Suez*, p. 327.

42. Eden, p. 374; Memorandum of a Conversation, January 30, 1956, *FRUS*, 1955–57, XV, 101–107; Summary of Eden Visit, February 7, 1956, Eisenhower Library, Ann Whitman File, International Series, Eden Visit, Box #20.

43. Eden, *Full Circle*, p. 373; Shuckburgh, *Descent to Suez*, pp. 329–330. In October 1955 the United Kingdom had withdrawn from an arbitration designed to resolve the dispute with Saudi Arabia over the Buraimi Oasis. Later the British forcefully reoccupied the area and declared "unilaterally a boundary." In so doing the British indicated their willingness to discuss minor rectifications with Saudi Arabia, but they opposed any withdrawal or resumption of arbitration. "The United Kingdom contend[ed] this absolute dependence on Persian Gulf oil [made] the preservation of their traditional position and prestige in the area imperative...." Eisenhower's response was that "the British [could] not maintain that every mile in every border area would be a matter of British prestige." Summary of Eden Visit, February 7, 1956, Ann Whitman File, International Series, Eden Visit, Box #20, Eisenhower Library, Abilene, Kans. (henceforth Eisenhower Library, Ann Whitman File, International Series).

44. *Ibid.* For the British reaction to the trip, see Public Records Office, CAB 128/30, C.M. (56)10, Eden and Lloyd Visit to the United States, February 9, 1956.

45. Sherman Adams, *Firsthand Report* (London, 1962), p. 196.

46. Public Records Office, FO 800/724, Duke to Foreign Office, March 1, 1956; see Sir John Bagot Glubb, *A Soldier with the Arabs* (London, 1957), pp.

426–427. When it was learned that Hussein had fired Glubb, Selwyn Lloyd was having dinner with Nasser in Cairo. Nasser told Lloyd he thought it was a useful move by the British, and that London had finally appreciated that figures like Glubb no longer served any useful purpose in the area. Lloyd thought it was absurd and saw it as a direct move to humiliate him. Heikal, *Cutting the Lion's Tail*, pp. 96–98. Heikal goes on to suggest that the CIA had Glubb removed as part of a policy designed to isolate Egypt from its Arab neighbors.

47. Carleton, *Anthony Eden*, pp. 395–398, discusses all of Eden's problems in detail.

48. Anthony Nutting, *No End of a Lesson: The Inside Story of the Suez Crisis* (New York, 1967), pp. 17–18. According to Nutting, Eden completely lost his touch. "Driven by impulse of pride and prestige and nagged by mounting sickness, he began to behave like an enraged elephant charging senselessly at invisible and imaginary enemies in the international jungle." Nutting, *No End of a Lesson*, p. 32; see Shuckburgh, *Descent to Suez*, p. 340.

49. Memorandum of a Conversation, February 10, 1956, *FRUS*, 1955–57, XV, 163–166; see Public Records Office FO 371/121724, Shuckburgh to Nicholls, February 18, 1956; *ibid.*, FO 371/121701, Hadow Foreign Office Minute, February 15, 1956.

50. See letter from Members of the House of Representatives, February 3, 1956, in Paul Zinner, ed., *Documents on American Foreign Relations, 1956* (New York, 1957), pp. 271–273, and Dulles's answer, *ibid.*, pp. 273–275. See Department of State Press Release #96, February 24, 1956, Seely G. Mudd Library, John F. Dulles Papers, Box #100.

51. Message to Central Intelligence Agency, #88, February 22, 1956, *FRUS*, 1955–57, XV, 203–204.

52. Message to the Director of Intelligence, #93, February 22, 1956, *ibid.*, p. 209.

53. Dulles to Byroade, February 29, 1956, Seely G. Mudd Library, John F. Dulles Papers, Box #100.

54. Special National Intelligence Estimate, SNIE 30-56, February 28, 1956, "Critical Aspects of the Arab-Israeli Situation," *FRUS*, 1955–57, XV, 248–254. Information from Lawson in Tel Aviv kept pointing to the Israelis being at the "end of their rope." Lawson to the Department of State, #861, February 29, 1956, *ibid.*, pp. 255–256; Lawson to the Department of State, #865, February 29, 1956, *ibid.*, pp. 257–260; Lawson to the Department of State, #868, March 1, 1956, *ibid.*, pp. 269–272.

55. Message from Cairo, #97, March 1, 1956, *ibid.*, pp. 262–263.

56. Message from Anderson to the Secretary of State, at Karachi, #110, *ibid.*, pp. 295–300.

57. Message from Anderson to the Secretary of State, at Karachi, #111, *ibid.*, pp. 302–307.

58. Message from Anderson to the Secretary of State, at Karachi, #115, *ibid.*, pp. 310–314.

59. Message from Anderson to the Secretary of State, at New Delhi, #121, *ibid.*, pp. 333–336; Ben-Gurion, *My Talks*, pp. 305–312.

60. Touval, *Peace Brokers*, p. 133. The author agrees with Touval's analysis presented pp. 131–133.

61. Public Records Office, PREM 11/1177, #1246, Foreign Office to Washington, March 5, 1956; see footnote, *FRUS*, 1955–57, XV, 294.

62. Eisenhower to Eden, March 9, 1956, Eisenhower Library, Ann Whitman File, Dulles-Herter Series, Box #5; Eisenhower to Eden, March 9, 1956, *FRUS*, 1955–57, XV, 337–338.

63. Diary Entry by the President, March 8, 1956, *ibid.*, pp. 326–328. Donald Neff argues that instead of trying to resolve America's differences with Britain, France, and Israel, the president chose the easiest course by picking on the weakest country involved, Egypt. Eisenhower, like his Atlantic allies, accepted the miscalculation that Nasser was the common author of all their woes in the Middle East. But the sole cause of their troubles was not Nasser but the decline of colonialism and the resurgence of Islam. Neff, *Warriors at Suez*, pp. 196–197. Neff is totally correct, but more emphasis must be placed on the United States' inability to accept and understand the economic and social factors that helped produce the indigenous nationalism at the heart of Middle East developments.

64. Dulles to Hoover, March 8, 1956, Eisenhower Library, Ann Whitman File, Dulles-Herter Series, Box #5; Dulles to Hoover, March 8, 1956, *FRUS*, 1955–57, XV, 325–326; see Memorandum of a Conversation with the President, March 13, 1956, Eisenhower Library, Ann Whitman File, Eisenhower Diaries, Box #9.

65. Hoover to Dulles, March 16, 1956, Eisenhower Library, John F. Dulles Papers, White House Memorandum Series, Box #4; Hoover to Dulles, March 16, 1956, *FRUS*, 1955–57, XV, 370–371; Memorandum by the Director of the Office of Near Eastern Affairs, March 14, 1956, *ibid.*, pp. 353–357.

66. Eden to Eisenhower, March 15, 1956, *ibid.*, pp. 364–365; Eisenhower's sympathetic response is provided in a footnote on p. 365.

67. Memorandum from the Secretary of State to the President, March 28, 1956, Eisenhower Library, Ann Whitman File, Dulles-Herter Series, Box #5; Memorandum from the Secretary of State to the President, March 28, 1956, *FRUS*, 1955–57, XV, 419–421; based on a Memorandum Prepared in the Bureau of Near Eastern, South Asian, and African Affairs, March 28, 1956, *ibid.*, pp. 409–418. It is interesting to note that while the United States was considering building up King Saud as a replacement for Nasser, its own intelligence analysis stated that as long as King Saud remained in power it was unlikely that American relations with Saudi Arabia could be improved. Saudi Arabia: A Disruptive Force in Western-Arab Relations: An Intelligence Report, January 19, 1956, Declassified Documents Reference System, DDRS (79) 318A.

68. Diary Entry by the President, March 28, 1956, *FRUS*, 1955–57, XV, 425; Ferrell, *The Eisenhower Diaries*, pp. 323–324.

69. Memorandum from the Secretary of State to the President, March 28, 1956, *FRUS*, 1955–57, XV, 419–421. The remainder of the memo is classified; but when one examines the British sources and hints dropped by Eveland and Copeland, "drastic action" included plotting a pro-Western coup in Syria and deposing Nasser. According to John Prados, Operation Straggle was designed to bring about a coup of Syrian officers to forestall the leftist Ba'ath party from increasing its power. The coup was scheduled to take place at the end of October 1956. John Prados, *President's Secret Wars: CIA and Pentagon Covert*

Operations from World War II Through Iranscam (New York, 1986), pp. 128–130.

70. Notes from Makins to Dulles, March 21, 1956, *FRUS*, 1955–57, XV, 383–387. Public Records Office, FO 371/118842, United Kingdom High Commissioner in Pakistan to Foreign Office, March 7, 1956.

71. Memorandum of a Conversation, April 1, 1956, *FRUS*, 1955–57, XV, 435–445; Memorandum Prepared in the Bureau of Near Eastern, South Asian, and African Affairs, March 28, 1956, *ibid.*, pp. 409–418.

72. Memorandum of a Conversation, March 27, 1956, Eisenhower Library, John F. Dulles Papers, White House Memorandum Series, Box #4.

73. Eveland, *Ropes of Sand*, p. 168.

74. Russell to Dulles, May 18, 1955, *FRUS*, 1955–57, XIV, 204–205.

75. Aldrich to the Department of State, #1603, October 20, 1955, *ibid.*, pp. 633–636. On May 23, 1955, Soviet Ambassador Daniel S. Solod supposedly offered Egypt $600 million in Soviet goods and services plus technical and economic assistance which included financing for the dam. Jernegan to Murphy, June 21, 1955, *ibid.*, pp. 261–262; National Intelligence Estimate, NIE 36.1.55, November 15, 1955, *ibid.*, pp. 750–772.

76. Department of State to the Delegation at the Foreign Ministers Meeting in Paris, October 25, 1955, *ibid.*, pp. 645–647.

77. Delegation at the Foreign Ministers Meetings to the Department of State, November 3, 1955, *ibid.*, pp. 707–710; Delegation at the Foreign Ministers Meetings to the Department of State, November 9, 1955, *ibid.*, pp. 728–732.

78. Memorandum of a Conversation, November 16, 1955, *ibid.*, pp. 777–780.

79. Memorandum of a Conversation, November 22, 1955, *ibid.*, pp. 798–801; Eden to Eisenhower, November 27, 1955, *ibid.*, pp. 808–809; Memorandum of a Discussion at the 268th Meeting of the National Security Council, December 1, 1955, *ibid.*, pp. 812–820.

80. Memorandum of a Conversation, December 12, 1955, *ibid.*, pp. 849–851; Department of State to London, #3346, December 14, 1955, *ibid.*, pp. 860–862; Department of State to Cairo, #1282, December 16, 1955, *ibid.*, pp. 868–870; see footnote 14 of this chapter.

81. Byroade to Hoover, #1236, January 1, 1956, *FRUS*, 1955–57, XV, 1–4; Hart (Cairo) to the Department of State, #1432, January 29, 1956, *ibid.*, pp. 98–100; Hart to the Department of State, #1450, January 31, 1956; *ibid.*, pp. 115–116.

82. Byroade to the Department of State, #1665, February 23, 1956, *ibid.*, pp. 227–229.

83. Hoover to Byroade, January 31, 1956, *ibid.*, p. 117. Nasser's distrust was mounting, and the United States wanted Black to reassure Nasser that after the initial phase of construction, after five years, money would be available for the continuation of the project. Message to Anderson at Athens, February 1, 1956, *ibid.*, pp. 119–120; Message to Washington, #67, February 2, 1956, *ibid.*, pp. 127–128.

84. Byroade to the Department of State, #1667, February 23, 1956, *ibid.*, pp. 230–232.

85. Byroade to the Department of State, #1668, February 24, 1956, *ibid.*, pp. 232–233.

86. Byroade to the Department of State, #1794, March 8, 1956, *ibid.*, pp. 330–331.

87. Heikal, *Cairo Documents*, p. 64; Lloyd, *Suez*, p. 69.

88. Department of State to Cairo, #2165, April 30, 1955, *FRUS*, 1955–57, XV, 588–589.

89. Delegation at the North Atlantic Council Ministerial Meeting to the Department of State, #11, May 4, 1956, *ibid.*, pp. 604–607.

90. Lloyd, *Suez*, p. 69; Aldrich to the Department of State, #5584, June 2, 1956, *FRUS*, 1955–57, XV, 705–706.

91. Delegation at the North Atlantic Council Ministerial Meeting to the Department of State, #2, May 3, 1956, *ibid.*, pp. 595–599; Dulles to the Department of State, May 3, 1956, *ibid.*, pp. 601–602; Delegation at the North Atlantic Council Ministerial Meeting to the Department of State, #29, May 6, 1956, *ibid.*, pp. 615–619; Dulles to Eisenhower, May 6, 1956, Eisenhower Library, Ann Whitman FIle, Dulles-Herter Series, Box #5.

92. Public Records Office, FO 371/118843, Trevelyan to Shuckburgh, May 26, 1956; Byroade to the Department of State, #2264, May 17, 1956, *FRUS*, 1955–57, XV, 644.

93. Memorandum of a Conversation, May 17, 1956, *ibid.*, pp. 645–650.

94. Memorandum from the Deputy Assistant Secretary of State for Near Eastern, South Asian, and African Affairs to Dulles, May 23, 1956, *ibid.*, pp. 658–667.

95. Public Records Office, PREM 11/1177, #2354, Foreign Office to Washington, May 1, 1956.

96. Public Records Office, FO 371/118862, Foreign Office to Trevelyan, May 15, 1956; *ibid.*, Shuckburgh to Middle East Embassies, May 29, 1956.

97. Aldrich to the Department of States, #5584, June 2, 1956, *FRUS*, 1955–57, XV, 705–706.

98. Allen W. Dulles to John F. Dulles, June 27, 1956, *ibid.*, pp. 751–754.

99. Memorandum of a Conversation, June 25, 1956, *ibid.*, pp. 748–751.

100. Allen W. Dulles to John F. Dulles, June 27, 1956, *ibid.*, pp. 751–754.

101. Memorandum of Discussion at the 289th Meeting of the National Security Council, June 28, 1956, *ibid.*, pp. 754–756.

102. Byroade to Dulles, #45, July 10, 1956, *ibid.*, pp. 806–807.

103. Memorandum of a Conversation with the President, July 13, 1956, Eisenhower Library, John F. Dulles Papers, White House Memorandum Series, Box #4.

104. Memorandum of a Conversation, July 10, 1956, *FRUS*, 1955–57, XV, 802–804.

105. Memorandum of a Conversation, July 13, 1956, *ibid.*, pp. 830–832; Public Records Office, CAB 21/3314, Suez Canal—UKG/GOF Intervention (8/56-12/58), undated.

106. Allen to Dulles, July 17, 1956, *FRUS*, 1955–57, XV, 849–853.

107. Public Records Office, CAB 128/30, C.M. (56)50, Discussion of Aswan Dam Loan, July 17, 1956.

108. Memorandum of a Conversation, July 18, 1956, *FRUS*, 1955–57, XV, 855.

109. Public Records Office, CAB 21/3314, Suez Canal—UKG/GOF Intervention (8/56–12/58), undated.

110. Memorandum of a Conversation, July 19, 1956, *FRUS*, 1955–57, XV, 861–862.

111. Memorandum of a Conversation, July 19, 1956, *ibid.*, pp. 863–864. For a full discussion of Dulles's motivation in withdrawing the loan, see Meyer, *Egypt and the United States*, pp. 143–146; Aronson, *From Sideshow to Center Stage*, pp. 176–178; Finer, *Dulles Over Suez*, pp. 51–52; Lyons, *Eisenhower*, pp. 734–735; Cooper, *Lion's Last Roar*, pp. 96–99; James, *Eden*, pp. 448–450; Speigal, *Other Arab-Israeli Conflict*, pp. 70–71; Neff, *Warriors at Suez*, pp. 257–262; and Ambrose, *Eisenhower*, pp. 328–330.

112. Dulles assumed that as he had not heard from the British during the five hours between his last meeting with them and the approaching visit of Hussein, they did not object to his plans. Allen Dulles–John F. Dulles Phone Conversation, July 19, 1956, *FRUS*, 1955–57, XV, 866. For a full description of the Dulles-Hussein meeting, see Memorandum of a Conversation, July 19, 1956, *ibid.*, pp. 867–873.

113. For extracts from Nasser's speech, see The Suez Canal Problem, July 26–September 22, 1956 (Washington, D.C., Department of State Publication #6392), pp. 25–32.

114. Eden, *Full Circle*, p. 470.

7. Conspiracy at Suez

1. Hoopes, *Devil and John Foster Dulles*, pp. 348–353, 361–362.

2. Of the total of seventy million tons of oil which passed from the Persian Gulf through the Suez Canal, sixty million tons were destined for Western Europe and represented two-thirds of its oil supplies. To move this amount of tonnage around Cape Horn would require twice the tonnage of existing tankers. At the time of nationalization the British only had a six-week supply of oil. Of the 14,666 ships which passed through the Canal in 1955, one-third were British. Public Records Office, CAB 128/30, C.M.(56)54, Cabinet Meeting Held in the Prime Minister's Room at the House of Commons, July 27, 1956.

3. *Ibid.* See Memorandum by the Assistant Legal Adviser for United Nations Affairs, July 27, 1956, *FRUS*, 1955–57, XVI, 16–18, for the American legal analysis of Nasser's actions.

4. Public Records Office, CAB 128/30, C.M.(56)54, Cabinet Meeting Held in the Prime Minister's Room at the House of Commons, July 27, 1956.

5. *Ibid.* At this cabinet meeting the "Egypt Committee" was appointed to formulate policy. The committee was composed of the prime minister (Eden), the lord president (Salisbury), the commonwealth secretary (Home), the chancellor of the exchequer (Macmillan), the foreign secretary (Lloyd), and the minister of defence (Monckton). Its purpose was to act as an "inner Cabinet and was also responsible for supervising the military operations and plans."

6. Eden, *Full Circle*, p. 479.

7. Heikal, *Cutting the Lion's Tail*, pp. 120–126; Heikal, *Cairo Documents*, pp. 86–89.

8. Aldrich to Dulles, #481, July 27, 1956, *FRUS*, 1955–57, XVI, 1–3.

Aldrich to Dulles, #481, July 27, 1956, Eisenhower Library, Ann Whitman File, Dulles-Herter Series, Box #5.

9. Public Records Office, PREM 11/1177, #3358, Foreign Office to Washington, July 27, 1956. Eden to Eisenhower, July 27, 1956, *FRUS*, 1955–57, XVI, 9–11.

10. Eisenhower to Eden, July 28, 1956, *ibid.*, p. 12. Eisenhower, *Waging Peace*, pp. 38–40. Eisenhower told Eden that he rejected the idea that "no one except the European technicians then operating the Canal were capable of doing so."

11. Notes on a Conversation with the President, July 28, 1956, Eisenhower Library, Eisenhower Diaries, Staff Memos, Box #16.

12. Public Records Office, #1609, Makins to Foreign Office, July 28, 1956. Later that day the Egypt Committee met for the second time to determine the best course of action to present to Pineau and Murphy when they arrived. The committee decided that any maritime conference should be delayed until military preparations were advanced to the point of possible forceful action. If Egypt rejected a proposal for international management of the canal, the United States, the United Kingdom, and France would inform the other maritime powers that action must be taken against Cairo. Egypt Committee Minutes, July 28, 1956, Meeting of the Egypt Committee Number 2, Public Records Office, London, United Kingdom (henceforth CAB 134/1216, E.C.(56) and meeting #).

13. Robert Murphy, *Diplomat Among Warriors* (Garden City, N.Y., 1964), p. 380.

14. Murphy to Dulles, #517, July 29, 1956, Eisenhower Library, Ann Whitman File, Dulles-Herter Series, Box #5.

15. Public Records Office, PREM 11/1098, Record of Conversation Between the French, United Kingdom, and United States Delegation, July 29, 1956. Pineau, who did not agree with the American approach to the problem, suffered from a greater sense of outrage than his British counterpart. Pineau stated, "If Nasser were able to get away with this, it would have incalculable consequences for the whole Western position. Like Hitler, Nasser had made no secret of his intentions. . . ."

16. Murphy, *Diplomat Among Warriors*, p. 381. In the afternoon Dulles telephoned Nixon and said, "The United Kingdom and French are really anxious to start a war and get us into it. I am doing the best I can to make them realize they may have to do it alone." Dulles-Nixon Phone Conversation, July 30, 1956, Eisenhower Library, John F. Dulles Papers, Telephone Conversation Memorandum, Box #5.

17. Public Records Office, FO 371/119080, #1613, Makins to Foreign Office, July 30, 1956.

18. Memorandum of a Conversation with the President, July 31, 1956, Eisenhower Library, Ann Whitman File, Eisenhower Diaries, Staff Memos, Box #16; Memorandum of a Conference with the President, July 31, 1956, *FRUS*, 1955–57, XVI, 62–68. For a full analysis of United States intelligence concerning Nasser's nationalization of the canal, see Nasser and the Middle East Situation, Special National Intelligence Estimate 30-3-56, July 31, 1956, *FRUS*, 1955–57, XVI, 78–93; Editorial Note, *ibid.*, pp. 2–3.

19. *Ibid.*

20. *Ibid.*

21. Public Records Office, PREM 11/1098, Eisenhower to Eden, July 31, 1956; Eisenhower to Eden, July 31, 1956, *FRUS*, 1955–57, XVI, 69–71.

22. Public Records Office, CAB 134/1216, E.C.(56)4, July 30, 1956. At the meeting the secretary of war stated that the Chiefs of Staff "were examining plans for an amphibious assault as a means of overthrowing 'the present regime in Egypt.'" In addition, Class A reservists were being activated. See Public Records Office, CAB 134/1216, E.C.(56)3. Eden stated that if Nasser refused to accept a resolution prepared by a maritime conference to internationalize control of the canal, "military operations could then proceed."

23. Public Records Office, PREM 11/1098, Record of a Meeting, August 1, 1956. Memorandum of a Conversation Between Eden and Dulles, August 1, 1956, *FRUS*, 1955–57, XVI, 98–100.

24. *Ibid.*; Public Records Office, CAB 128/30, C.M.(56)56, Discussion of Suez Situation, August 1, 1956. See Eden, *Full Circle*, pp. 486–492. Eden writes, "Nasser must be made, as Mr. Dulles put it to me, 'to disgorge.' These were forthright words. They would ring in my ears for months."

25. Public Records Office, PREM 11/1098, Record of a Meeting, August 1, 1956. Dulles to Department of State, August 2, 1956, *FRUS*, 1955–57, XVI, 100–105.

26. Public Records Office, CAB 128/30, C.M.(56)57, Discussion of Suez Situation, August 1, 1956. See Zinner, *Documents on American Foreign Relations 1956*, pp. 292–294, for the Joint Statement Issued by the United States, United Kingdom, and France at London, August 2, 1956; see Public Records Office, CAB 134/1261, E.C.(56), August 2, 1956.

27. Eden, *Full Circle*, p. 486.

28. Alistair Horne, *Macmillan, 1894–1956* (London, 1988), pp. 407–408; see Cooper, *Lion's Last Roar*, p. 151.

29. Radio-Television Address by the President and Secretary of State, August 3, 1956, Seely G. Mudd Library, John F. Dulles Papers, Box #102.

30. Public Records Office, FO 800/726 or PREM 11/1177, #3568, Foreign Office to Washington, August 5, 1956. Eden to Eisenhower, August 5, 1956, *FRUS*, 1955–57, XVI, 146–148.

31. See Public Records Office, CAB 134/1216, E.C.(56)6, August 7, 1956; Public Records Office, T236/4635, France and the Middle East, August 3, 1956. A British treasury analysis prepared by Macmillan called for the removal of Nasser and stressed that the Baghdad Pact was "still the basis of our Middle East policy and the model for future relations with countries in the area." France did not favor the Baghdad Pact because it wanted Lebanon and North Africa oriented toward the Mediterranean, not the Arab world. Paris believed that Iraq was too unreliable to unify the Arab states. Public Records Office, FO 371/118871, Record of a Meeting in M. Joxe's Room at the Quai D'orsay, August 11, 1956. Both France and the United Kingdom agreed that the United States should be kept in the dark about their discussions. Public Records Office, FO 371/11887, Foreign Office to Jebb, August 11, 1956.

32. Memorandum of a Conversation at the 292nd Meeting of the National Security Council, August 9, 1956, Eisenhower Library, Ann Whitman File, National Security Council Series, Box #8; Memorandum of Discussion at the

292nd Meeting of the National Security Council, August 9, 1956, *FRUS*, 1955–57, XVI, 165–176; Eisenhower, *Waging Peace*, pp. 43–44.

33. Notes on Presidential-Bipartisan Legislative Meeting, August 12, 1956, Eisenhower Library, Ann Whitman File, Legislative Series, Box #2; Memorandum of a Conversation, August 12, 1956, *FRUS*, 1955–57, XVI, 185–187; Memorandum of a Conversation, August 12, 1956, *ibid.*, pp. 186–196; Eisenhower, *Waging Peace*, pp. 44–45.

34. *Ibid.*; Spiegal, *Other Arab-Israeli Conflict*, p. 73.

35. Memorandum of a Conversation with the President, August 14, 1956, Eisenhower Library, John F. Dulles Papers, White House Memorandum Series, Box #5.

36. Public Records Office, CAB 128/30, C.M.(56)59, Discussion of the Suez Problem, August 14, 1956.

37. Public Records Office, PREM 11/1099, Record of a Conversation Between Lloyd and Dulles, August 15, 1956. Dulles to Department of State, August 16, 1956, *FRUS*, 1955–57, XVI, 203–205; James, *Eden*, p. 501.

38. Dulles Statement of United States Position at the First London Conference, August 16, 1956, Seely G. Mudd Library, John F. Dulles Papers, Box #110; Public Records Office, CAB 134/1216, E.C.(56)17, August 17, 1956; James, *Eden*, p. 501.

39. Public Records Office, PREM 11/1099, Record of a Conversation Between Lloyd, Dulles, and Pineau, August 18, 1956.

40. Eisenhower to Dulles, August 19, 1956, Eisenhower Library, Ann Whitman File, Dulles-Herter Series, Box #5. The papers for the American delegation at the London Conference are contained in Department of State Conference files, Lot 61D 181. An edited verbatim record is printed in *The Suez Canal Problem, July 26–September 22, 1956*, pp. 255–293. Other important documents appear in *FRUS*, 1955–57, XVI, 213–283.

41. Public Records Office, CAB 134/1216, E.C.(56)18, August 20, 1956. Later in the meeting military planning was discussed as it related to the overthrow of "Nasser's regime."

42. Statement by John F. Dulles in Submitting Paper by United States Delegation, August 20, 1956, Seely G. Mudd Library, John F. Dulles Papers, Box #110.

43. Public Records Office, PREM 11/1099, Record of a Meeting Between Lloyd, Dulles, and Pineau, August 20, 1956. Dulles to Department of State, August 20, 1956, *FRUS*, 1955–57, XVI, 242–245.

44. The complete text of the eighteen-power proposal can be found in the John F. Dulles Papers, Box #110, at the Seely G. Mudd Library.

45. Public Records Office, PREM 11/1099, Record of a Meeting Between Lloyd, Dulles, and Pineau, August 23, 1956.

46. Public Records Office, CAB 134/1216, E.C.(56)19, August 22, 1956. Townsend Hoopes's criticism of Dulles is accurate. Hoopes writes that "although he had invented, presented, argued for, and dragooned others into accepting what became the majority proposal, Dulles now wished to slip away from further responsibility. Caught between distasteful choices, his tactical sense prevailed. He cabled Eisenhower saying, "think it is preferable that we should become less conspicuous," and returned home after agreeing that Menzies

should lead the mission to Cairo." Hoopes, *Devil and John Foster Dulles*, p. 355.

47. McCardle to Department of State, August 21, 1956, *FRUS*, 1955–57, XVI, 249–250; Memorandum of a Conversation between Dulles and Eden, August 22, 1956, *ibid.*, pp. 256–257. Before the Menzies Mission departed for Cairo the Egypt Committee concluded that if Nasser rejected the proposals, "The United Nations machinary did not seem to provide any means of redress for the threat which Egyptian action constituted to the vital interests of the United Kingdom." Public Records Office, CAB 134/1216, E.C.(56)20, August 23, 1956.

48. Public Records Office, PREM 11/1177, #3913, Foreign Office to Washington, August 27, 1956; Eden to Eisenhower, August 27, 1956, *FRUS*, 1955–57, XVI, 304–305.

49. Memorandum of a Conversation between the President and the Secretary of State, August 29, 1956, *ibid.*, pp. 314–315; Memorandum of Discussion at the 295th Meeting of the National Security Council, August 30, 1956, *ibid.*, pp. 324–332.

50. Memorandum of a Conversation Between the President and the Secretary of State, August 30, 1956, *ibid.*, pp. 334–335.

51. While reviewing the Middle East scene, Dulles remarked to presidential assistant Emmet Hughes, "I really don't know how much we can do. Every day that goes by without some gain, and I just keep trying to buy that day. I don't know anything to do but keep improvising." Hughes, *Ordeal of Power*, pp. 177–178.

52. Public Records Office, CAB, 134/1216, E.C.(56)22, August 22, 1956; Public Records Office, CAB 128/30, C.M.(56)62, August 28, 1956.

53. Public Records Office, CAB 134/1216, E.C.(56)23, August 28, 1956.

54. Public Records Office, PREM 11/1100, #3931, Foreign Office to Washington, August 28, 1956.

55. Department of State Press Release #450, August 28, 1956, Seely G. Mudd Library, John F. Dulles Papers, Box #110.

56. Public Records Office, PREM 11/1100, #1761, Makins to Foreign Office, August 29, 1956.

57. Public Records Office, PREM 11/1121, #1788, Trevelyan to Foreign Office, August 30, 1956.

58. Eisenhower was not sympathetic to Nasser per se, he was simply obsessed with the colonial issue. Dulles's conversation with Eisenhower on August 30 summed up the American viewpoint. Dulles stated, "I could not see any end to the situation that might be created if the British and the French occupied the Canal and parts of Egypt. They would make bitter enemies of the entire population of the Middle East and Africa. . . . The Soviet Union would reap the benefit of a greatly weakened Western Europe and would move into a position of predominant influence in the Middle East and Africa. The President said he entirely agreed with me on this basic analysis." Memorandum of a Conversation with the President, August 30, 1956, Eisenhower Library, John F. Dulles Papers, White House Memorandum Series, Box #4.

59. Memorandum of a Discussion at the 295th Meeting of the National Security Council, August 30, 1956, *FRUS*, 1955–57, XVI, 324–332.

60. Public Records Office, PREM 11/1100: Eisenhower to Eden, September

2, 1956; Public Records Office, FO 800/726; Eisenhower to Eden, September 2, 1956, *FRUS*, 1955–57, XVI, 355–358.

61. Public Records Office, PREM 11/1177, #4061, Foreign Office to Washington, September 6, 1956; Eden, *Full Circle*, pp. 516–521.

62. Public Records Office, FO 800/726, Eisenhower to Eden, September 8, 1956; Eisenhower to Eden, September 8, 1956, *FRUS*, 1955–57, XVI, 434–435. Dulles did not believe the letter from Eden was very well thought out and pointed out to the president that you could not go to war to preserve influence. Eisenhower told Dulles "that the British had gotten themselves into a box in the Middle East. They have been choosing the wrong player with which to get tough." The president mentioned Buraimi "where they had only succeeded in incurring the hatred of the Saudis." The president's position remained that Egypt could not be attacked so long as they did not hinder the running of the canal. Memorandum of a Conversation with the President, September 7, 1956, *ibid.*, pp. 403–404.

63. Accounts of the Menzies mission vary. The Egyptian view is presented by Heikal in *Cutting the Lion's Tail*, pp. 147–153, and by Mahmoud Fawzi in *Suez 1956: An Egyptian Account* (London, 1986), pp. 59–62. The Western viewpoint is provided by Sir Robert Menzies, *Afternoon Light* (New York, 1967), pp. 161–167. See a daily summary of meetings prepared by the State Department, entitled Menzies Mission Report, located in the Eisenhower Library, Ann Whitman File, International Series, Suez Summary, Box #43.

64. Memorandum of a Conversation with the President, September 7, 1956, Eisenhower Library, John F. Dulles Papers, White House Memorandum Series, Box #4. SCUA was first named CASCU. But the Portuguese pointed out that it meant "balls" in their language; and in French it sounded like "breaking-arse." Thus Dulles had to alter the name of his plan. Horne, *Macmillan*, p. 414.

65. Public Records Office, PREM 11/1100, #1823, Makins to Foreign Office, September 7, 1956. The United States position is detailed in Outline Proposal for a Voluntary Association of Canal Users, September 9, 1956, *FRUS*, 1955–57, XVI, 451–458.

66. *Ibid.* Dulles argued that we do not, "as of today know whether the Egyptian government has 'refused' to negotiate." Public Records Office, PREM 11/1100, #1830, Makins to Foreign Office, September 7, 1956.

67. Public Records Office, PREM 11/1100, #1832, Makins to Foreign Office, September 7, 1956.

68. Hoopes, *Devil and John Foster Dulles*, p. 359.

69. Public Records Office, PREM 11/1100, #4102, Foreign Office to Washington, September 8, 1956.

70. Public Records Office, PREM 11/1100, #1838, Makins to Foreign Office, September 8, 1956.

71. Memorandum of a Conference with the President, September 8, 1956, Eisenhower Library, John F. Dulles Papers, White Memorandum Series, Box #4.

72. James, *Eden*, p. 511.

73. Public Records Office, CAB 134/1216, E.C.(56)26, September 10, 1956.

74. Public Records Office, PREM 11/1101, #4159, Foreign Office to Washington, September 11, 1956; Public Records Office PREM 11/1101,

#1878, Makins to Foreign Office, September 11, 1956. Foreign Minister Pineau was highly distrustful of Dulles; he told Ambassador Jebb on September 9 "that we are really wasting our time talking with the Americans. They will never authorize any action likely to overthrow Nasser, at least until after their elections, if ever. Thus it is essential that our two countries should now go firmly ahead on our chosen path." Public Records Office, PREM 11/1100, Jebb to Foreign Office, September 9, 1956.

75. Eden, *Full Circle*, pp. 535–536; Nutting, *No End of a Lesson*, p. 62.

76. Eden, *Full Circle*, pp. 539–540; Public Records Office, PREM 11/1101, #1910, #1917, Makins to Foreign Office, September 13, 1956; James, *Eden*, pp. 514–515.

77. See Department of State Press Release #498, September 19, 1956, Seely G. Mudd Library, John F. Dulles Papers, Box #110.

78. Nutting, *No End of a Lesson*, p. 63.

79. Dulles to Eisenhower, September 20, 1956, *FRUS*, 1955–57, XVI, 544–545.

80. Public Records Office, PREM 11/1102, Record of a Conversation between Lloyd and Dulles, September 21, 1956.

81. Public Records Office, PREM 11/1102, #1979, Makins to Foreign Office, September 22, 1956.

82. Public Records Office, PREM 11/1102, #4389, Foreign Office to Washington, September 22, 1956.

83. Public Records Office, PREM 11/1102, Macmillan Private Notes to Eden, September 25 and 26, 1956. Ambassador Makins, who was in the room with Macmillan when he met with Eisenhower, claims the chancellor of the exchequer was overoptimistic about gaining Eisenhower's support. Makins argues that Macmillan misunderstood his conversations with the president. Public Records Office, PREM 11/1102, #2000, #2001, Makins to Foreign Office, September 25, 1956.

84. Department of State Press Release, #508, Seely G. Mudd Library, John F. Dulles Papers, Box #110.

85. Cooper, *Lion's Last Roar*, p. 138. Cooper states that "Eden appeared to be functioning on a level of 10% removed from reality." Anthony Nutting and David Carleton support Cooper's assessment. In addition, Donald Neff describes Eden's temper tantrums and volatile behavior accurately in *Warriors at Suez*, pp. 315–316. Robert Rhodes James provides a useful synopsis of Eden's medical history in *Eden*, pp. 362–366.

86. Public Records Office, PREM 11/1174, #2046, Makins to Foreign Office, October 2, 1956; Zinner, *Documents on American Foreign Relations 1956*, pp. 337–338; Eden, *Full Circle*, pp. 556–557. Makins reported to the Foreign Office that Dulles "drew me over this evening... and said that he wanted me to know how very unhappy he was about his press conference yesterday. In the first place he had been drawn into a line of discussion which was in itself undesirable. Secondly, his remarks had been given a connexion which he did not intend, between the colonial question and the Suez affair.... This second mistake had aggravated the effects of the first, as it limited his ability to repair the damage, though he had done what he could.... Dulles added that he thought this was the only time that he had made 'a really bad

blunder.'" Dulles's assessment is rather inaccurate. Public Records Office, FO 371/120318, #2052, Washington to Foreign Office, October 3, 1956.

87. Carleton, *Anthony Eden*, pp. 427–428.

88. Public Records Office, PREM 11/1177, #4540, Foreign Office to Washington, October 1, 1956. Eden to Eisenhower, October 1, 1956, *FRUS*, 1955–57, XVI, 618–619.

89. Memorandum of a Conversation with the President, October 2, 1956, Eisenhower Library, John F. Dulles Papers, White House Memorandum Series, Box #4.

90. *Ibid.*; Memorandum of a Conversation with the President, October 8, 1956, Eisenhower Library, Ann Whitman File, Eisenhower Diaries, October 1956, Staff Papers, Box #19.

91. *Ibid.*

92. The six principles were incorporated into the Anglo-French resolution submitted to the UN Security Council on October 13, 1956. They consisted of the following:

(1) There should be free and open transit through the canal without discrimination, overt or covert—this covers both political and technical aspects.

(2) The sovereignty of Egypt should be respected.

(3) The operation of the canal should be insulated from the politics of any country.

(4) The manner of fixing tolls and charges should be decided by agreement between Egypt and the users.

(5) A fair proportion of the dues should be allotted to development.

(6) In case of disputes, unresolved affairs between the Suez Canal Company and the Egyptian government should be settled by arbitration with suitable terms of reference and suitable provisions for the payment of sums to be due. Nutting, *No End of a Lesson*, pp). 184–186. For the course of United Nations debate, see Public Records Office, CAB 134/1216, E.C.(56)33, October 8, 1956; Public Records Office, PREM 11/1102, E.C.(56)34, October 10, 1956.

93. Dulles to Dillon, October 4, 1956, *FRUS*, 1955–57, XVI, 634–637. Dulles continued that "the Western European nations have been preserving their political divisions which keep them weak, partly because they felt they could afford this luxury so long as they had more or less a blank check on the United States, or economic, military, and political support elsewhere in the world." Suez brought out in the open the fact that Britain and France could not count upon the United States outside the NATO treaty. The Secretary of State concluded that "under those circumstances they feel weak and frustrated. . . . We should not try and buy pro-Americanism by providing blanket support."

94. Public Records Office, PREM 11/1102, #1078, Foreign Office to New York, October 8, 1956.

95. Public Records Office, PREM 11/1102, Record of a Conversation Between Lloyd, Dulles, and Pineau, October 5, 1956; Memorandum of a Conversation, October 5, 1956, *FRUS*, 1955–57, XVI, 639–645.

96. Public Records Office, W032/16709, #801, Lloyd to Eden, October 8, 1956.

97. Public Records Office, PREM 11/1121, #847, Dixon to Foreign Office, October 13, 1956.

98. Summary of Developments in the Suez Situation, #29, October 12,

1956, Eisenhower Library, Ann Whitman File, International Series, Suez Summary, Box #43.

99. Memorandum from the Secretary of State's Special Assistant for Intelligence to the Secretary of State, December 5, 1956, *FRUS*, 1955–57, XVI, 1249–1271, is a retrospective analysis of Anglo-French-Israeli collusion leading up to Suez, particularly pp. 1252–1263. The Israeli-French connection, which had developed two years earlier, was reinforced during the spring of 1956. With Nasser's activity in Algeria and his refusal to end the blockade of the canal against Israel, the two nations found a community of fate. In addition, the French believed that Israel could be useful in counterbalancing the British in the region. During meetings with Israeli officials in June and September the French agreed to supply the Israelis with massive amounts of weapons, including two hundred AMX tanks, seventy-two Mystere IV planes, forty thousand 75 mm. shells, and ten thousand SS-10 antitank missiles at a cost of $80 million. The French also agreed to exchange intelligence information as well as military planning. Bar-Zohar, *Ben-Gurion*, pp. 228–229; Dayan, *Story of My Life*, pp. 190–191. For an excellent summary of the evolution of Israeli-French relations, see Crosbie, *France and Israel from Suez to the Six Day War*.

100. Bar-Zohar, *Ben-Gurion*, pp. 230–232; Dayan, *Story of My Life*, pp. 193–196.

101. Nutting, *No End of a Lesson*, p. 93; Cooper, *Lion's Last Roar*, p. 147. In January 1987 the Public Records Office in London made available to historians numerous documents dealing with the Suez crisis. But they included few dealing with the period October 14 through 24.

102. Public Records Office, FO 800/75, Meeting in Paris Between Eden, Mollet, Pineau, and Lloyd, October 16, 1956; Eden, *Full Circle*, pp. 569–572; Lloyd, *Suez*, pp. 173–174.

103. *Ibid.*; see Memorandum from the Secretary of State's Special Assistant for Intelligence to the Secretary of State, December 5, 1956, *FRUS*, 1955–57, XVI, 1263–1266; Memorandum by the Director of Central Intelligence, November 16, 1956, *ibid.*, pp. 1135–1137.

104. *Ibid.*

105. Dayan, *Story of My Life*, p. 212.

106. *Ibid.*

107. Public Records Office, CAB 128/30, C.M.(56)71, October 18, 1956.

108. Dayan, *Story of My Life*, pp. 219, 181–185; Nutting, *No End of a Lesson*, pp. 101–102.

109. Public Records Office, FO 800/75, Lloyd Foreign Office Minute, October 23, 1956; Dayan, *Story of My Life*, pp. 222–223.

110. The Sevres Protocol consisted of the following:

"On the afternoon of October 29th Israeli forces would launch a full-scale attack on Egyptian forces.

"On October 30th the British and French governments would appeal to Egypt for an absolute ceasefire, the withdrawal of forces ten miles from the Canal, and acceptance of the temporary occupation of the key positions on the Canal by Anglo-French forces.

"There would, simultaneously, be an appeal to the Government of Israel for an absolute ceasefire and withdrawal of forces to ten miles east of the Canal.

"If either of the two governments rejected the appeal, or failed to give its agreement within twelve hours, the Anglo-French forces would intervene; if the Egyptians refused, the Anglo-French forces would attack early on October 31st.

"Israel agreed not to attack Jordan, but if Jordan attacked Israel the British would not go to Jordan's assistance, as the Anglo-Jordanian Treaty referred specifically to the defence of Jordan against Israeli (or other) attack.

"Israeli forces would seize the western shore of the Gulf of Aqaba and ensure the control of the Gulf of Tiran." The protocol is reprinted in James, *Eden*, p. 531.

111. Public Records Office, CAB 128/30, C.M.(56)73, October 24, 1956.

112. Public Records Office, CAB 128/30, C.M.(56)74, October 25, 1956.

113. James, *Eden*, pp. 532–533.

114. Memorandum of a Discussion at the 300th Meeting of the National Security Council, October 12, 1956, *FRUS*, 1955–57, XVI, 701–704. See Hahn, *The United States, Great Britain, and Egypt*, pp. 224–230, for an excellent synthesis explaining why the U.S. appeared to be caught by surprise by the Israeli invasion and subsequent action by the British and French.

115. Memorandum from the Secretary of State's Special Assistant for Intelligence to the Secretary of State, December 5, 1956, *FRUS*, 1955–57, XVI, 1264; See *ibid.*, p. 1271, for a detailed discussion of the American view of Anglo-French deception from October 16 through October 29, 1956.

116. Memorandum of a Conversation with the President, October 15, 1956, Eisenhower Library, John F. Dulles Papers, White House Memorandum Series, Box #4. The Israelis effectively used misinformation and troop movements to make the United States believe that if there was to be an attack, it would be against Jordan, not Egypt.

117. John F. Dulles–Allen W. Dulles Phone Conversation, October 18, 1956, Eisenhower Library, John F. Dulles Papers, Telephone Conversation Memorandum, Box #5. Throughout October preparations continued for a CIA-arranged coup against the Syrian government. According to Wilbur Eveland, the target date was October 29. See Eveland, *Ropes of Sand*, pp. 223–230; and Neff, *Warriors at Suez*, pp. 317–318, 338–339, 352–354.

118. Memorandum of a Conversation with the President, October 21, 1956, Eisenhower Library, John F. Dulles Papers, White House Memorandum Series, Box #4.

119. Memorandum from the Director of the National Indications Center to the Intelligence Advisory Committee, NIC #6-2237, October 26, 1956, *FRUS*, 1955–57, XVI, 787–788.

120. Memorandum From the Director of the National Indications Center to the Intelligence Advisory Committee, NIC #T5-6-372, October 28, 1956, *ibid.*, pp. 799–800.

121. Dillon to Department of State, #1853, *ibid.*, pp. 760–761.

122. Eisenhower to Ben-Gurion, October 27, 1956, Eisenhower Library, Ann Whitman File, International Series, Israel, Box #29.

123. Dulles to Dillon, #1537, October 29, 1956, *FRUS*, 1955–57, XVI, 815–816.

8. American Ascendancy

1. Public Records Office, FO 371/121783, #3780, Foreign Office to Cairo, October 30, 1956.

2. Public Records Office, FO 371/121783, #2590, Foreign Office to Cairo, October 30, 1956; Trevelyan, *The Middle East in Revolution*, pp. 114–115.

3. Dulles's anger with the British stemmed in part from events in Hungary. He informed the British embassy, "Just when the Soviet orbit was crumbling and we could point to a contrast between the western world and the Soviets, it looked as though the west was producing a similar situation." All of Dulles's beliefs concerning the Russians and their Eastern European empire were now being realized—but they were obscured by the Suez War. Public Records Office, PREM 11/1105, #2206, Washington to Foreign Office, October 30, 1956.

4. Eveland, *Ropes of Sand*, pp. 225–227. On October 29, 1956, Eveland's contact in Syria told him, "The Israelis invaded Egypt and are right now heading for the Suez Canal! How could you have asked us to overthrow our government at the exact moment when Israel started a war with an Arab state." P. 227. On October 30, in a phone conversation with Roundtree, Dulles informed him that the United States should not proceed with the coup. Roundtree-Dulles Phone Conversation, October 30, 1956, Eisenhower Library, John F. Dulles Papers, Telephone Conversation Memorandum, Box #5. A few minutes later Dulles called his brother Allen and said, "Our people feel that the conditions are such it would be a mistake to try and pull it off." The British, who were also involved with the coup, wanted to proceed. John F. Dulles–Allen W. Dulles Phone Conversation, October 30, 1956, Eisenhower Library, John F. Dulles Papers, Telephone Conversation Memorandum, Box #5.

5. Memorandum of a Conference with the President, October 29, 1956, Eisenhower Library, John F. Dulles Papers, White Memorandum Series, Box #4. It was obvious from the start that the British had chosen to go their own way. During the evening of October 29, Henry Cabot Lodge, the American representative at the United Nations, spoke with his British counterpart Piers Dixon. Lodge asked if London intended to honor the Tripartite Declaration. He was taken aback when Dixon stated, "Don't be silly and moralistic. We have got to be practical. . . . The United Kingdom would never go along with action against Israel in the Security Council." Dulles-Lodge Phone Conversation, October 29, 1956, Eisenhower Library, John F. Dulles Papers, Telephone Conversation Memorandum, Box #5.

6. Memorandum of a Conference with the President, October 29, 1956, Eisenhower Library, Ann Whitman Files, Eisenhower Diaries, October 1956, Staff Memos, Box #19.

7. For the text of the resolution, see *FRUS*, 1955–57, XVI, 881. The full text of the British ultimatum to the Egyptians reads:

"The Governments of the United Kingdom and France are resigned to do all in their power to bring about the early cessation of hostilities and to safeguard the free passage of the canal.

"They accordingly request the Government of Egypt:

"(a) to stop all warlike action on land, sea and air forthwith;

"(b) to withdraw all Egyptian military forces to a distance ten miles from the canal;

"(c) in order to guarantee freedom of transit through the canal for the ships of all nations and in order to separate the belligerents, to accept the temporary occupation by Anglo-French forces of key positions at Port Said, Ismailia and Suez.

"The United Kingdom and French governments request an answer to this communication within 12 hours. If at the expiration of that time one or both governments have not undertaken to comply with the above requirements, United Kingdom and French forces will intervene in whatever strength may be necessary to secure compliance.

"A similar communication has been sent to the government of Israel."

Public Records Office, FO 371/121783, #3780, Foreign Office to Cairo, October 30, 1956.

8. Dulles-Eisenhower Phone Conversation, October 30, 1956, Eisenhower Library, Ann Whitman Files, Eisenhower Diaries, Telephone Conversation Memorandum, Box #19.

9. Public Records Office, PREM 11/1105 or 11/1177, #5025, Foreign Office to Washington, October 30, 1956.

10. Eisenhower, *Waging Peace*, p. 77. Three hours before it was presented in the House of Commons, Eden sent a telegram to Eisenhower to inform him of the ultimatum announcement. Due to decoding delays it did not reach the president in time. This mistake just fueled Eisenhower's anger with and mistrust of Eden. Eden to Eisenhower, October 30, 1956, *FRUS*, 1955–57, XVI, 871–872.

11. Memorandum of a Conference with the President, October 30, 1956, Eisenhower Library, Ann Whitman Files, Eisenhower Diaries, Box #19. Eisenhower's true feelings emerge in a letter to his friend Swede Hazlett, in which he wrote, "I think that the French and British have made a terrible mistake. Because they have such a poor case, they have isolated themselves from the good opinion of the world and it will take them many years to recover. France was perfectly cold-blooded about the matter. She was anxious to get someone else fighting the Arabs from the east, due to her war in Algeria, and was ready to do anything to get England and Israel in that affair. . . . We have handed the Soviet Union opportunities because of this and have an additional chance to embarrass the western world beyond measure." Robert Griffith, ed., *Ike's Letters to a Friend* (Lawrence, Kans., 1984), pp. 174–175.

12. Hughes, *Ordeal of Power*, p. 219.

13. Public Records Office, CAB 130/28, C.M.(56)75, October 30, 1956.

14. Leslie Rowan Treasury Minute, October 30, 1956, Records of the Treasury Department, T236/4188, Public Records Office, London, United Kingdom (henceforth Public Records Office, Treasury Office, followed by file #). American approval was needed to obtain funds from the IMF. In addition, see Diane B. Kuntz, "The Importance of Having Money: The Economic Diplomacy of the Suez Crisis," in William Roger Louis and Roger Owen, ed., *Suez 1956: The Crisis and Consequences* (Oxford, 1989), pp. 216–225.

15. Public Records Office, CAB 128/30, C.M.(56)76, October 30, 1956.

16. Robert A. Divine, *Eisenhower and the Cold War* (New York, 1981), p. 85.

17. Nixon-Dulles Phone Conversation, October 31, 1956, Eisenhower Library, John F. Dulles Papers, Telephone Memorandum Series, Box #5.

18. Dulles Address to the General Assembly, November 1, 1956, Department of State Publication #6505, pp. 151–157; Public Records Office, FO 371/118902, #1008, Dixon to Foreign Office, November 1, 1956. Zinner, *Documents*, p. 346; for the November 2 resolution, see *ibid.*, pp. 350–351.

19. Eisenhower to Dulles, November 1, 1956, Eisenhower Library, Ann Whitman Files, Dulles-Herter Series, Box #6; Memorandum of a Discussion at the 302nd Meeting of the National Security Council, November 1, 1956, Eisenhower Library, Ann Whitman Files, NSC Series, Box #8.

20. Public Records Office, T236/4188, Leslie Rowan Treasury Minute, November 2, 1956.

21. Public Records Office, PREM 11/1105, E.C.(56)36, November 3, 1956; Memorandum of a Conversation, November 3, 1956, *FRUS*, 1955–57, XVI, 953–954.

22. Public Records Office, PREM 11/1105, E.C.(56)38, November 3, 1956.

23. Public Records Office, PREM 11/1105, E.C.(56)40, November 4, 1956; CAB 128/30, C.M.(56)79, November 4, 1956. The United Kingdom had to act immediately, because if it "postponed the attack for even 24 hours world opinion would make it difficult to resume it."

24. Eden wrote Eisenhower, "I am convinced that, if we had allowed things to drift, everything would have gone from bad to worse. Nasser would have become a kind of Moslem Mussolini and our friends in Iraq, Jordan, Saudi Arabia, and even Iran would gradually have been brought down. His efforts would have spread westwards, and Lybia and all of North Africa would have been brought under his control." Public Records Office, PREM 11/1105, #5181, Foreign Office to Washington, November 5, 1956; Eden to Eisenhower, November 5, 1956, *FRUS*, 1955–57, XVI, 984–986.

25. Memorandum of a Conference with the President, November 5, 1956, Eisenhower Library, Ann Whitman Files, November 1956 Staff Papers, Box #19.

26. Eisenhower to Eden, November 5, 1956, *FRUS*, 1955–57, XVI, 989–990.

27. Public Records Office, CAB 128/30, C.M.(56)80, T236/4190, Note of a Meeting at 11 Downing Street, November 6, 1956; Lloyd, *Suez*, pp. 209–211; Nutting, *No End of a Lesson*, pp. 144–146; Kuntz, "Importance of Having Money," p. 227.

28. Kuntz, "Importance of Having Money," p. 228.

29. James, *Eden*, p. 573; Horne, *Macmillan*, p. 442.

30. "The implied Soviet threat to employ rockets was hardly a credible one. The Soviets in 1956 had only one long-distance rocket in large quantity—the T-1 (M-101), a single-stage, liquid-fueled rocket of the German V-2 type, capable of delivering an eight-hundred-pound nuclear warhead some 450 miles. Longer-range IRBMs had been tested but had not yet been deployed on any scale." Jon D. Glassman, *Arms for the Arabs* (New York, 1975), p. 16.

31. In their memoirs both Eden and Macmillan argue that the United Kingdom agreed to a cease-fire because "we had intervened to divide and, above all, to contain the conflict. The occasion for our intervention was over,

264 NOTES TO CHAPTER EIGHT

the fire was out." Eden, *Full Circle*, p. 557. Macmillan commented, "There was no escape from this conclusion." Harold Macmillan, *Riding the Storm* (New York, 1971), p. 165.

32. Public Records Office, FO 371/121274, Eden to Eisenhower, November 6, 1956, Telephone Conversation Between Eisenhower and Eden, November 6, 1956, *FRUS*, 1955–57, XVI, 1025–1027.

33. Memorandum for the Record, November 7, 1956, Declassified Documents Reserve System, (81) 275A WH.

34. Public Records Office, T236/4190, The Foreign Exchange Market, November 8, 1956.

35. Public Records Office, T236/4189, #2271, #2272, Caccia to Foreign Office, November 8, 1956.

36. Memorandum of a Discussion at the 303rd Meeting of the National Security Council, November 8, 1956, Eisenhower Library, Ann Whitman Files, NSC Series, Box #8.

37. *Ibid.*

38. *Ibid.*; Special National Intelligence Estimate, "Outlook for the Syrian Situation," SNIE 36.7-56, November 6, 1956, CIA, Freedom of Information Act. The Soviet Union was now focusing on Syria. Intelligence reports stated that leftist-oriented, extreme nationalist, anti-Western politicians and their counterparts in the army were overshadowing pro-Western forces in Syria. Due to the Suez situation the locus of power seemed to be in the hands of a pro-Egyptian "little RCC" group headed by Lieutenant Colonel Sarraj, the head of Syrian intelligence. Pro-Soviet elements were moving close to consolidating their hold on the government. The pro-Western forces were divided and had weak leadership. The report concluded that Syria was ripe for a pro-Soviet coup.

39. Public Records Office, CAB 128/30, C.M.(56)82, November 8, 1956.

40. *Ibid.*

41. Ferrell, *Eisenhower Diaries*, pp. 333–334; Cole Christian Kingseed, "Eisenhower and Suez: A Reappraisal of Presidential Activism and Crisis Management," Ph.D. dissertation, Ohio State University, 1983, pp. 184–185.

42. Public Records Office, CAB 134/1216, E.C.(56)83, November 12, 1956; CAB 128/30, C.M.(56)83, November 13, 1956.

43. Public Records Office, FO 371/118873 or PREM 11/1106, #1216, Dixon to Foreign Office, November 14, 1956.

44. The secretary-general's position was summed up in a November 13 internal memorandum. Hammarskjöld wrote that "the United Nations force had no function in the Canal area after the withdrawal of the Anglo-French forces," and they could not return without the "consent of the Egyptian government." Public Records Office, CAB 134/1217, Hammarskjöld Internal Memorandum, November 13, 1956. Hammarskjöld's position was clear: there would be no link between the UNEF, clearance of the canal, and an arrangement for a future canal regime. Public Records Office, PREM 11/1106, #1218, Dixon to Foreign Office, November 14, 1956.

45. Public Records Office, CAB 134/1216, E.C.(56)44, November 15, 1956.

46. *Ibid.*

47. Aldrich to the Department of State, #2782, *FRUS*, 1955–57, XVI, 1142–1143.

48. Public Records Office, T236/4190, Message from Macmillan to Humphrey, November 19, 1956. Macmillan was exceptionally open with Humphrey, who was one of the leaders in the Eisenhower administration advocating economic pressure on the United Kingdom. Perhaps Macmillan thought to improve Anglo-American relations in the hope he would benefit should he one day become prime minister.

49. Public Records Office, T236/4190, Macmillan's Statement in Cabinet, November 19, 1956; T236/4190, Notes of a Meeting at the Treasury, November 19, 1956.

50. Public Records Office, CAB 134/1216, E.C.(56)45, November 16, 1956.

51. Public Records Office, FO 371/120342, D. A. H. Wright Foreign Office Minute, U.S.A. and the Middle East, November 15, 1956.

52. Memorandum of a Conversation with the President, November 17, 1956, Eisenhower Library, John F. Dulles Papers, White Memorandum Series, Box #4.

53. Aldrich to the Department of State, #2791, November 19, 1956, *FRUS*, 1955–57, XVI, 1150–1152.

54. Aldrich-Hoover Phone Conversation, November 19, 1956, Eisenhower Library, Ann Whitman Files, Dulles-Herter Series, Box #6.

55. *Ibid.*

56. Aldrich to the Department of State, #2814, November 19, 1956, *FRUS*, 1955–57, XVI, 1163.

57. Humphrey-Eisenhower Phone Conversation, November 19, 1956, Eisenhower Library, Ann Whitman Files, Dulles-Herter Series, Box #6.

58. Neff, *Warriors at Suez*, pp. 424–426. I agree with Neff that "the conservative leaders and the Eisenhower administration now began a secret collusion of their own. Its purpose was to keep the Conservative government in power in Britain." *Ibid.*, p. 425.

59. Memorandum of a Conference with the President, November 20, 1956, Eisenhower Library, Ann Whitman Files, Eisenhower Diaries, November 1956, Staff Memos, Box #19.

60. *Ibid.*

61. *Ibid.*

62. Memorandum of a Conference with the President, November 21, 1956, Eisenhower Library, Ann Whitman Files, Eisenhower Diaries, November 1956, Staff Memos, Box #19.

63. Public Records Office, CAB 128/30, C.M.(56)85, November 20, 1956. Treasury officials wanted the United States to realize this "confidence" was based on their reserves. Washington knew that after increasing by $265 million in the first half of the year, London's dollar reserves had fallen by $318 million during the July-October period. Even without a further loss of confidence, reserves might fall below $1.75 billion. The reserves had been hit by the persistent drawing down of sterling balances by nonsterling countries. The treasury pointed out that between the end of 1954 and September 1956, the holdings of the nonsterling countries fell some 160 million pounds sterling. In the third quarter of 1956 alone they fell 35 million pounds sterling.

64. Hoover to Aldrich, November 23, 1956, #3666, Eisenhower Library, Ann Whitman Files, Subject Series, Suez Crisis, Box #82. Eisenhower told Hoover to inform Caccia that "we will help them out with oil if they are '4

square' with the UN." Memorandum of a Conversation with the President, November 23, 1956, Eisenhower Library, Ann Whitman Files, Eisenhower Diaries, November 1956, Staff Memos, Box #19. Public Records Office, PREM 11/1106, #2334, Caccia to Foreign Office, November 23, 1956; T236/4190, #2335, Caccia to Foreign Office, November 23, 1956.

65. Public Records Office, T236/4190, #2355, #2356, Caccia to Foreign Office, November 27, 1956.

66. Public Records Office, CAB 128/30, C.M.(56)90, November 28, 1956.

67. Public Records Office, T236/4190, Rowan to Makins, November 30, 1956.

68. Public Records Office, CAB 128/30, C.M.(56)93, Draft Statement for the Foreign Secretary, November 30, 1956. Lloyd rationalized, "Our two main objectives have been met: stopping the fighting and stopping the spread of a small into a major war. We have helped create an international police force for the Canal. We made it clear that all resources we have will be made available to the team created by the Secretary-General to help clear the Canal. It appears to us that the clearance of the Canal will begin as soon as technically possible and will not be dependent upon other considerations." Lloyd seems to have forgotten American pressure to obtain British withdrawal.

69. Horne, *Macmillan*, p. 452.

70. Public Records Office, T236/4190, Record of Discussion at the Hotel Talleyrand, December 11, 1956.

71. A major controversy which emerged during the period is whether the Eisenhower administration, in alliance with Harold Macmillan, arranged the removal of Anthony Eden from office. Although the documentation is not clear-cut, there is sufficient evidence to suggest that Washington was heavily involved behind the scenes. Donald Neff supports this view; others, including David Carleton, Alistair Horne, and Richard Lamb in *The Failure of the Eden Government* (London, 1987), do not.

72. Horne, *Macmillan*, p. 458.

73. Thomas G. Paterson, *Meeting the Communist Threat: Truman to Reagan* (New York, 1988), p. 177.

74. Ferrell, *Eisenhower Diaries*, pp. 334–335.

75. Eisenhower to Dulles, December 12, 1956, Eisenhower Library, Ann Whitman Files, Eisenhower Diaries, Box #20.

76. *Ibid.*

77. Dulles-Eisenhower Phone Conversation, December 8, 1956, Eisenhower Library, John F. Dulles Papers, Telephone Memorandum Series, Box #11.

78. *Ibid.*

79. Bipartisan Meeting of Congressional Leaders, January 1, 1956, Eisenhower Library, Ann Whitman Files, Legislative Meeting Series, Box #2.

80. *Ibid.* Miles Copeland's reaction to the Eisenhower Doctrine is interesting. Copeland writes, "To this day, I do not know who originated the idea. . . . All of us were quite prepared to believe that the plan might have made sense in some subtle and delicate domestic political context beyond the ken of us 'field people,' but in the light of extant intelligence on the Arab world it made no sense at all. As I remember, the Middle East hands were fairly unanimous about this. When the CIA representative on the MEPPC [Middle East Policy

Planning Council] was asked, 'Would you fellows like to send someone along on the mission that was going out to explain it to Arab chiefs of state?' he replied, 'We can't afford to associate ourselves with every lunatic scheme that comes along.'" Copeland, *Game of Nations*, pp. 215–216.

81. U.S. Department of State Bulletin, #6505, Eisenhower Address to the Joint Session of the 85th Congress, January 5, 1957, pp. 15–23. A copy of House Joint Resolution 117, 85th Congress, 1st Session, can be found in Eisenhower Library, John F. Dulles Papers, Subject Series, Box #5.

82. See Nadav Safran, *Saudi Arabia: The Ceaseless Quest for Security* (Cambridge, Mass., 1985), pp. 82–85.

83. Eisenhower's Notes from Talks with Saud, January 30, 1957, Eisenhower Library, Ann Whitman Files, Dulles-Herter Series, Box #6.

84. Joint Chiefs of Staff, Memorandum for Admiral Radford, August 14, 1957, Declassified Documents Reserve System 1979 Collection, 380C. See also U.S. Department of State, Draft Statement Resulting from Discussions Between King Saud and President Eisenhower, February 7, 1957, Declassified Documents Reserve System, 1982 Collection, 000329; Eisenhower, *Waging Peace*, p. 120.

85. Memorandum of Discussion at the 310th Meeting of the National Security Council, January 24, 1957, *FRUS*, 1955–57, XVII, 47–51.

86. Eisenhower, *Waging Peace*, p. 184.

87. Eisenhower to Ben-Gurion, February 3, 1957, *FRUS*, 1955–57, XVII, 82–84.

88. Ben-Gurion to Eisenhower, February 8, 1957, *ibid.*, pp. 109–112.

89. Aide-Memoire to Israel, February 11, 1957, Eisenhower Library, John F. Dulles Papers, Subject Series, Box #7.

90. Memorandum of a Conversation at Thomasville, Ga., February 16, 1957, Eisenhower Library, John F. Dulles Papers, Subject Series, Box #7; Eisenhower, *Waging Peace*, p. 185. American private gifts to Israel were about $40 million a year; sales of Israel bonds in the United States were between $50 million and $60 million a year. *Ibid.*, p. 186.

91. See Abba Eban, *An Autobiography* (New York, 1977), pp. 245–256; Eban Visits Dean, February 18, 1957, Eisenhower Library, John F. Dulles Papers, Telephone Conversation Memorandum, Box #6; Dean-Dulles Phone Conversation, February 19, 1957, *ibid.*; Draft Talks with Eban, February 24, 1957, *ibid.*; Bipartisan Legislative Meeting, February 20, 1957, Eisenhower Library, Ann Whitman File, Legislative Meeting Series, January–February 1957, Box #2.

92. David Ben-Gurion, *Israel: A Personal History*, pp. 531–532.

Epilogue

1. Meyer, *Egypt and the United States*, p. 192.
2. Paterson, *Meeting the Communist Threat*, pp. 186–189.
3. *Ibid.*, pp. 180–181.
4. Hoopes, *Devil and John Foster Dulles*, p. 362.

A Note on Sources

The Suez crisis was a seminal event of the post–World War II era. Its complex workings involved superpower confrontation, a major split among the Atlantic allies, Third World nationalism, the Arab-Israeli conflict, and the possibility of pro-Western military coups in the Middle East. In trying to make sense of these events, the historian has had to wait more than thirty years for the necessary sources to become available. Only recently have the United States and United Kingdom released important documents which bear directly on Anglo-American relations and the crisis itself.

In 1987, when the British opened their files on Suez, historians flocked to the Public Records Office in London. The materials are voluminous. If one examines the Administrative Files, the Cabinet Papers, Cabinet Minutes, Defence Files, Foreign Office Files, Prime Minister's Papers, Treasury Papers, War Office Files, and, most important, the Egypt Committee papers, one hopes to emerge with a complete picture. Yet certain important files are still closed. Subjects such as Anglo-Egyptian negotiations, the Baghdad Pact, and Project ALPHA can be accurately assessed, and the Suez crisis itself can be easily pieced together. But the most glaring deficiency involves the Egypt Committee materials. After sifting through the Egypt Committee files and minutes, one is left with the feeling that another archive is hidden away and will be made available at a future date. The most disconcerting gap is the period October 14 through 24, 1956, on which few documents have been released.

On the American side, during the past two years significant new archival materials have been made public. Particularly important has been the appearance of the *Foreign Relations of the United States* volumes dealing with the Middle East between 1952 and 1957. The background material for the crisis receives major coverage in *FRUS*, 1952–54, XIV (Washington, D.C., 1986). The Baghdad Pact or northern-tier option, relations with Egypt, and Project ALPHA are explored in *FRUS*, 1955–57, XIV, (Washington, D.C., 1989). The development and failure of the Anderson mission and the American withdrawal of the Aswan Dam loan are featured in *FRUS*, 1955–57, XV (Washington, D.C., 1989). The negotiations leading to the invasion of Suez, the invasion itself, and American pressure on the British culminating in the resignation of Anthony Eden are dealt with in *FRUS*, 1955–57, XVI (Washington, D.C., 1990). Finally, the Eisenhower Doctrine, the Saudi option, and Israeli withdrawal from Sinai are presented in *FRUS*, 1955–57, XVII (Washington, D.C., 1990). Other important volumes in the series include *FRUS, 1949–51* (Washington, D.C., 1957); *FRUS, The Suez Canal Problem, July 26–September 22, 1956: Documents* (Washington, D.C., 1957); and *FRUS, United States Policy in the Middle East, September 1956–June, 1957* (Washington, D.C., 1957).

The Eisenhower Presidential Library, located in Abilene, Kansas, is an excellent archival resource for Anglo-American relations during the period. After examining the Ann Whitman File (Administrative Series and Ann Whitman Diary Series), Cabinet Series, Dulles-Herter Series, Eisenhower Diaries, International Series, Legislative Series, National Security Council Series, Subject Series, and oral histories, the historian emerges with a reasonably complete picture of American policymaking. The John Foster Dulles Papers (Subject Series, Telephone Memorandum Series, and White House Memorandum Series) are also of interest. Of major importance in following the ebb and flow of American strategy are the White House Office, National Security Council Staff: Papers, 1948–1961, and the White House Office: Office of the Special Assistant for National Security Affairs, Records, 1952–1961 NSC Series, Policy Papers Subseries.

The John Foster Dulles Papers and oral histories housed at the Seely G. Mudd Library, Princeton, New Jersey, are also invaluable. Of interest are the General Correspondence and Memoranda Series, Selected Correspondence and Related Materials, Telephone Conversations Memoranda, White House Memoranda Series, and Meetings with the President. The use of the *Declassified Documents Reference System* (Washington, D.C., 1975–1981) and *Declassified Documents Reference System* (Woodbridge, Conn., 1982–1989) are also helpful.

Diaries and memoirs have appeared from most of the major participants in the Suez crisis. On the British side, Anthony Eden, *Full Circle* (Boston, 1960) is a self-serving account. Selwyn Lloyd, *Suez 1956: A Personal Account* (London, 1978) is both inaccurate and distorted in several areas. For insight into Eden's behavior, Anthony Nutting, *No End of a Lesson: The Inside Story of the Suez Crisis* (New York, 1967) is interesting. Harold Macmillan, *Riding the Storm, 1956– 1959* (New York, 1969) is a justification of his position and is not always reliable. Humphrey Trevelyan, *The Middle East in Revolution* (New York, 1970) is useful, but perhaps the most valuable memoir is Evelyn Shuckburgh, *Descent to Suez: Diaries 1951–1956* (London, 1986).

On the American side, Dean Acheson, *Present at the Creation: My Years in the State Department* (New York, 1969) is helpful for an understanding of the infighting in the Truman administration. Winthrop Aldrich, "The Suez Crisis: A Footnote to History," *Foreign Affairs*, January 1967, provides insights into behind-the-scenes events during the November 1956 discussions of Anthony Eden's status. Sherman Adams, *Firsthand Report* (London, 1962) provides some of the internal debate in the White House. Dwight D. Eisenhower, *Mandate for Change, 1953–1956* (New York, 1963) and *Waging Peace, 1956–1961* (New York, 1965), and Robert Ferrell, ed., *The Eisenhower Diaries* (New York, 1981) are particularly useful in presenting the correspondence between Eden and the president. But, as in most presidential memoirs, Eisenhower's focus is rather narrow. Other accounts which should be explored are Waldemar J. Gallman, *Iraq Under General Nuri: My Recollections of Nuri al-Said, 1954–1958* (Baltimore, 1964); Robert Murphy, *Diplomat Among Warriors* (New York, 1964); and Archie Roosevelt, *For Lust of Knowing: Memoirs of an Intelligence Officer* (Boston, 1988).

The French contribution includes André Beaufre, *The Suez Expedition, 1956* (New York, 1969), and Christian Pineau *1956 Suez* (Paris, 1976), which expresses French anger and frustration toward the United States. For Israel, David Ben-Gurion, *Israel: A Personal History* (Tel Aviv, 1971) and *Israel: Years of Challenge* (New York, 1963) has relevant chapters, and *My Talks with Arab Leaders* (New York, 1973) presents a daily account of the Anderson mission which has been substantiated by later documentation. Moshe Dayan, *Diary of the Sinai Campaign* (New York, 1965) and *Story of My Life* (New York, 1976) are useful in putting together the Sevres conspiracy. Abba Eban, *An Autobiography* (New York, 1977) and Gideon Rafael, *Destination Peace: Three Decades of Israeli Foreign Policy* (New York, 1981) should be consulted. For Egypt, Mohammed Naguib, *Egypt's Destiny* (New

York, 1955), and Gamal Abdel Nasser, "The Egyptian Revolution," *Foreign Affairs*, January 1955, are useful for the early years. Of major importance in understanding Nasser's mind-set are the books of his trusted confidant, Mohamed Heikal—*The Cairo Documents* (New York, 1973) and *Cutting the Lion's Tail: Suez Through Egyptian Eyes* (London, 1986). Lastly, Mohammad Fawzi, *Suez 1956: An Egyptian Perspective* (London, 1956) repeats the Egyptian viewpoint.

In trying to gain an understanding of the attitudes of the historical actors involved, I suggest a number of works. For Eisenhower and Dulles, see H. W. Brands, Jr., *Cold Warriors: Eisenhower's Generation and American Foreign Policy* (New York, 1988); "What Eisenhower and Dulles Saw in Nasser: Personalities and Interests in U.S.-Egyptian Relations," *American-Arab Affairs*, Summer 1986; and David Mayers and Richard A. Melanson, *Reevaluating Eisenhower: American Foreign Policy in the 1950s* (Chicago, 1987). For Dulles, see John Foster Dulles, *War and Peace* (New York, 1965) and "A Policy of Boldness," *Life*, May 19, 1952. For the development of Dulles's ideological perspective, Mark Toulouse, *The Transformation of John Foster Dulles: From Prophet of Realism to Priest of Nationalism* (Atlanta, 1985) is without peer. A closeup of Anthony Eden's thought processes is presented by Owen Harries, "Anthony Eden and the Decline of Britain," *Commentary*, June 1987. Robert Rhodes James, *Anthony Eden* (London, 1986) is very sympathetic to Eden; Nutting, *No End of a Lesson*, and Shuckburgh, *Descent to Suez*, present a more balanced appraisal. To understand Nasser, Gamal Abdel Nasser, *The Philosophy of Revolution* (New York, 1959) is essential as is Miles Copeland, *The Game of Nations* (New York, 1969).

Biographies of the major participants abound. Among the most important are Stephen Ambrose, *Eisenhower the President* (New York, 1984); Piers Brendon, *Ike: His Life and Times* (New York, 1986); William Bragg Ewald, *Eisenhower the President* (Englewood Cliffs, N.J., 1981); Peter Lyons, *Eisenhower: Portrait of a Hero* (Boston, 1974); and Herbert Parmet, *Eisenhower and the American Crusades* (New York, 1972). For Dulles, the most convincing account is Townsend Hoopes, *The Devil and John Foster Dulles* (Boston, 1973). Others include J. R. Beal, *John Foster Dulles* (New York, 1957); Andrew Berding, *Dulles on Diplomacy* (Princeton, 1965); Louis L. Gerson, *John Foster Dulles* (New York, 1967); Richard Goold-Adams, *John Foster Dulles: A Reappraisal* (New York, 1962), and Michael Guhin, *John Foster Dulles: A Statesman and His Times* (New York, 1972). Ronald W. Pruessen, *John Foster Dulles: The Road to Power* (New

York, 1982) is essential for understanding Dulles's background before becoming secretary of state. Richard Immerman has edited an excellent collection of articles, *John Foster Dulles and the Diplomacy of the Cold War* (Princeton, 1990).

Historians have long argued whether Dulles or Eisenhower was in charge of foreign affairs. The latest works all seem to agree that Eisenhower was responsible for American Middle East policy. For this viewpoint, consult Richard Immerman, "Eisenhower and Dulles: Who Made the Decisions?" *Political Psychology*, Autumn 1979; Barton J. Bernstein, "Foreign Policy in the Eisenhower Administration," *Foreign Service Journal*, May 1973; Robert A. Divine, *Eisenhower and the Cold War* (New York, 1981); and Cole Christian Kingseed, "Eisenhower and Suez: A Reappraisal of Presidential Activism and Crisis Management," Ph.D. dissertation, Ohio State University, 1983.

Two major biographies of Anthony Eden have appeared. The best is David Carleton, *Anthony Eden* (London, 1981), but Robert Rhodes James, *Anthony Eden* (London, 1986) is helpful because of its discussion of Eden's medical history and the publication of the Sevres agreement. The only useful biography of Selwyn Lloyd is D. R. Thorpe, *Selwyn Lloyd* (London, 1988). Alistair Horne, *Macmillan, 1894–1956* (London, 1988) is well done and explores Macmillan's role in the removal of Eden. The best secondary works on Nasser include Anthony Nutting, *Nasser* (New York, 1972); Jean Lacouture, *Nasser* (New York, 1973); and Keith Wheelock, *Nasser's Egypt* (New York, 1960). For Ben-Gurion, the best work in English is Michael Bar-Zohar, *Ben-Gurion* (New York, 1977).

Secondary works on events leading up to the Suez crisis and beyond are numerous; not all are worthwhile. The most up-to-date is Peter L. Hahn, *The United States, Great Britain, and Egypt, 1945–1956* (Chapel Hill, N.C., 1991). Hahn does an excellent job in developing Anglo-American relations during the period and provides a fine understanding of why the United States was caught by surprise by the Israeli invasion in October 1956. A useful synthesis is provided by David Carleton, *Britain and the Suez Crisis* (London, 1988). Other useful works which deal with the same subject matter are Geoffrey Aronson, *From Sideshow to Center Stage: United States Policy Toward Egypt, 1946–1956* (Boulder, Colo., 1986); Gail E. Meyer, *Egypt and the United States: The Formative Years* (Madison, Wisc., 1980); and Donald Neff, *Warriors at Suez* (New York, 1981).

Anyone dealing with the events surrounding the Suez crisis owes a debt of gratitude to former *New York Times* reporter Kennett Love for his monumental work *Suez: The Twice-Fought War* (New York, 1969). The book appears to have been the answer to the more polemical anti-Dulles presentation of Herman Finer, *Dulles Over Suez* (Chicago, 1964). Hugh Thomas, *Suez* (New York, 1967) is a surprisingly accurate account considering the lack of documentation available when the book was written. Other important monographs include Terence Robertson, *Crisis: The Inside Story of the Suez Conspiracy* (New York, 1965); Chester L. Cooper, *The Lion's Last Roar: Suez, 1956* (New York, 1978); and Michael Scott Bornstein, "From Revolution to Crisis: Egypt-Israel Relations, 1952–1956," Ph.D. dissertation, Princeton University, 1985). Two important edited works by scholars and participants in the crisis are William Roger Louis and Roger Owen, *Suez 1956: The Crisis and Its Consequences* (New York, 1989), and Anthony Moncrieff, *Suez: Ten Years After* (New York, 1966).

Works dealing with the pre-1953 period which should be consulted include Alan Bullock, *Ernest Bevin: Foreign Secretary* (New York, 1983); Elizabeth Monroe, *Britain's Moment in the Middle East, 1914–1956* (London, 1963); William R. Louis, *The British Empire in the Middle East, 1945–1951* (New York, 1984); Ritchie Ovendale, *The English-Speaking Alliance: Britain, The United States, The Dominions and the Cold War, 1945–1951* (London, 1985); and Wilbur Terry Lindley, "The Tag End of Diplomacy: American Policy in the Near East, 1949–1953," Ph.D. dissertation, Texas Christian University, 1985. The most recent contribution to this area is Peter L. Hahn, "Containment and Egyptian Nationalism: The Unsuccessful Effort to Establish the Middle East Command, 1950–1953," *Diplomatic History*, Winter 1987.

Because the intelligence community was heavily involved in Washington's Middle East policy, several books are important. The CIA's chief Egyptian operative, Miles Copeland, in *The Game of Nations*, offers an accurate account of our relations with Nasser. Wilbur Crane Eveland, who was heavily involved in the Syrian coup planned for October 1956, has written *Ropes of Sand: America's Failure in the Middle East* (New York, 1980). Other accounts which are useful include Blanche Wessen Cook, *The Declassified Eisenhower: A Divided Legacy* (New York, 1981); John Ranelagh, *The Agency: The Rise and Decline of the CIA* (New York, 1986); and John Prados, *President's Secret Wars* (New York, 1986).

The influence of American oil interests on Middle East policy is explored in Irvine H. Anderson, *Aramco, the United States and Saudi Arabia* (Princeton, 1981); David S. Painter, *Oil and the American*

Century: The Political Economy of U.S. Foreign Oil Policy, 1941–1954
(Baltimore, 1986); Benjamin Shwadran, *The Middle East, Oil and the
Great Powers* (New York, 1973); and Deborah Polster, "The Need for
Oil Shapes the American Diplomatic Response to the Invasion of
Suez," Ph.D. dissertation, Case Western Reserve University, 1985.

Numerous books have appeared analyzing American-Israeli rela-
tions. The best of these include Nadav Safran, *Israel: The Embattled
Ally* (Cambridge, Mass., 1978); Cheryl A. Rubenberg, *Israel and the
American National Interest* (Urbana, Ill., 1986); Yaacov Bar Simon-Tov,
Israel, the Superpowers and the War in the Middle East (New York,
1987); Ernest Stock, *Israel on the Road to Sinai, 1949–1956* (Ithaca,
N.Y., 1967); and Steven Spiegel, *The Other Arab-Israeli Conflict:
Making America's Middle East Policy, from Truman to Reagan* (Chi-
cago, 1985). Israel Yungher's Ph.D. dissertation, "United States-Israel
Relations, 1953–1956," University of Pennsylvania, 1985, provides
many useful insights.

American-Arab relations have produced a great many books, the best
of which is Robert W. Stookey, *America and the Arab States: An
Uneasy Encounter* (New York, 1975). Other works worth consulting are
John S. Badeau, *The American Approach to the Arab World* (New
York, 1968); William Stivers, *America's Confrontation with Revolution-
ary Change in the Middle East, 1948–1983* (New York, 1986); David E.
Long, *The United States and Saudi Arabia: Ambivalent Allies* (Boulder,
Colo., 1985); John C. Campbell, *Defense of the Middle East* (New
York, 1960); Barry Rubin, "America and the Egyptian Revolution,"
Political Science Quarterly, Spring 1982; and Robert J. McMahon,
"Eisenhower and Third World Nationalism," *Political Science Quarter-
ly*, Fall 1986.

Inter-Arab relations have not produced a wealth of materials; significant is Patrick Seale, *The Struggle for Syria* (New Haven, Conn.,
1987). Others available include Nadav Safran, *Saudi Arabia: The
Ceaseless Quest for Security* (Cambridge, Mass., 1985), and Barry
Rubin, *The Arab States and the Palestine Conflict* (Syracuse, 1981).

Because Anglo-American policy was predicated on the Soviet threat,
the following books are recommended: Thomas G. Paterson, *Meeting
the Communist Threat: Truman to Reagan* (New York, 1988) argues
that Washington's Middle East policy failed because it could not
understand Arab nationalism. Jon D. Glassman, *Arms for the Arabs:
The Soviet Union and War in the Middle East* (Baltimore, 1975); Paul
Jabber, *Not by Arms Alone: Security and Arms Control in the Middle
East* (Berkeley, Calif., 1981); and Uri Ra'anan, *The USSR Arms the*

Third World: Case Studies in Soviet Foreign Policy (Cambridge, Mass., 1969) discuss the origins of the Czech arms deal and Soviet penetration of the Middle East. The debate among these books centers on the influence of the American refusal to sell military equipment to Egypt, the Gaza raid, and Nasser's domestic political situation in motivating the Egyptian president to purchase Soviet weapons. Other important monographs include Mohrez Mahmoud El-Hussini, *Soviet-Egyptian Relations, 1945–1985* (New York, 1987); Mohamed Heikal, *The Sphinx and the Commissar: The Rise and Fall of Soviet Influence in the Middle East* (New York, 1978); and Walter Laqueur, *The Soviet Union in the Middle East* (New York, 1959).

Books which do not fall easily into a specific category nonetheless offer important contributions. Saadia Touval, *The Peace Brokers: Mediators in the Arab-Israeli Conflict, 1948–1979* (Princeton, 1982) has an excellent chapter on the failure of the Anderson mission. Richard Lamb, *The Failure of the Eden Government* (London, 1987) argues that there was no conspiracy to remove Anthony Eden from office. Elie Kedourie, *Islam in the Modern World* (New York, 1980) has a useful chapter which evaluates the memoirs of the Suez participants. Jay Gonen, *A Psychohistory of Zionism* (New York, 1975) provides interesting psychological insights into Israel's policies toward the Arabs. Sylvia K. Crosbie, *A Tacit Alliance: France and Israel from Suez to the Six-Day War* (Princeton, 1974) traces the development of the Franco-Israeli alliance. Michael Brecher, *Decisions in Israel's Foreign Policy* (New Haven, Conn., 1975) is a superb study of the Israeli foreign policy establishment. Finally, Brian Urquhart, *Hammarskjöld* (New York, 1972) explores the role of the UN secretary-general in the Suez crisis.

Index

A NOTE ON THE AUTHOR

Steven Z. Freiberger was born in Brooklyn, New York, and studied at Pace University and at West Virginia University, where he received an M.A. in history. After teaching social studies in Virginia and New Jersey high schools, he was awarded a Fulbright Fellowship and began work toward a Ph.D. in history at Rutgers University, where he was awarded the degree in 1990. He is now associate professor of history at Franklin Pierce College in Rindge, New Hampshire, and lives there with his wife and two children.